John Storrs

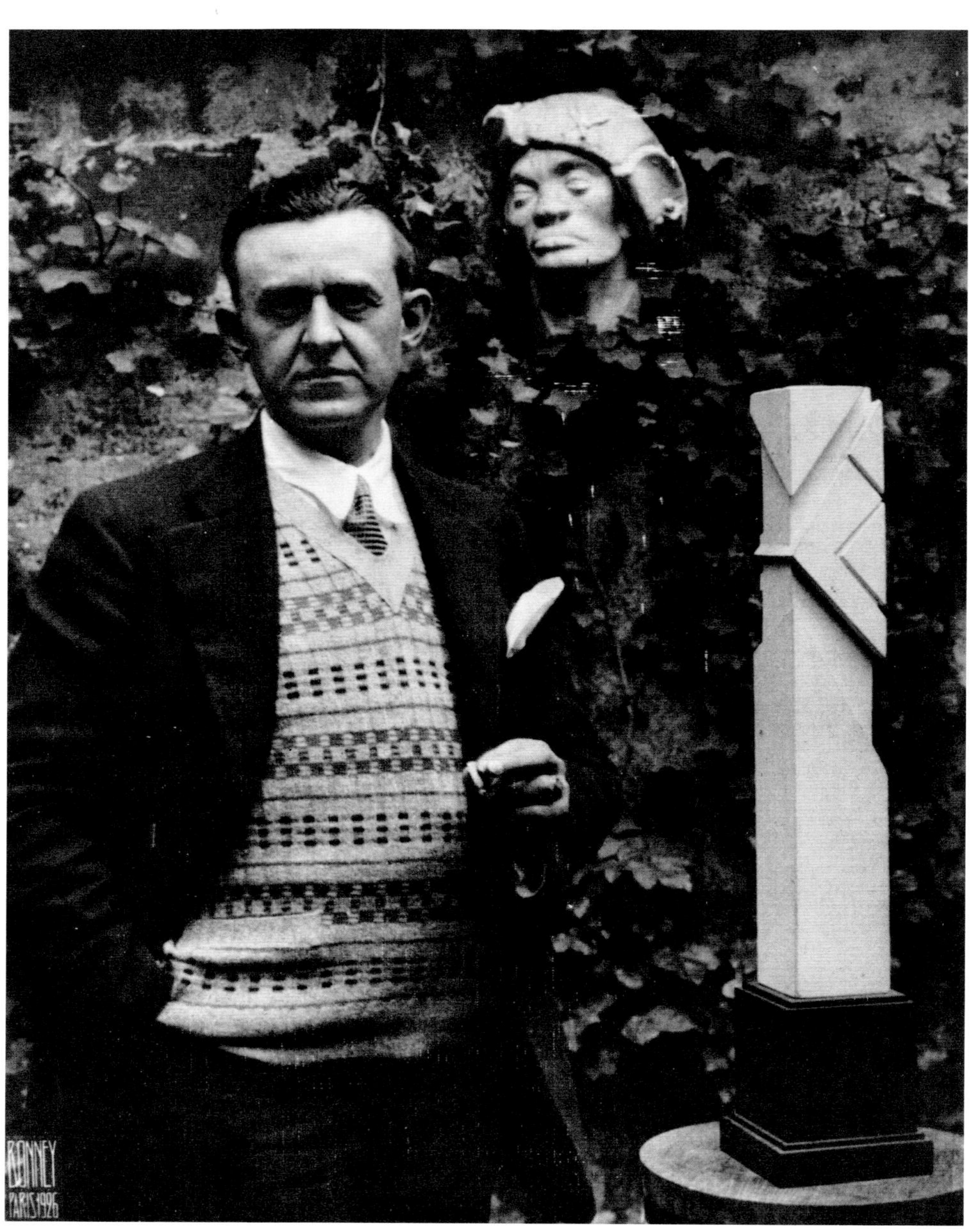
BONNEY
PARIS 1926

John Storrs

Noel Frackman

Whitney Museum of American Art, New York

Dates of the exhibition:

Whitney Museum of American Art, New York
December 11, 1986–March 22, 1987

Amon Carter Museum, Fort Worth, Texas
May 2–July 5, 1987

J. B. Speed Art Museum, Louisville, Kentucky
August 28–November 1, 1987

This exhibition is sponsored by the Howard and Jean Lipman Foundation,
Elaine and Henry Kaufman, Stephen E. O'Neil, an anonymous donor,
and the National Endowment for the Arts.

Curator of the exhibition: Patterson Sims, Associate Curator,
Permanent Collection, Whitney Museum of American Art

Library of Congress Cataloging-in-Publication Data
Frackman, Noel.
    John Storrs.

    Bibliography: p.
    1. Storrs, John Henry Bradley, 1885–1956—
Exhibitions. I. Storrs, John Henry Bradley,
1885–1956. II. Whitney Museum of American Art.
III. Title.
NB237.S67A4   1986   730'.92'4   86–26687
ISBN 0–87427–051–0

Frontispiece: John Storrs. Paris, 1926.
Cover: *Study for Architectural Sculpture*, 1929 (Fig. 85).

This publication was organized at the Whitney Museum of American Art by
Doris Palca, Head, Publications and Sales; Sheila Schwartz, Editor;
Deborah Lyons, Associate Editor; and Vicki Drake, Secretary/Assistant

John Storrs was designed by Katy Homans, Homans | Salsgiver;
typeset in Monotype Walbaum by Michael & Winifred Bixler;
and printed in Connecticut by Rembrandt Press, Inc.

Contents

Acknowledgments

The late Professor H.W. Janson encouraged my initial research on John Storrs at the Institute of Fine Arts, New York University. Conversations with Monique Storrs Booz during her lifetime were invaluable, as were the time and assistance graciously given by her children, Michelle Storrs Booz and John Storrs Booz. Robert and Jane Schoelkopf of the Robert Schoelkopf Gallery, Ltd., along with their assistants William Buechler and Patricia Baird, have aided in every possible way with unstinting effort.

At the Whitney Museum of American Art, Patterson Sims, curator of the exhibition, has for many years shared my enthusiasm for John Storrs. The "John Storrs" retrospective and its accompanying catalogue would not have become a reality without the commitment of the Museum and its director, Tom Armstrong. Through the enthusiastic support of the Amon Carter Museum, particularly of Jan Keene Muhlert, director, and Linda Ayres, curator of paintings and sculpture, and the J.B. Speed Art Museum and its director, Peter Morrin, John Storrs' work will be made accessible to a national audience.

My family has been strongly supportive throughout this project. Many years ago, in Paris, London, and New York, Ruth Kaufmann opened my eyes to Art Deco. I also cite with gratitude the names of friends, scholars, and experts who assisted in the research and development of this catalogue: Colonel Frederick C. Badger, James Berenson, George Blow, Sam Carini, Anne Daniel, Henri Delgove, Anita Duquette, Martin Eidelberg, Cheryl Epstein, Alex Ettl, Philip Evola, Ronald Feldman, George Gurney, Vivian Harquail, Bernard Heineman, Jr., Linda D. Henderson, John Hunisak, James Hyde, Jim M. Jordan, Mr. and Mrs. Robert J. Kaufman, Mr. and Mrs. Charles Suddarth Kelly, John R. Lane, Martin Leifer, Yulla Lipchitz, Joan Mickelson Lukach, Deborah Lyons, Ann MacNary, Richard Masters, Garnett McCoy, Lacy McDearmon, Grant Carpenter Manson, Edgar Miller, Robert Moskowitz, Isamu Noguchi, Tom Norton, Bruce Brooks Pfeiffer, Suzanne Quinson, Robert Rosenblum, Timothy Rub, Jennifer Russell, Alice W. Schlessinger, Beatrice N. Schuetz, Sheila Schwartz, Elisabeth Stevens, Susan Teller, Marianne Thomas, Daniel Vannier, Joan Washburn, Martin Weyl, Dan Wheeler, Mrs. George B. Young, Virginia Zabriskie, Larry Zgoda, and Judith Zilczer.

N.F.

Introduction

It is in the area of advanced abstract sculpture that John Storrs makes the most serious claim for a significant place in the history of twentieth-century American art. As a member of the first generation of modernists, Storrs was a pioneer in his efforts to create abstract and non-objective sculpture of originality and geometric simplicity.

Until recently, American sculpture between the two World Wars has suffered from critical neglect. In the past few years, however, there has been a new appreciation of such American sculptors as Elie Nadelman and Gaston Lachaise, artists whose most inventive work was not achieved through public or private commissions, but rather evolved in the struggle to advance sculpture from statuary to conceptualized abstraction. Of this group of sculptors, it is John Storrs who worked most consistently toward developing a personal vocabulary of abstract forms and who pursued the direction of non-objective art in the most dedicated manner.

Because of his devotion to advanced abstraction, Storrs received some attention from avant-garde publications. Prior to 1925, his art was discussed and reproduced in experimental magazines such as *Playboy* and *The Little Review*. But within the establishment, the critical reception of his work generally suffered from his ambivalent nationality. Since he married a French writer and owned a château in the Loire Valley, his life was almost equally divided between France and the United States. Thus, the French considered him to be an American artist while Americans thought of his art as Europeanized. American critics reviewing Storrs' work before 1925 objected that his art showed too much influence of the Vienna Secession and too many of the new Cubist tendencies. While his craftsmanship was admired, his experimentation with abstract forms in sculpture was considered a weakness or, at the very least, puzzling. The French critic André Salmon, trying to come to terms with avant-garde tendencies in what he considered to be the work of an American, asked what American critics had been asking, though for different reasons: "Why the sensible modeler of realistic busts, the pupil of Rodin, was led to carve those recent 'constructions' with their geometrical appearance."[1]

Storrs' thrust toward abstraction was manifested not only in sculpture but in drawings, prints, and paintings. Although he considered himself first and foremost a sculptor and it is on this basis that his reputation must finally be assessed, his achievements in other media are of such high quality as to support the evaluation that Storrs was an artist of unquestioned talent, inventiveness, and versatility.

1. André Salmon in *Exhibition of Sculpture by John Storrs*, exhibition brochure (New York: Société Anonyme, 1923), unpaginated.

I. Early Years

John Henry Bradley Storrs was born on June 28, 1885, the last of seven children and, as it turned out, the only surviving son. Storrs' older brother, William, died at the age of nine and, as a result, Hannah Bradley Storrs pampered, spoiled, and protected her youngest son. For fear that he would contract a disease, Hannah Storrs did not send John to school until he was nine years old. He entered school unable to read or write and his spelling remained atrocious.[1]

Storrs' father, David W. Storrs (always called "D.W.") was a Chicago architect and real estate developer, the only member of an old, prestigious New England family who was not a minister, lawyer, or farmer.[2] Many New England towns boast a Storrs Avenue and the family founded Storrs, Connecticut. Through investments in real estate, the fortunes of the D.W. Storrs family continued to rise. D.W. was a thoroughly pragmatic man who believed in thrift and hard work. Although he tried, he could never understand the more contemplative and meandering ways of his artist-son.

When the Storrs family moved from their home on Wentworth Avenue to an apartment in 1900, John Storrs was enrolled in the Chicago Manual Training School (part of University High School), where he took to the woodworking shops—the smell of the wood shavings and the feel of the tools. There was a machine shop, a foundry, and a studio where one could study freehand, architectural, and mechanical drawing. Storrs recollected with enthusiasm:

It was not it would seem until my entrance into Manual Shool that the connection was really istablished between my brain and my eyes & hands, thereby awakening for the first time my immagination & my immotions—and culmenating in an intrest, not merly to learn, but to create.

To make things, things that I could see & touch, and in this making to be free & perhaps able to express something which inside myself had, until now, very little chance to escape.

But I was still to young to think of all these things. I just liked it and enjoyed for the first time, really, being able to do things as well—often better—than the other fellows.[3]

Storrs' talent for drawing was in demand and he became staff artist for *The University High School Weekly* and art editor for *The Correlator*, the yearbook of University High School. Although he was a member of the class of 1904, Storrs could not garner enough credits to graduate that year, despite an earlier summer school session at Culver Naval Academy. He was able to graduate in 1905 because he persuaded his drawing teacher, Frederick Newton Williams, to let him teach an advanced class of his own devising in architectural drawing.

When Storrs finally graduated, his parents were so relieved that they sent him on a promised trip to Europe. Once abroad, John and his friend Sidney Jenkins traveled to England, Holland, Belgium, and Germany. When they arrived in Berlin, they visited Storrs' older sister, Mary, who had been living there since 1904, studying voice, piano, French, and German. Soon, Storrs was taking voice lessons too, but he balked at the idea of becoming an opera singer; what he enjoyed most was drawing.

It was through his sister Mary's close friend, the interpretive dancer Maud Allan, that John Storrs heard about the sculptor Arthur Bock. On Allan's recommendation, Storrs went to Hamburg to study with Bock, then thirty years old and known for his funerary monuments. During Storrs' six-month tenure, Bock was working on a fifteen-foot-high statue of Christ for a mausoleum and chapel, for which he also designed the architecture and all of the interior decorations, including doorknobs, tiles, frescoes, and even face towels. This concept of harmony and unity of design in all the related arts— *Gesamtkunstwerk*—was one that Storrs himself adopted, although circumstances rarely allowed him to put it into practice.[4]

Later, reflecting on his early experiences in Germany, Storrs felt that he was impressed not so much by German painting and sculpture as by German design and architecture.[5] There seems little question that Storrs responded strongly to the architectural and design concepts of the Vienna Secession group. Such concepts reinforced his natural predisposition for simplicity, geometric order, symmetry, and for art as a totality—conceived as a unity rather than as an aggregate of detail. The Vienna Secession movement was seminal for the development of what has come to be termed Art Deco.[6] The striving for an absolute unity of design, as stressed in the concept of the *Gesamtkunstwerk*, found further expression in Art Deco interiors and would, some years later, be captured in the holistic quality of Storrs' architectural sculpture, where every detail functioned within a total idea. Storrs would also have noticed especially the geometric forms used most frequently by Secession architects and designers, the square, rectangle, and circle. As Bock's student, Storrs was absorbing these concepts, although he did not yet have the maturity, confidence, or skill to put them into practice.

Convinced of Storrs' talent, Arthur Bock had encouraged him to continue with his studies at the Berlin Academy, but in the summer of 1906 he instead toured Germany, Switzerland, and France with his family. By November 1906, he was enrolled in the Académie Julian, Paris; however, he seems to have withdrawn almost immediately, perhaps due to his scant knowledge of French and fears that he would not be able to do the work.[7] By January 1907, he had enrolled in the Académie Franklin. That summer he traveled with his friend Irving Heitkamp to Spain, Italy, Greece, Turkey, and Egypt.

At his parents request (and not their first), Storrs returned to

America, arriving in New York City en route to Chicago in November 1907. New York was a heady experience for Storrs: "New Yorkers don't spare pains or money to do a thing right. New buildings going up all over, a great deal more than in Chicago."[8] None of the architectural landscape, including the early skyscrapers, was lost on Storrs as he roamed the city until late at night.

Back in Chicago, Storrs went to work in his father's real estate business in the winter of 1908, under instructions to collect delinquent payments and to try to rent flats without bed or table linens if possible. While collecting rents, Storrs would probably have seen any number of tenements. Although overprotected as a young child, this exposure to conditions of poverty may have initiated Storrs' concerns for uplifting the masses, justice for the poor, and his espousal of socialism.

Attempting to keep up with his art studies, Storrs took day and evening classes at the School of the Art Institute of Chicago through the summer of 1909.[9] By the fall, it had become obvious to his family that he was not cut out to be a real estate tycoon and so he was enrolled at the School of the Museum of Fine Arts, Boston. His chief instructor was Bela Pratt, who had studied with Henri Chapu and Alexandre Falguière and was at one time an assistant to Augustus Saint-Gaudens.[10] Pratt seemed to have felt that sculpture should develop from knowledge of a particular part to a satisfactory whole.[11] However, Storrs' own method of working was quite opposite: he blocked out the whole concept first and simplified or eliminated the details. Pratt's students were pushed to strive for perfection of detail, and after working for four weeks from a live model Storrs was discouraged: "I didn't seem to get as far as most of the students some of whom got even the wavelets in her toe nails."[12]

Impatient with Bela Pratt's classes, Storrs changed art schools, enrolling in the fall of 1910 at the school of the Pennsylvania Academy of the Fine Arts. He studied sculpture with Charles Grafly, who as a teacher seemed less concerned with the problem of "finish," for Storrs wrote, "I am trying to forget for the time being, any knoledg I may have of technque or surface modeling and am going in for absolutly nothing but movement, character, masses—well, I'll have to get them this year or I'll never be what *I call* a sculptor."[13]

Storrs' attempts to concentrate on the entirety of each sculpture must have helped him win the Edmund Stewardson Prize given by the Department of Sculpture at the Pennsylvania Academy of the Fine Arts, for at one level, the contest depended on swiftness in blocking out a figure. Ten students competed in modeling a half life-sized full figure from the living model within a time limit of eighteen hours.[14] Encouraged by the award, Storrs absolutely determined to return to Paris for more study. Before he left, he obtained a letter of introduction from Charles Grafly to Paul Bartlett, the American sculptor who was then teaching in Paris. Although he had studied painting at the Pennsylvania Academy, Storrs had decided to make sculpture the center of his life: "No amount of painting can give me the sensation which, I receive in creating forms—all of my own."[15]

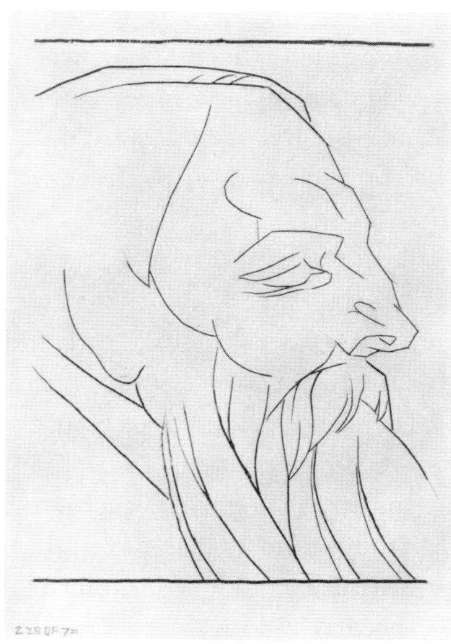

1. *Head of Rodin*, 1919
Drypoint
9⁵⁄₁₆ x 6¼ (23.7 x 15.9)
Private collection

In Paris, in the fall of 1911, Storrs enrolled at the Académie Colarossi, where he studied with Paul Bartlett and Jean-Antoine Injalbert, and at the Académie de la Grande Chaumière, where his teacher was Lucien Simon.[16] As of the fall 1912, he was still enrolled in both academies.

Then Storrs was given the opportunity to study with Rodin. According to a newspaper article of the period, Rodin saw some of Storrs' studies and said, "I would like to give this student some criticism. He can be my pupil."[17] Perhaps Rodin saw some of Storrs' student work when Storrs was studying with Paul Bartlett in 1911–12.[18] The first correspondence between Rodin's atelier and Storrs is a letter of June 1913 in which Rodin's secretary writes that Rodin will be happy to see him.[19] However, it is likely that Storrs' studies with Rodin started in 1912.[20] He revered Rodin both as a teacher and as a person and many of his sculptures of this period show an effort to absorb Rodin's thumbed surfaces, to reiterate his renowned art of "hollows and mounds,"[21] and respond to Rodin's emphasis on light and on the light-reflecting qualities of sculpture. The most important lessons Storrs felt he learned from Rodin were:

Work by the volume and not by the surface, from inside to outside. It is by density that you create form and not by the exterior.
A sculpture is constructed by carving and not by adding. It is complete in the primitive mass. What's left is a selection.[22]

So much do these statements agree with Storrs' conception of sculpture as a totality that one suspects he interpreted Rodin's lessons according to his own ideas. For Storrs, sculpture always remained a selection of elements from an envisioned whole, a work built from the inside out. From this concept results the inner strength of his art. Moreover, he never used slick surface detail just to display his craftsmanship but rather employed his surfaces to reflect light.

The outbreak of World War I interrupted Storrs' studies with Rodin but he kept in touch with the master as best he could. When Rodin was old and ill, Storrs visited him in Meudon and brought him news of the reception of his works in the United States, particularly of those Storrs had been able to see at the 1915 Panama-Pacific International Exposition in San Francisco.

The emotional bond with Rodin remained strong and when Rodin died in 1917, Storrs was asked by Rodin's cousins and by the director of the Musée du Luxembourg, Léonce Bénédicte (who later became director of the Musée Rodin), to execute a drawing of Rodin on his deathbed. Two years later, Storrs made a drypoint etching of Rodin, partly based on memory and partly on the deathbed portrait, in which Rodin resembles an oriental sage (Fig. 1). The spareness of form, abrupt cropping, and asymmetrical composition reflect Storrs' early admiration for Japanese prints. In about 1908, he bought out an entire exhibition of Japanese prints shown at the Carson Pirie Scott department store in Chicago, including works by Hiroshige, Hokusai, and Utamaro.[23]

Rodin's talent and achievement were simultaneously an inspiration and a frustration to younger sculptors in his orbit. Storrs thought of Rodin as the Michelangelo of modern times and asked, "Are we who come after Rodin the froth that comes after the wave? Is it going to be our lot to degenerate into Jean de Bolognes . . . that followed Michel Angelo?"[24]

Storrs seems to have answered the question for himself by taking an entirely different, modernist course. At the same time he began to study with Rodin, he was also becoming acquainted with Cubism and Futurism. He probably visited the Salon des Indépendants in the spring of 1912, where a Cubist exhibition included the works of Archipenko, Gleizes, Gris, Léger, and Le Fauconnier.[25] Moreover, it was at just about this point that Storrs gained a new friend, one whom he had met in art school, Jacques Lipchitz. At the time that they met, probably in the fall of 1911, neither Lipchitz nor Storrs had advanced very much in their attempts to apply Cubism to sculpture. By 1913, according to Lipchitz, there was little sculpture that could be regarded as purely Cubist; Lipchitz and Storrs would have been acquainted with Cubism chiefly through the paintings of Picasso, Braque, and others.[26] For ambitious sculptors like Lipchitz and Storrs the challenge was to translate Cubism, which began as a revolution in painting, into three-dimensional form.

Notes

1. No attempt has been made to correct Storrs' spelling in quotations from his letters and notes, and the use of *sic* would constantly interrupt the text.

2. Much information about John Storrs' life and the Storrs family has emerged during the author's conversations with Storrs' daughter, Monique Storrs Booz (d. 1985).

3. John Storrs' recollections of the Chicago Manual School are in the Archives of American Art, Smithsonian Institution, Washington, D.C., John Storrs Papers, 2, Writings 1946–1947, "The Scribble-in Book," pp. 102–03. (These archives will hereafter be cited as AAA, JSP, followed by the box number and folder identification.) In dating letters and notes, Storrs sometimes used the American sequence of month, day, and year, and sometimes the European sequence of day, month, and year. Unless otherwise indicated, these latter have been transposed to the American system. In cases where the system used cannot be determined, the date is given as it appears on the document.

4. Storrs writes about Bock's concept of totality of design and "how difficult it was & still is to get cooperation on an idea of this kind" in AAA, JSP, 2, Writings 1947, brown book, marked Vol. IV, pp. 25–26.

5. Ibid., pp. 43–44.

6. For the definition and chronology of Art Deco, see Judith Applegate, "What is Art Deco?" *Art News*, 69 (December 1970), pp. 38–42. Applegate demonstrates that the roots of Art Deco are in Art Nouveau soil and that the movement grows in the first few years after the turn of the century. She considers Art Deco "as including activity from about 1909 through 1939," a time span that will be followed here. In other words, while the Paris Exposition des Arts Décoratifs of 1925 gave rise to the term Art Deco, the movement actually had its origins much earlier.

7. Entry, September 1908, AAA, JSP, 1, Diary 1906 (this diary contains entries through 1908): "I had in tended starting at Julien's and even paid a months tuition. But it seemed to me then that they were all so far advanced and that there were apt to be so many distractions for a beginer, & as I had only had the few months in Hamburg,

I felt that a smaller place were I could put my whole attencion on my work would be much the better.'' A receipt for payment of tuition to the Académie Julian, from November 5 to December 2, 1906, is in AAA, JSP, 9, Tax & Insurance.

8. John Storrs to his parents, AAA, JSP, 6, Family correspondence, 1906 (4th folder thus marked). The letter is incorrectly dated ''10.29.06'' in pencil in another hand. Clearly, it was written in 1907, on the day after Storrs' arrival in New York City.

9. Registrar's records from the School of the Art Institute of Chicago reveal that John Storrs attended the day school from January 4 to May 10, 1909, and the summer session from May 28 to August 18, 1909; he attended evening classes from February 19 to May 18, 1909. Storrs also attended a summer session of the school in 1910. Courtney Donnell and Marita Maginson of the Art Institute of Chicago, and Mary McIsaac of the School of the Art Institute of Chicago kindly assisted in the researching of these records.

10. For Bela Pratt, see ''Artists' Biographies'' by Libby W. Seaberg, assisted by Cherene Holland, in *200 Years of American Sculpture*, exhibition catalogue (New York: Whitney Museum of American Art, 1976), pp. 298–99.

11. John Storrs to his parents, November 7, 1909, AAA, JSP, 6, Family correspondence, 1909.

12. John Storrs to his parents, fragmentary letter that appears to belong to another fragment dated February 6, 1910, AAA, JSP, 6, Family correspondence, 1910 (1st folder thus marked).

13. John Storrs to his parents, 12/11/10, AAA, JSP, 6, Family correspondence, 1910 (2nd folder thus marked).

14. A description of the type of competition for the Stewardson Prize is in an unidentified newspaper article, AAA, JSP, 10, Clippings (1st folder thus marked), where the jurors are listed as Alexander Stirling Calder of Croton-on-Hudson, Samuel Murray of Philadelphia, and Edward Berge of Baltimore, described as ''three well known sculptors.''

15. John Storrs to his mother, dated 1911 in pencil but not necessarily in Storrs' hand, AAA, JSP, 6, Family correspondence, 1911 (1st folder thus marked).

16. John Storrs to Miss Cross (Louise Cross), August 16, 1932, AAA, JSP, 1, Biography & Chronology, lists his schooling in part as follows: ''in Paris under Paul Bartlett, Angelbert, Bouchard, Landowsky and Rodin.'' Storrs' ''Angelbert'' is Injalbert. Possibly Storrs studied with Bouchard and ''Landowsky'' in the evenings, for a letter to his parents, 13/3/11, AAA, JSP, 6, Family correspondence, 1911, mentions that he ''changed to Simon's class in the morning'' and needs ''15 per month for nights.'' Storrs' ''Landowsky'' is probably the sculptor Paul Landowski.

17. ''American Sculptor Chosen to Design French War Medal,'' *Buffalo Express*, datelined Paris, April 26, John Storrs Scrapbook, Robert Schoelkopf Gallery, Ltd., New York, p. 6. Although no year appears on the clipping, the article refers to Storrs' work ''In the last Beaux Arts salon held in the spring of 1914.'' The scrapbook is also on microfilm, AAA, Downtown Gallery Papers, microfilm no. 70, frames 588–765.

18. Paul Bartlett's father, Truman Howe Bartlett, a sculptor and critic, had published a most significant interview with Rodin; see Albert E. Elsen, *Rodin* (New York: The Museum of Modern Art, 1963), p. 25 n. 4 and p. 191. The Bartletts had made their home in France since Paul Bartlett was nine years old; probably the family remained friendly with Rodin.

19. Letter dated June 18, 1913, signed ''Son Secrétaire,'' AAA, JSP, 3, Correspondence, 1913.

20. A list in John Storrs' handwriting, AAA, JSP, 1, Biography & Chronology, gives the dates of study with Rodin as ''1912–14.''

21. Quoted in Elsen, *Rodin*, p. 57.

22. During some informal instruction from Rodin one evening, Rodin asked Storrs if he had ever seen a statue illuminated by artificial light, whereupon Rodin took a lamp and held it next to the stomach of a small marble copy of the Medici Venus in his studio. Storrs noticed how the light underlined, accentuated, and deepened certain details of form; his comments as quoted here were written after he described this experience. The evening and Storrs' comments are recorded by his wife, Marguerite, AAA, JSP, 2, Writings (undated).

23. Two prints by Hokusai and one by Hiroshige remain in the Monique Storrs Booz estate. One is marked as having been purchased in c. 1890 by D.W. Storrs and another came from John Storrs' château in France. These prints may not have come from Storrs' purchase at the Carson Pirie Scott store, but they attest to his continuing exposure to Japanese prints. Storrs mentions his 1908 or 1909 purchase of Japanese prints in AAA, JSP, 2, Writings 1942–1943, ''The Scribble Book,'' p. 118.

24. Storrs' musings on the influence of Rodin and a description of Rodin on his deathbed are in Storrs' reminiscences, ''Last Moments of Rodin,'' AAA, JSP, 2, Writings (undated).

25. An excellent listing of the various Cubist exhibitions of the period is found in Robert Rosenblum, *Cubism and Twentieth-Century Art* (New York: Harry N. Abrams, 1960), pp. 307–11. That Storrs almost surely saw the 1912 Salon des Indépendants is indicated in his letter to his parents, May 5, 1912, AAA, JSP, 6, Correspondence 1912, where he writes from Paris, ''Both the Salons are open now —but I will try & say something about them in my next letter.''

26. Jacques Lipchitz with H.H. Arnason, *My Life in Sculpture* (New York: The Viking Press, 1972), p. 17. See also p. 7: ''Among my friends at school I remember an American, John Storrs, from Chicago, a good sculptor and a very nice man, who lived most of his life in France. He is one of the American pioneers of modern art and is only now beginning to be recognized in his own country.'' Like Storrs, Lipchitz also attended the Académie Colarossi and the two young artists may have initially met there.

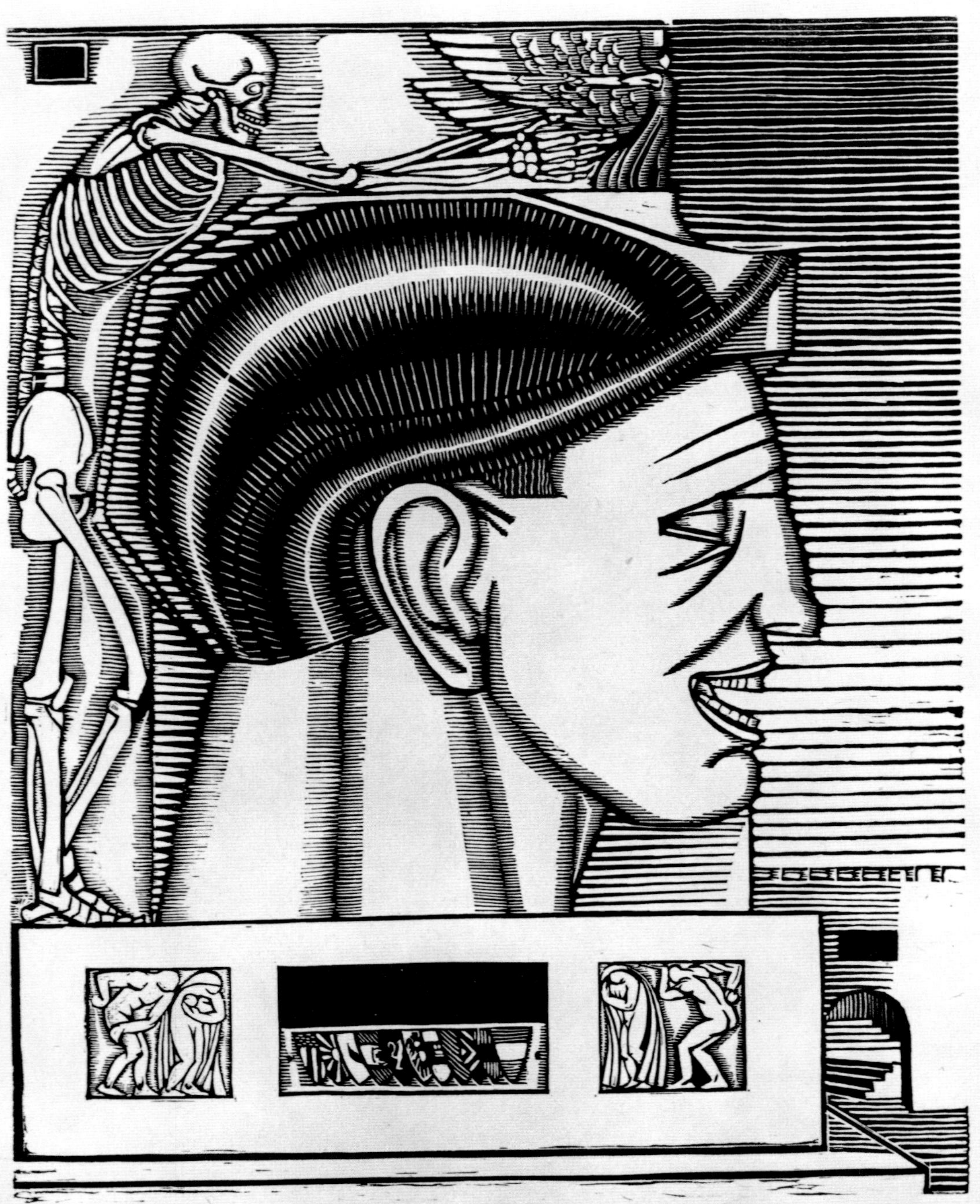

II. Themes of the War

The year 1914 was a crucial one for John Storrs. In that year he married, exhibited at the 1914 Salon of the Société Nationale des Beaux-Arts, and the onset of the war terminated his studies with Rodin.

Storrs married Marguerite De Ville Chabrol, a sophisticated French woman, five years his senior, whose family lived in Orléans. Author of the popular novel *La Route Choisie* (written under the pseudonym Marc Debrol),[1] at the age of twenty she became a front-page correspondent for *Paris Temps*. Storrs' serious commitment to writing poetry seems to have begun with this romance. An unpublished love poem he wrote to Marguerite is significant in terms of understanding the evolution of his art toward an ever increasing purity of geometry. The poem is striking in its intense expression of passion and in the simple but revealing sketches (Fig. 3). In a columnar series of parallel lines, sexual release is metaphorically expressed by means of pure geometry. It is clear from the sketches that geometry for Storrs was never merely intellectual but deeply ingrained in his poetic, passionate nature.

In the evolution of his sculpture, Storrs was to achieve a stylistic mode that allowed him to express through geometry the deepest emotions and sensations of purity and spirituality. In Cubism, whose planar and proportional structuring appealed to him, Storrs found a way to geometrize the human figure. However, in his earliest personalized works, he relied on thematic content to serve as a carrier for emotions and used traditional themes as a means of providing ready-made spiritual symbols.

A comparison between two of the sculptures he exhibited in the Salon of 1914, the bronze statuette of *Howard E. Smith* (Fig. 4) and *Portrait of My Mother* (Fig. 6), shows Storrs caught in a dichotomy—wishing to follow in the Rodinesque tradition on the one hand, and, on the other, trying to forge a more simplified, geometrized individual style.

Storrs chose to depict two people with whom he was extraordinarily close—his adored mother and his close friend. *Portrait of My Mother* was executed as an homage to Hannah Storrs, who had died suddenly in Paris in July 1913 while visiting her son; Storrs was devastated by her death. As in so many of Rodin's marble portrait busts, Storrs has captured an honest, informal likeness; the roughened marble simultaneously substitutes for clothing and also suggests an emerging mythic birth from cleft rock.[2] By contrast, in the bronze *Howard E. Smith*, we sense the first true impress of a personal style. Storrs began to work on the plaster for this sculpture in the spring of

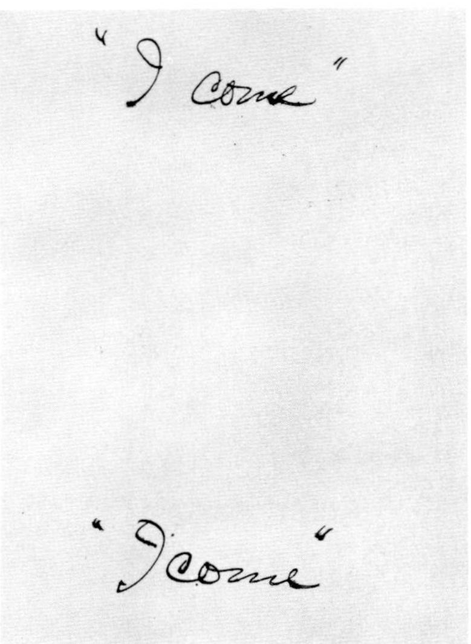
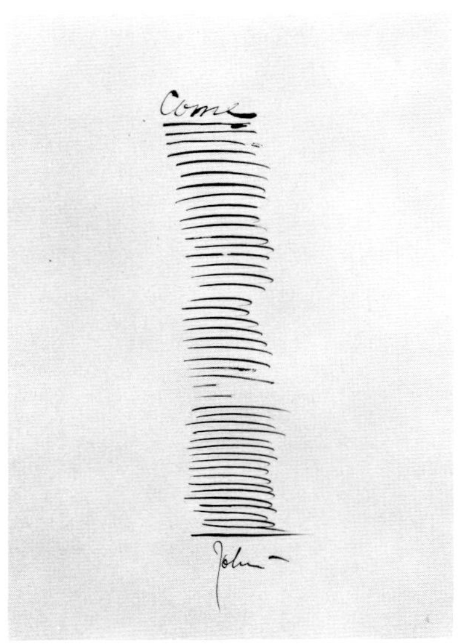

3. Handwritten text of a poem
by John Storrs, c. 1914,
recto and verso, with
accompanying drawing
John Storrs Papers,
Archives of American Art,
Smithsonian Institution,
Washington, D.C.;
Gift of Monique Storrs Booz

1912, when Howard Smith, a young painter in Paris on a scholarship from the School of the Museum of Fine Arts, Boston, was sharing his studio. Casual in pose and naturalistic, Storrs' sculpture of Smith is nevertheless stylistically advanced in its simplification of contour lines and elimination of detail. Storrs is beginning to conceive of his figures in terms of basic geometries. Three interlocking triangles join to form the figure: one articulated in the space from spread feet to groin; an inverted triangle formed by the upper body and cape; and a smaller triangle formed by the head and flat cap.[3] Yet in *Howard E. Smith*, Storrs has still not applied what he was learning from Cubism, for the figure shows no changes in planes or proportions that could not be explained as aspects of realism.

A figure that shows the influence of Rodin in its theme but which also carries the unmistakable stamp of Storrs' developing personal style during this period is the 1915 bronze *Morning* (Fig. 5). This seated nude, a young, nearly androgynous figure who stretches as if awakening, combines the favorite Symbolist themes of the times of day and the phases of life. Clearly, "morning" is made to coincide with adolescence and budding youth. However, the figure sits on a stepped rectangular block, as stiffly upright as a statue of an Egyptian queen on a throne. As with Brancusi, whose bases act as sculptural objects themselves, so the stepped cubic form of the base in *Morning* is a portent of Storrs' geometric sculpture derived from architecture.[4]

It is difficult to trace the precise stylistic development of Storrs' sculpture between 1914 and 1919 because exact dates are not always known and Storrs seems to have tried a number of different approaches at the same time. Nevertheless, it is clear from *Howard E. Smith* and other works that his first formal experiments were for the most part only gentle attempts to "cubify" the human figure. However, a turning point seems to have come about 1915. In September of that year,

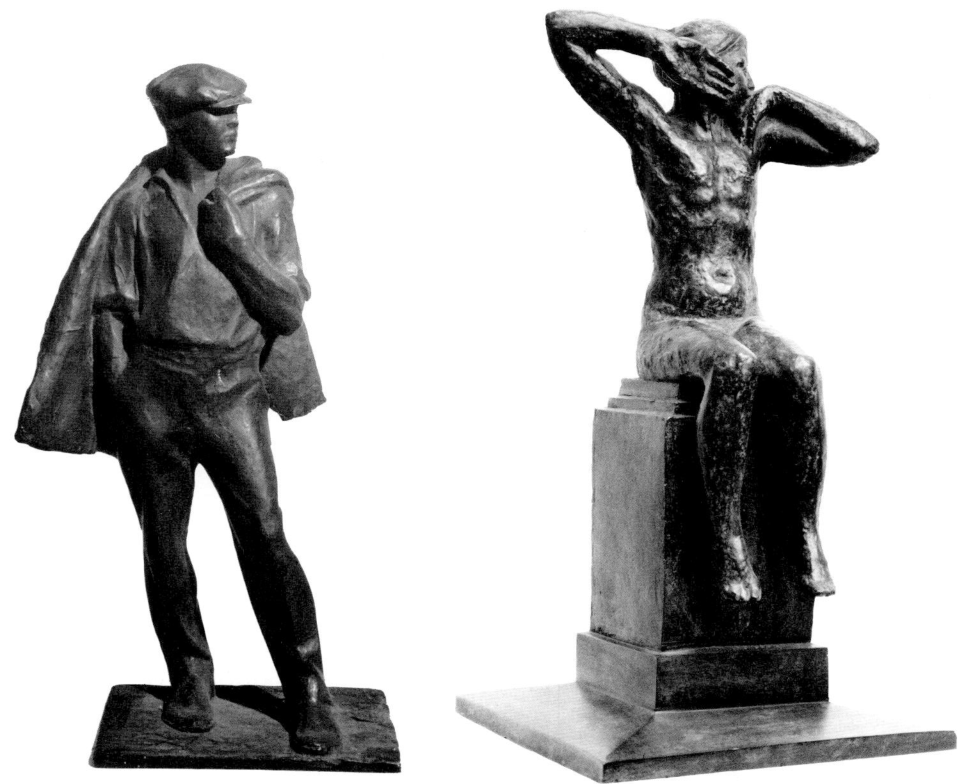

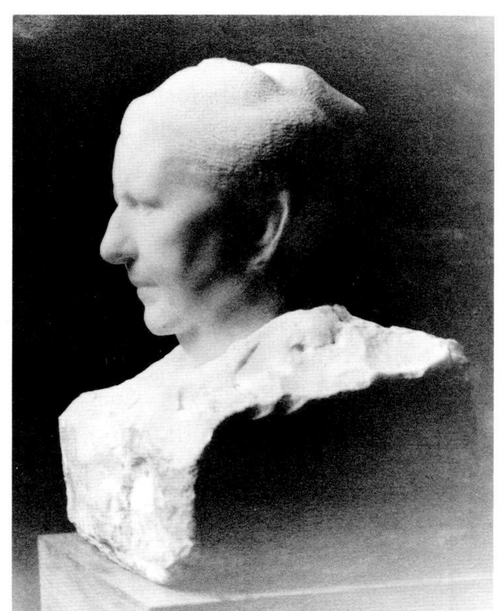

4. *Howard E. Smith*, 1913
Bronze
14½ x 6 x 4½
(36.8 x 15.2 x 11.4)
Private collection

5. *Morning*, 1915
Bronze
16¾ x 8¾ x 9
(42.5 x 22.2 x 22.9)
Estate of Monique Storrs Booz;
courtesy of Robert Schoelkopf
Gallery, Ltd., New York

6. *Portrait of My Mother*, 1913
Marble
14½ x 12¼ x 9¼
(36.8 x 31.1 x 23.5)
Musée, Mer, France

John and Marguerite Storrs returned to the United States for a much
delayed honeymoon trip, and D.W. Storrs took the couple on a three-
month cross-country excursion. They traveled over the Canadian
Rockies to San Francisco, where Storrs' *Portrait of My Mother* (Fig. 6)
was shown at the Panama-Pacific International Exposition,[5] as were
Rodin's work and Futurist sculpture. Exposure to such advanced

19   **Themes of the War**

sculpture as Boccioni's *Development of a Bottle in Space* (now The Museum of Modern Art, New York) may have made Storrs feel that his own marble portrait bust of his mother was rather old-fashioned.

Of equal or greater importance, during this cross-country trip Storrs became intensely interested in American Indian art and began to collect it. His initial curiosity concerning tribal art of all types no doubt predated this trip—his friend Lipchitz collected African sculpture[6] and Storrs had probably visited the African and Oceanic collections of the Musée d'Ethographie du Trocadero in Paris.

Storrs' own collection would eventually encompass Eskimo, African, and Mexican Indian art as well.[7] He responded not only to the formal characteristics of this primitive art, but also to its emotional and religious content. Raised as a Catholic, although his father was Protestant, he felt he was part of a universal religion:

If some one should ask me to what church I belong I should reply in this wise—there were times—when I didn't know what I was—but I was born and now am an active member of the Roman Catholic Church— which accoarding to my ideas of the Catholic faith is as much as to say that I am also very much of an accultist of the Western school—something of a Christian Scientist and Buddhist—in short I am probably a great deal of any and all religions that have to do with the love of God, yourself and your fellow consciousness.[8]

Deeply moved in 1915 by the vastness of the West and its natural wonders, Storrs began to see in all nature, in its basic forms and configurations, a potent symbolism that he applied to the man-made landscape. He sought to express ideas that combined notions of primitive nature worship with Christianity and concepts of pure form in art, while at the same time he perceived certain shapes and even lines as more spiritual than others. In 1915, Storrs wrote:

In America there is too much of the classic and not enough of the Gothic. Too much of the horisontal and not enough of the vertical. To much of the cube & not enough of the piramid. To much of the "box" and not enough of the mountain peak. The Animal in life & all that is low & of the earth. All that is heavy and brutal is well expressed by the horisontal. While the perpindicular in nature is the animal erect. It is the growth towards the sun & the sky. It is the line projected into infinity. . . .[9]

Such spiritual endeavors are not easy to pinpoint in works of art. However, we can say with certainty that beginning in 1915, American Indian art offered Storrs solutions for stylizing, geometrizing, and simplifying the human figure. After 1915, his "young Cubist" or "cubifying" sculptures followed an unpierced, rectangular format, replacing issues of concavity and convexity with a stress on a generalized flattening of planes. Iconographically, most of these works deal with themes that existed in tribal art and were also a heritage from the nineteenth century: the mother and child, war themes, and the winged figure or winged animal.

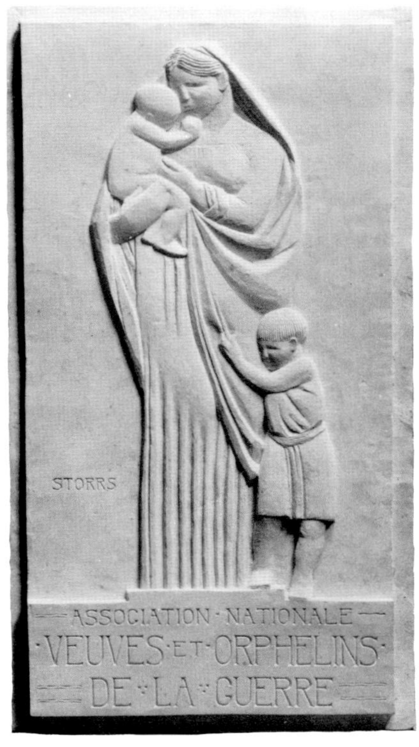

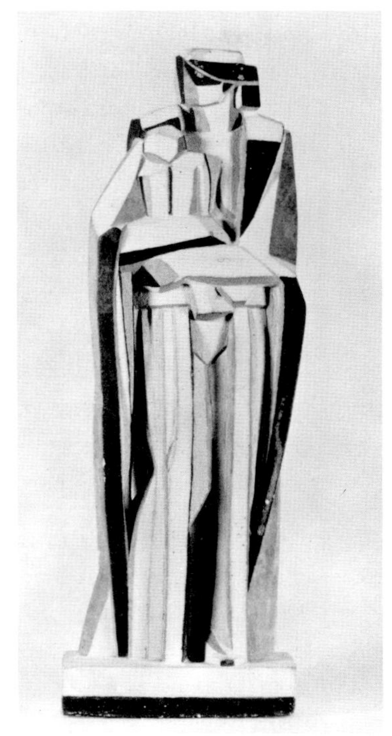

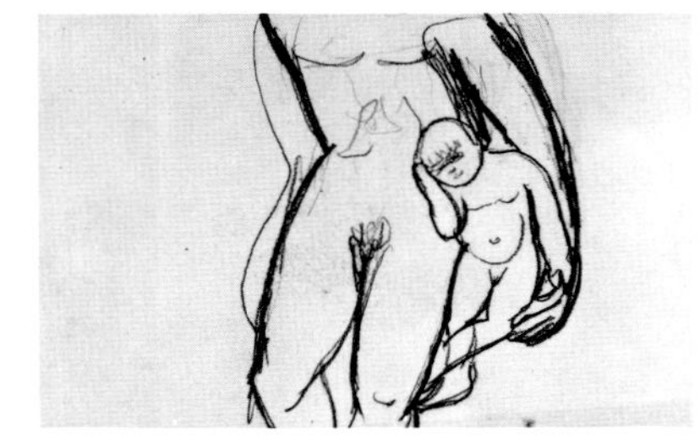

7. Maquette for medal,
*Association Nationale pour
la Protection des Veuves et
Orphelins de la Guerre*, 1915
Clay
Whereabouts unknown

8. *Modern Madonna*, c. 1918
Polychromed terra-cotta
11⅛ x 3¾ x 2⅜
(28.3 x 9.5 x 6)
Collection of Mr. and Mrs.
Alvin S. Lane

9. *Mother and Child*, c. 1918
Pencil on paper
3½ x 5 (8.9 x 12.7)
Archives of American Art,
Smithsonian Institution,
Washington D.C.;
Gift of Monique Storrs Booz

Mother and Child

The exploration of the mother and child theme in Storrs' art of this period seems to have been prompted by the death of his beloved mother in 1913, a commission to design a war medal for the Association Nationale pour la Protection des Veuves et Orphelins de la Guerre, and the birth of his only child, Monique, in 1918.

The Paris-based association for widows and orphans commissioned a medal from Storrs, to be sold in a fund-raising effort. A photograph of the maquette for the medal, which he created in 1915, is all that survives (Fig. 7). The figures in the maquette—based on the age-old theme of Caritas with her children—were two-thirds life-size (as was common in French medallic art from the later nineteenth century, a reducing machine would be used to make the die).[10] In his own words, Storrs aimed for "light, simplicity and grace of the ensemble"; to achieve these effects, he strove for unbroken surfaces and the elimination of intermediate lines because "Today, we of the modern school, try to put light into our thought, our art."[11]

After his daughter was born in 1918, Storrs reworked the traditional mother and child theme in a more formally advanced manner, this time appropriating the type of the Madonna and Child; Storrs referred to these works as his *Modern Madonna* sculptures. They were executed in several sizes and some were polychromed (Fig. 8). Many quick sketches of his wife and child served as studies for these

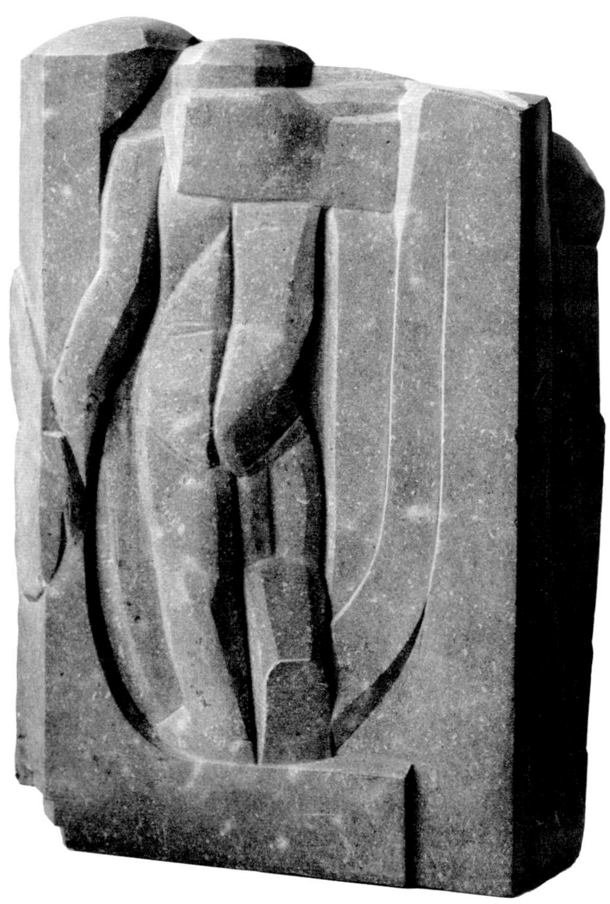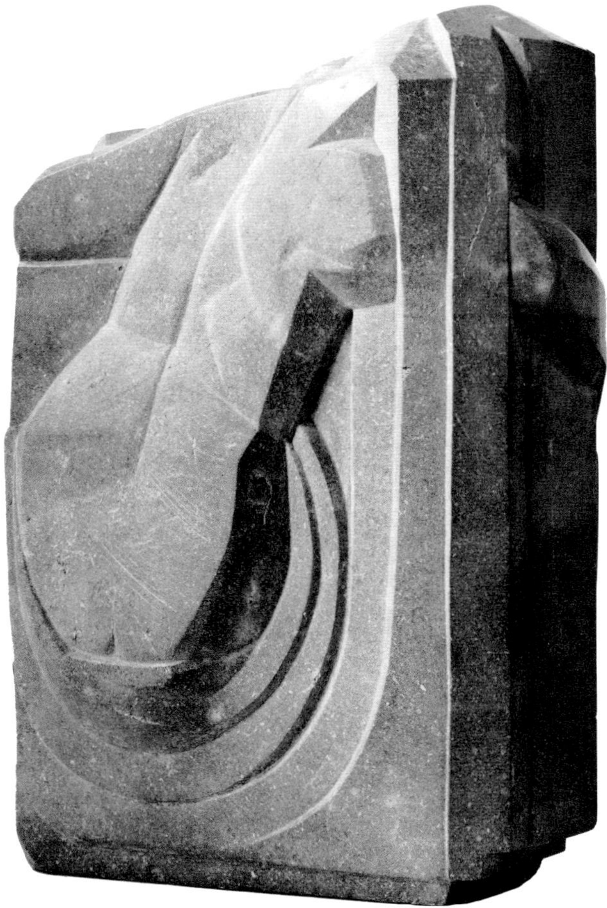

sculptures (Fig. 9). Compared to the woman on the 1915 maquette, the figure of the Madonna has become elongated and altogether more svelte, approximating the boyishly slim figure so popular in this period. But the Madonna's draperies retain the column character of those in the maquette, giving the later figure an architectonic verticality. The Christ Child's head, the arms of the Madonna, and other body parts are planar and angled in a manner not easily reconciled with the human form; rather, Storrs has superimposed a casing of sharp edges and slices.

Figurative Abstraction of c. 1919 (Figs. 10a, 10b) is more complex in the formal relationship of the figures, the mother's embrace creating an actual connecting link to the child. Like Storrs' *Modern Madonna* sculptures, where the Madonna cradles the child in her arms, *Figurative Abstraction* is both architectonic and tender, for the mother's loving gesture encompasses the block of marble. Although the mother's embrace in *Figurative Abstraction* connects the figures, Storrs has separated mother and child spatially—each appears on one side of the block. The viewer is as aware of the solid geometry as of the figures themselves. A recognition of this dual perception may have

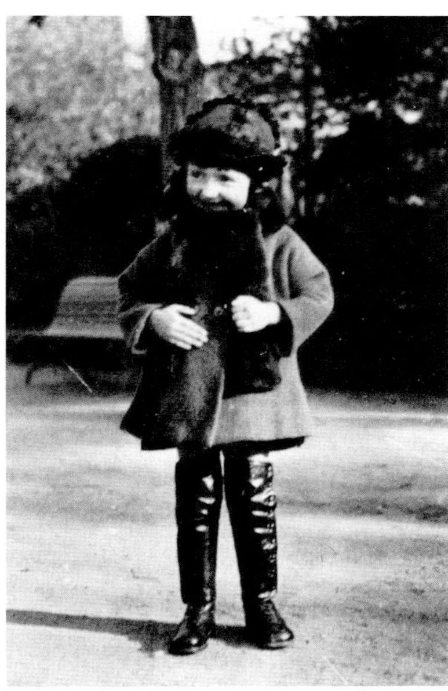

11. Photograph of John Storrs'
daughter, Monique, c. 1922
Estate of Monique Storrs Booz

12. *My Daughter in Winter
Costume*, c. 1922
Stone
17 x 6½ x 5
(43.2 x 16.5 x 12.7)
Collection of John P. Axelrod

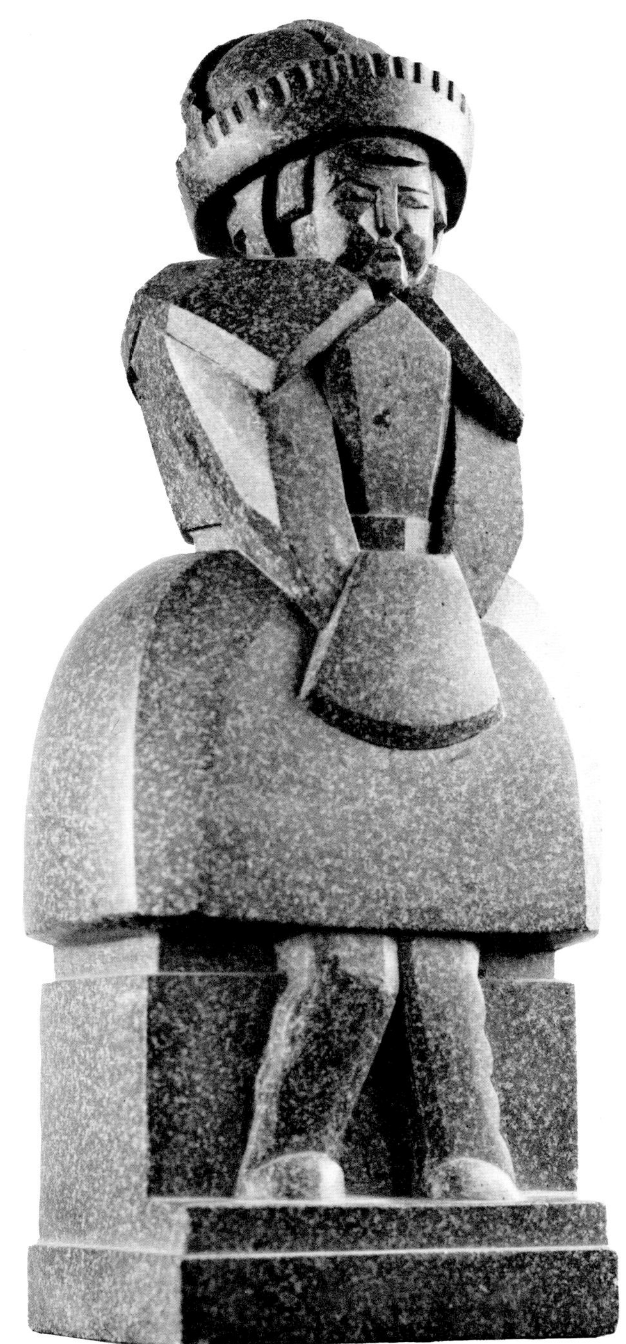

been the true beginning of Storrs' eventual separation of his architectural sculptures from his figurative ones.

On into the 1920s, Storrs continued to dwell on images of his
wife and daughter. One of his most delightful pieces is the black
granite *My Daughter in Winter Costume* (Fig. 12), where the figure of
Monique stands as innocent and frontal as the children depicted in
American folk art paintings by itinerant limners. Monique's costume
is a stylization of the garments she actually wore (Fig. 11)—leggings,
high rounded hat, muff and scarf fixed squarely in front of her.

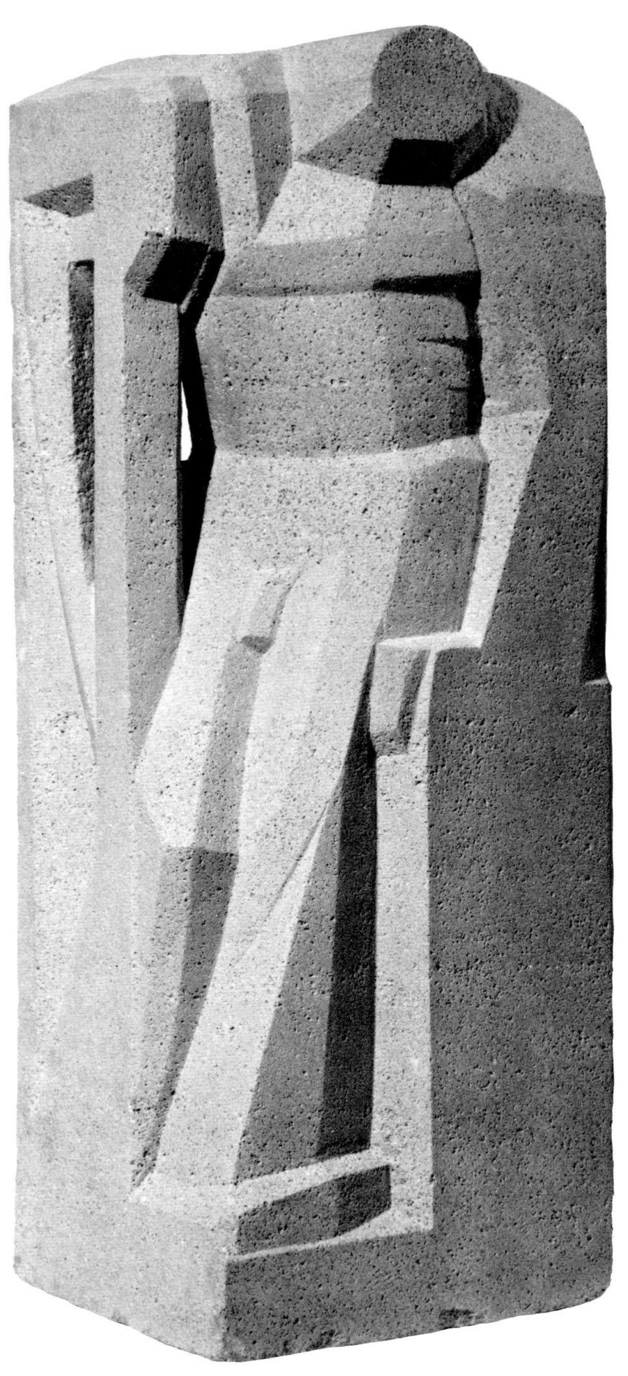

13. *Nude Man*, c. 1919
Stone
30¾ x 10½ x 10½
(78.1 x 26.7 x 26.7)
Des Moines Art Center;
James D. Edmundson Fund

Men at War

Unlike the Futurists, who glorified warfare, John Storrs found little
excitement or dynamism in it. His pantheism and sense of universal
brotherhood, combined with his wartime hospital work in Orléans
made him all the more cognizant of the horrors of war, the weariness,
wounds, and destruction.

Storrs' sculptures dealing with victims of the war relate to his
mother and child sculptures in that they are geometrized, the human
figure divided into angles and planes. The subject matter of the *Nude*

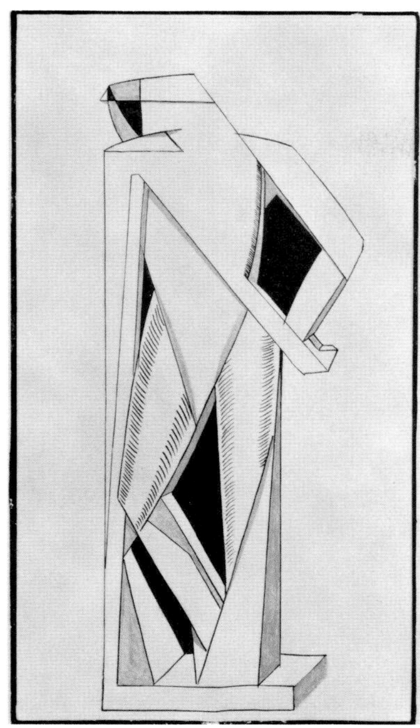

14. *Man with the Crutch*, c. 1919
Ink and watercolor on paper
9¾ x 5¾ (24.8 x 14.6)
Private collection

15. *Man with the Crutch*, c. 1919
Stone
Formerly in
the American Hospital,
Neuilly-sur-Seine, France
Whereabouts unknown

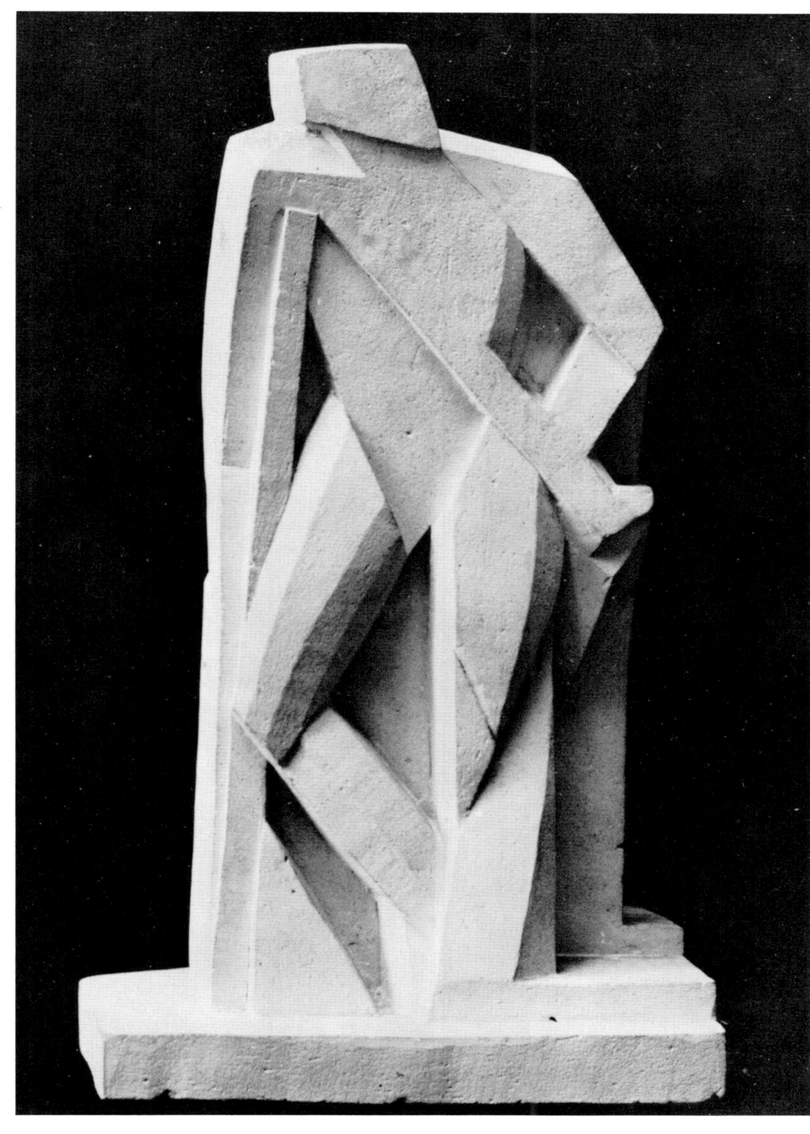

Man (Fig. 13), however, has remained somewhat mysterious. It
relates to a sculpture, now lost, that Storrs created for the American
Hospital in Neuilly called *Man with the Crutch* (Fig. 15).[12] Once
the shape of the crutch is identified, it is clear that the *Nude Man* also
leans on a crutch and does not merely rest on some type of stanchion.
Drawings for the work, one of c. 1919 (Fig. 14), help further clarify
the iconography of Storrs' sculptures of the wounded. A comparison
between the c. 1919 drawing and the sculpture *Man with the Crutch*
shows that in this sculpture Storrs has added a sling for the man's
injured arm, while in *Nude Man*, a crutch is under his right arm and
his left arm helps support his weary body. The sagging body and bent
head of *Nude Man*, a sculpture not intended for a hospital or public
space, also suggest depression.

Still another victim of war, a soldier who supports his weight with
a cane, is shown on a four-sided column (Fig. 16a) of approximately

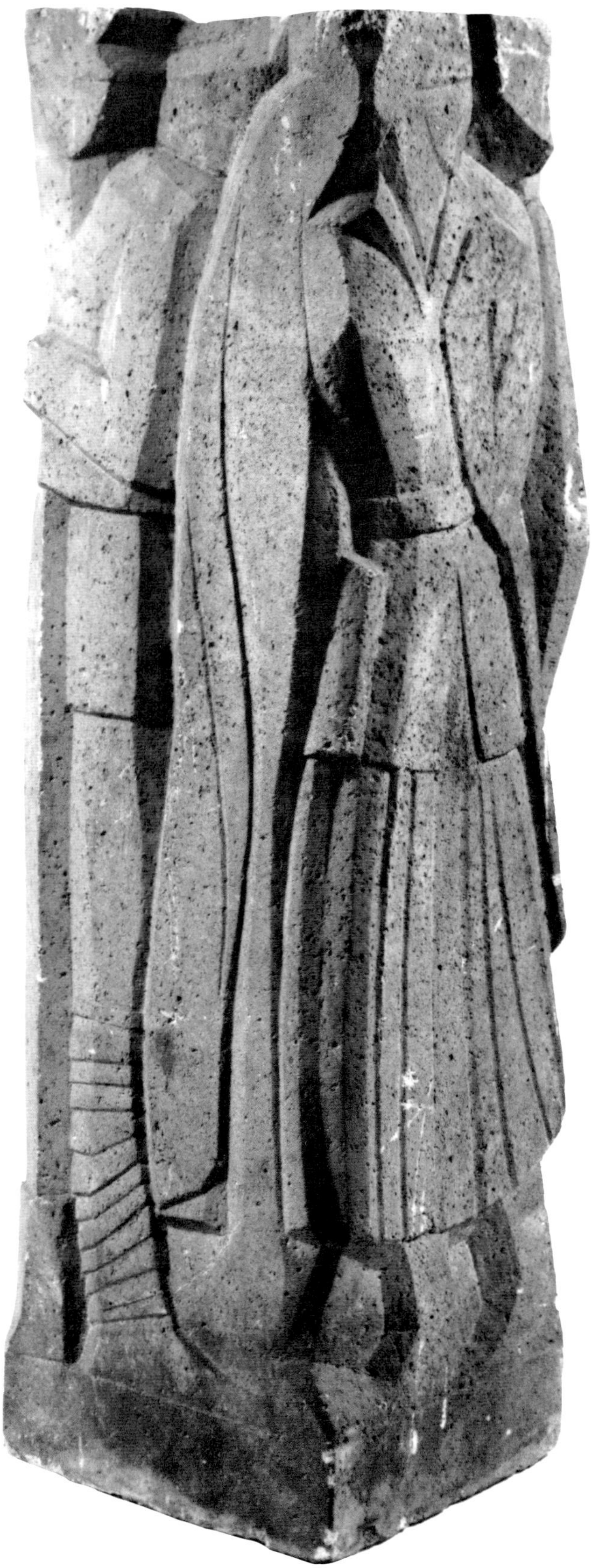

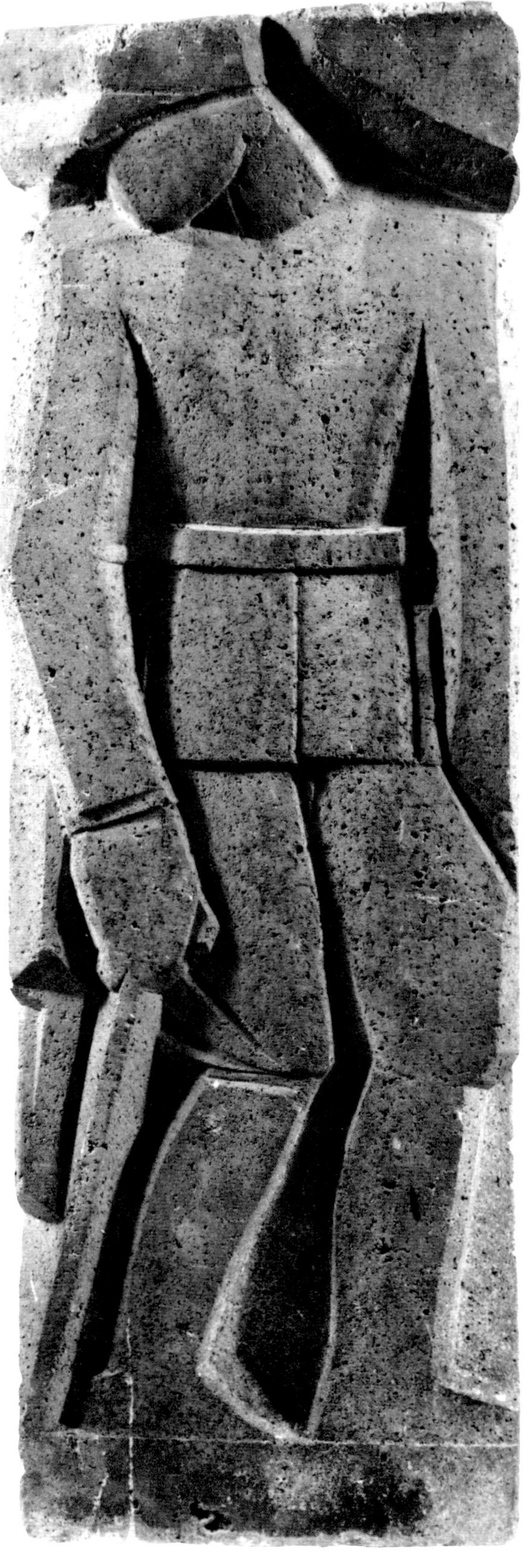

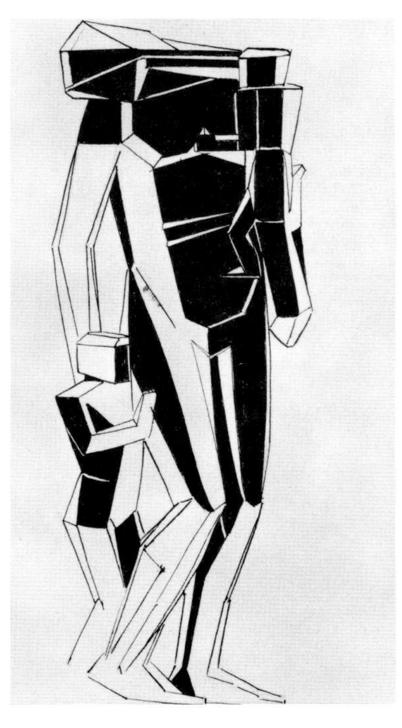

the same period. Another side of the column shows a World War I nurse carrying a crutch, and a second soldier in puttees who leans his tired body on a support (Fig. 16b). The sorrows, desolation, and losses of war are also seen in Storrs' drawing *War Widow* (Fig. 17), where the mother and child theme is transposed into the mourning survivors of a family decimated by war. In his 1918 woodcut *Three Soldiers* (Fig. 20) the men are anonymous, with machine-tooled physiognomies. Like the soldiers depicted by Léger in 1915–16, these comrades-in-arms are robots in the mechanics of war.

Perhaps Storrs' most powerful anti-war graphic is the woodcut *War* (Fig. 2). Early in 1918, Storrs sent a trial proof of *War* to Max Eastman, former editor of *The Masses*, and at that time editor of *The Liberator*, both anti-war publications.[13] In the woodcut, the chief themes Storrs had been dealing with during the war years coalesce. The central image is a huge simulacrum of a sculpture, a giant monument representing the head of a fierce warrior who wears a classicizing helmet. On the base of the "sculpture," and functioning like the predella of an altarpiece, is a further explication of the theme of war: the flags of nations, transformed into shields or medieval banners, are flanked by mourning families. A skeleton stands behind the head of the warrior, and a small winged female figure barely eludes his bony hands. At the bottom right, Storrs included the architectural motifs of an arched wall and steps that suggest an entrance to a medieval fortress. The use of figures of vastly different scales within the same work of art creates a further medievalizing effect. Like a morality tale, *War* is intended to instruct; creativity borne on the wings of inspiration must escape from the mindlessness of war and its deathly clutches.

Storrs' anti-war sympathies were in keeping with his Socialist leanings, and it was chiefly due to the efforts of the charismatic Louise Bryant, John Reed's lover and later his wife, that Storrs' poetry and graphics were published in *The Masses* and *The Liberator*.[14] Bryant had entrée to literary and liberal circles; Storrs sent her his graphics and she attempted to sell them to advance his reputation. Always a champion of his work, Bryant even wanted Storrs to create a sculpture for the square in front of the Winter Palace in Petrograd in celebration of the Russian Revolution, an idea he enthusiastically embraced.[15] The project never went beyond the correspondence stage, but, given his interest in the Russian Revolution, Storrs could scarcely have avoided a knowledge of the art of the Russian Constructivists and, surely, of Tatlin's architectural geometric abstraction, the model for a monument to the Third International. Malevich's Suprematist paintings as well would have deeply attracted him for their formal purity and their spiritual and humanistic content.

Since Storrs had spent most of the war years in Orléans, it is not surprising that he wished to celebrate a famous female warrior-saint, the Maid of Orléans, Joan of Arc. Beginning about 1918, he did many sketches, a print, and several reliefs of the subject; one example of such a relief (Fig. 19) shows an angular, bold figure, dressed in medieval armor. Storrs adopted the costume of St. Joan in Ingres'

18. *Joan of Arc*, c. 1920
Woodcut:
sheet, 7⅞ x 11⅛ (20 x 28.3);
image, 5¹⁄₁₆ x 5¹³⁄₁₆ (12.9 x 14.8)
National Museum of American
Art, Smithsonian Institution,
Washington, D.C.;
Museum Purchase

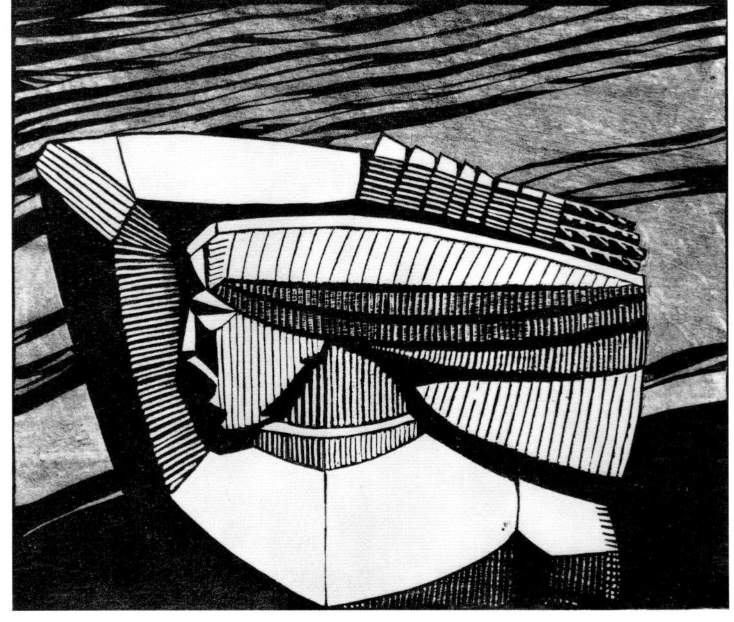

19. *Joan of Arc*, 1919
Terra-cotta with traces of gilding
9¹³⁄₁₆ x 4¼ x 2¼
(24.9 x 10.8 x 5.7)
Allen Memorial Art Museum,
Oberlin College, Ohio;
Friends of Art Fund

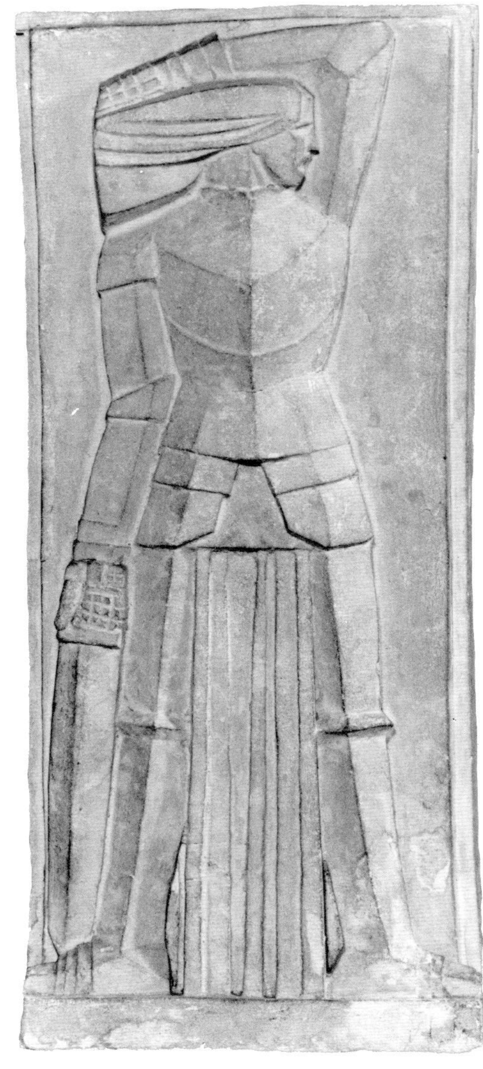

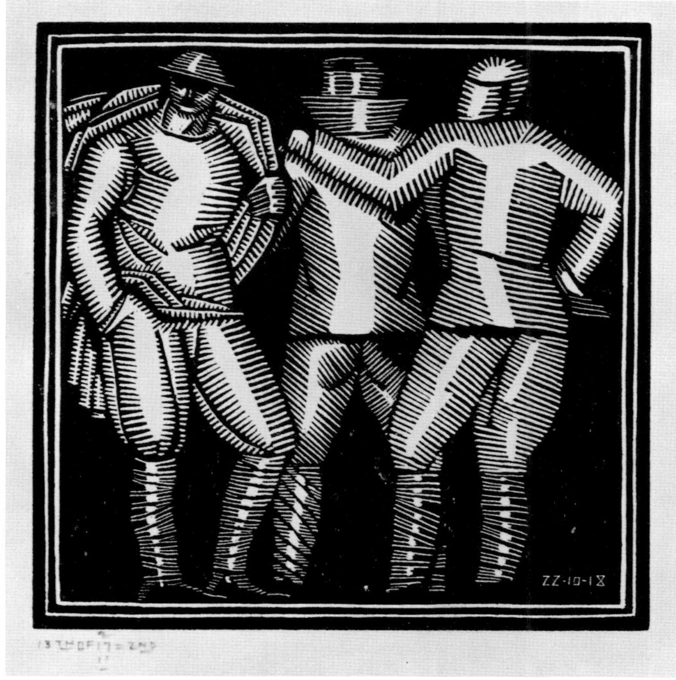

Joan of Arc at the Coronation of Charles VII. A postcard reproduction of that work remains among the John Storrs Papers.[16] Storrs probably had also studied the original painting on one of his many visits to the Louvre.

The terra-cotta relief of *Joan of Arc* reveals a physical gesture that became characteristic in several of Storrs' works; an arm flung back sharply across the top of the head, like a bent wing. A related woodcut of the same period (Fig. 18) repeats this gesture; the striations in the sleeve and glove and the configuration of the hair create a simulacrum of a winged figure.

Winged Figures

As was the case with his images of St. Joan, Storrs associated winged figures with spirituality—but also with freedom, liberation of the soul, the soaring of the creative imagination, and the new technology of flight: "Wings that fly and help one's soul climb to higher worlds grow from the inside out & are not mearly a colection of feathers glued to the back."[17]

Storrs began to treat the theme of the winged figure in his sculpture as early as 1913.[18] One rather traditional, tender example of an early winged figure is a small, grieving plaster angel (Fig. 21), probably dating from 1914.[19] If enlarged, this angel would make a suitable mourning figure for a funerary monument. By contrast, a wood relief of c. 1918 conveys a bold and distinctly archaizing effect (Fig. 22). Here Storrs uses a Gauguinesque earth goddess to signify a creature of

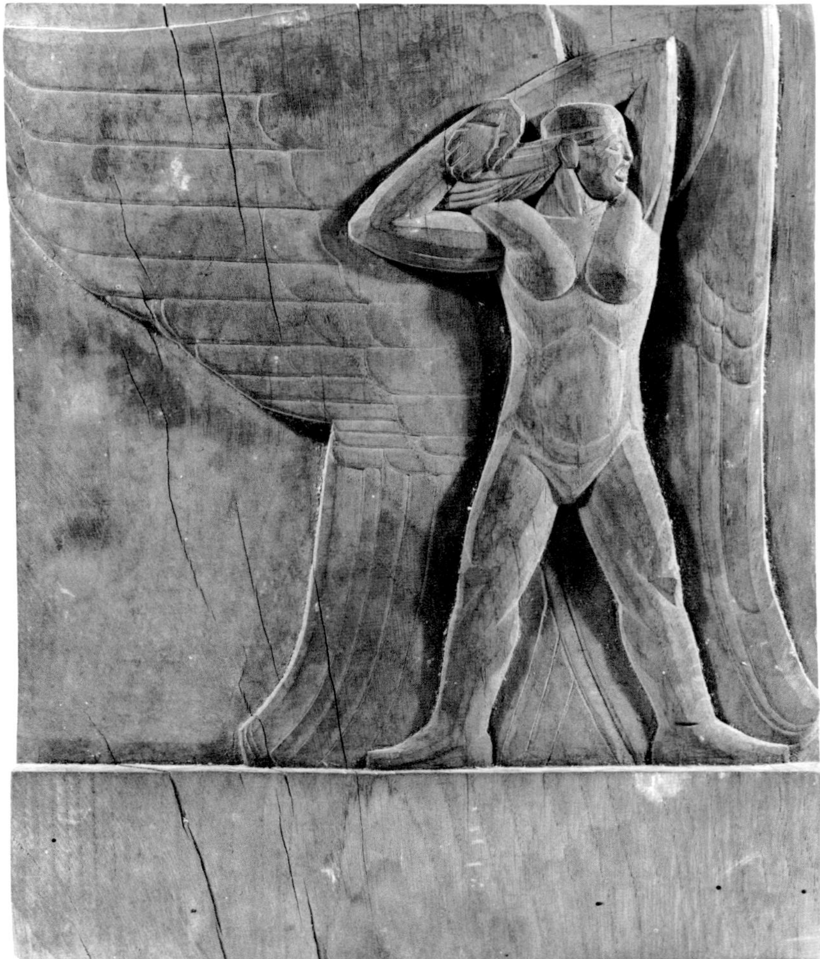

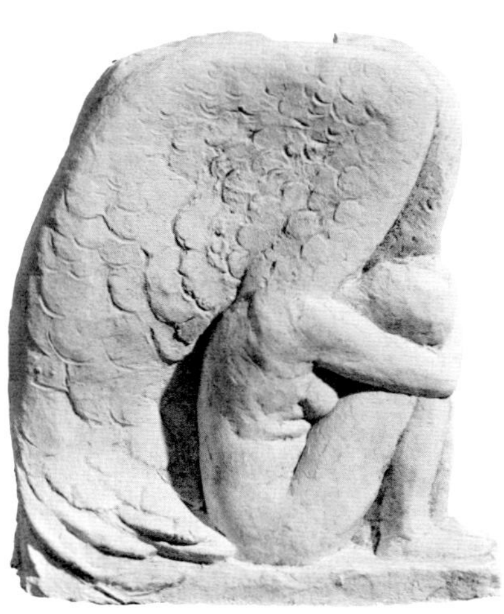

21. *Angel*, c. 1914
Plaster
8 x 7¼ x 2½ (20.3 x 18.4 x 6.4)
Estate of Monique Storrs Booz;
courtesy of Robert Schoelkopf
Gallery, Ltd., New York

22. *Winged Woman*, c. 1918
Wood
14⅛ x 11¼ x 3⅛
(35.9 x 28.6 x 7.9)
Estate of Monique Storrs Booz;
courtesy of Robert Schoelkopf
Gallery, Ltd., New York

the air. Her flung-back arms, echoing the gesture of Storrs' St. Joan, define a wingspan as huge as that of a giant eagle.

In 1920, Storrs' interest in the winged figure was intensified when he received a commission from the Aero Club of France to create sculpture for a monument to commemorate Wilbur Wright's early trial flights in Europe. The granite monument was originally erected in 1922 near the military Camp d'Auvours in Le Mans and is now in that city on the Avenue Léon Bollée.[20] Storrs' relief celebrates the exploits of a fellow American by using an emblematic American eagle (Fig. 23), yet one that bears a family resemblance to Egyptian falcons or Southwest Indian thunderbirds.

Storrs also chose the image of a winged horse and rider to honor one of his heroes, Walt Whitman. It was an idea that had been long developing. In Paris on May 31, 1919, Storrs attended a centennial celebration of Whitman's birth that included a reading of his poems and musical selections from Bach, Beethoven, and Handel. As early as 1914, Storrs had done a study for the head of Whitman and now he became totally committed to honoring the poet in some way.[21]

In a draft letter to Horace Traubel, Whitman's biographer and

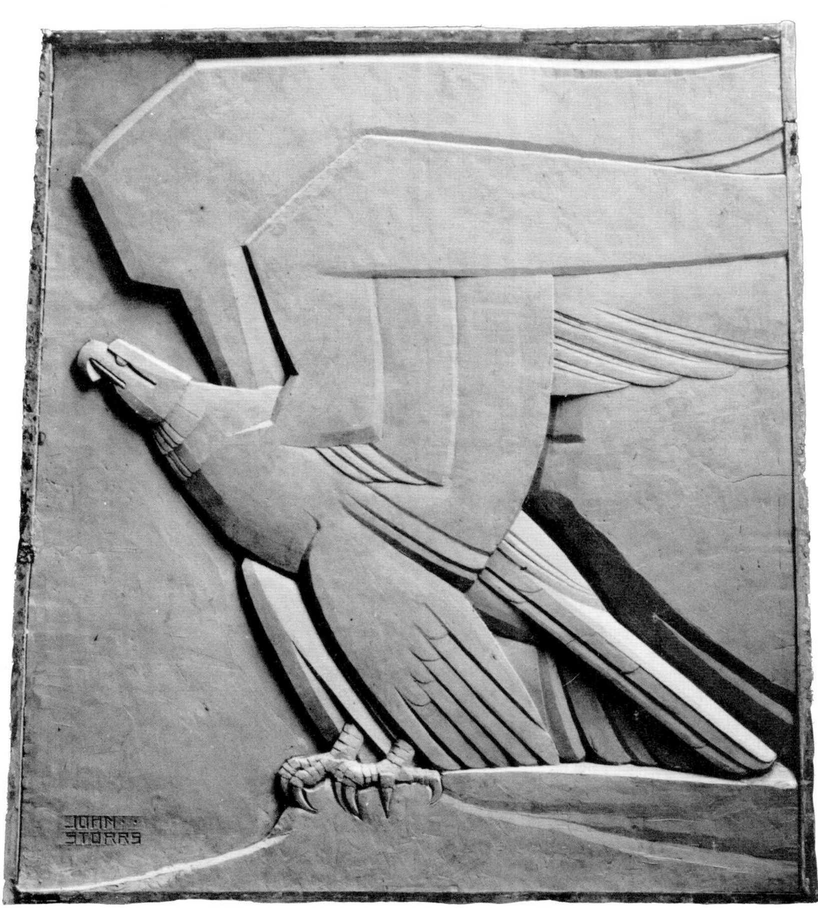

23. *Model for Monument to
Wilbur Wright*, c. 1918
Plaster
46 x 38¾ x 2
(116.8 x 98.4 x 5.1)
Musée Régional, Arts et
Traditions de l'Orléanais, Château
Dunois, Beaugency, France

close friend, Storrs wrote that he wished to create "a sincere and a complete expression of the soul of our United States. . . . Aside from a few of our designers of bridges, grain elevators, steel mills etc. Walt Whitman stands practically alone as one who has discovered a national soul and has given it expression in a form that can be called beautiful —that can be called art."[22] What Storrs had in mind to honor Whitman was not merely a small bronze sculpture but a monumental ensemble. Although such a monument was never commissioned, several bronzes and a plaster version of the model for the monument survive.[23] As one bronze version entitled *Winged Horse* reveals (Fig. 24), Storrs has fused horse and rider in the unfurled wings of Pegasus, which also form the backward flowing tresses of the rider.

In his diary, Storrs noted the lines from Whitman's poem "Song of Myself," which inspired this model: "Form complete is / worthier far— / The female equally / to the male I sing— / Of life immense in Passion, pulse / and power, / The modern man / I sing—."[24]

Storrs had earlier experimented with both a male and a female rider for Pegasus. A 1917 woodcut with a male rider was used on the front cover of the October 1918 issue of *The Liberator*. Printed in an

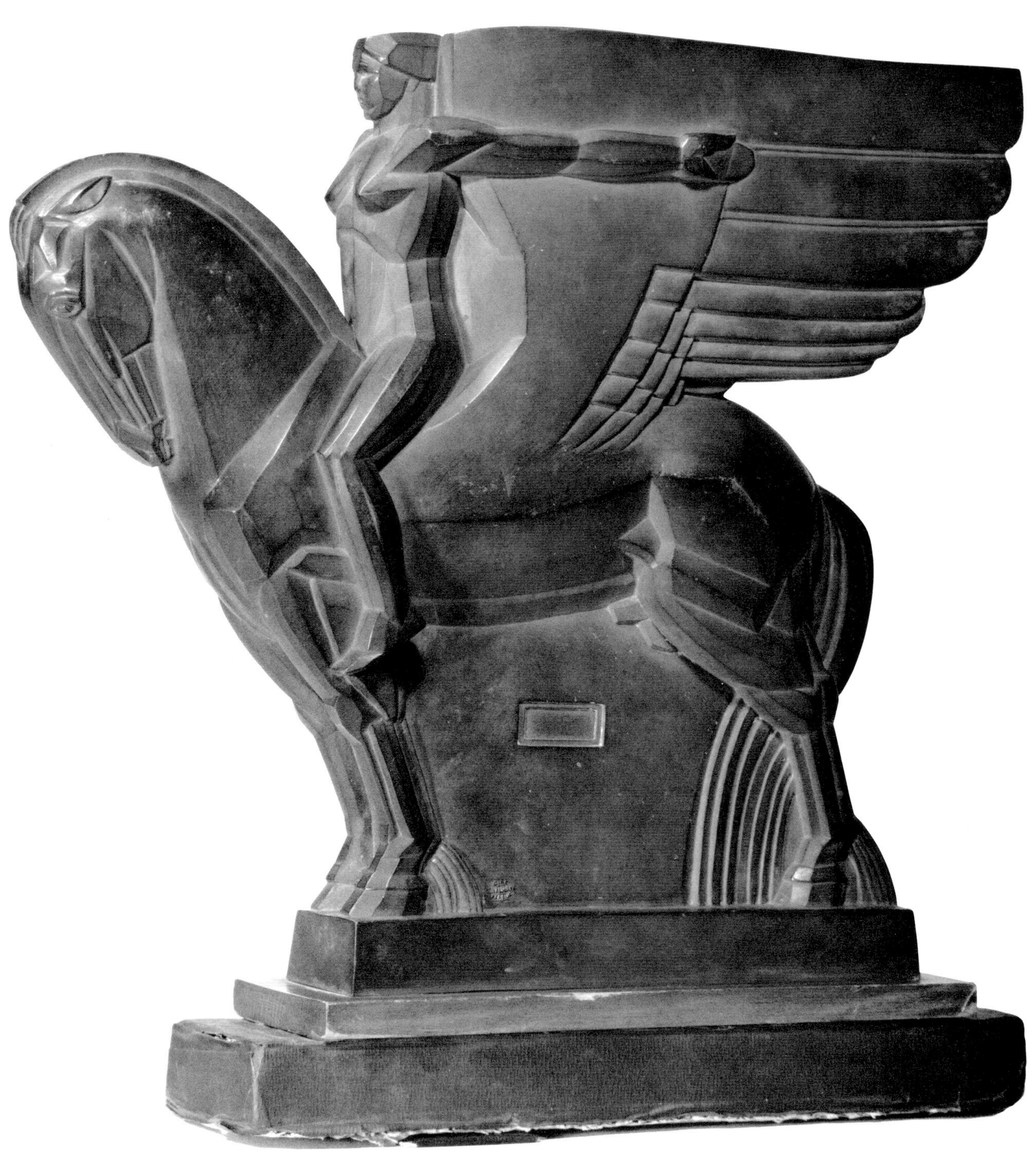

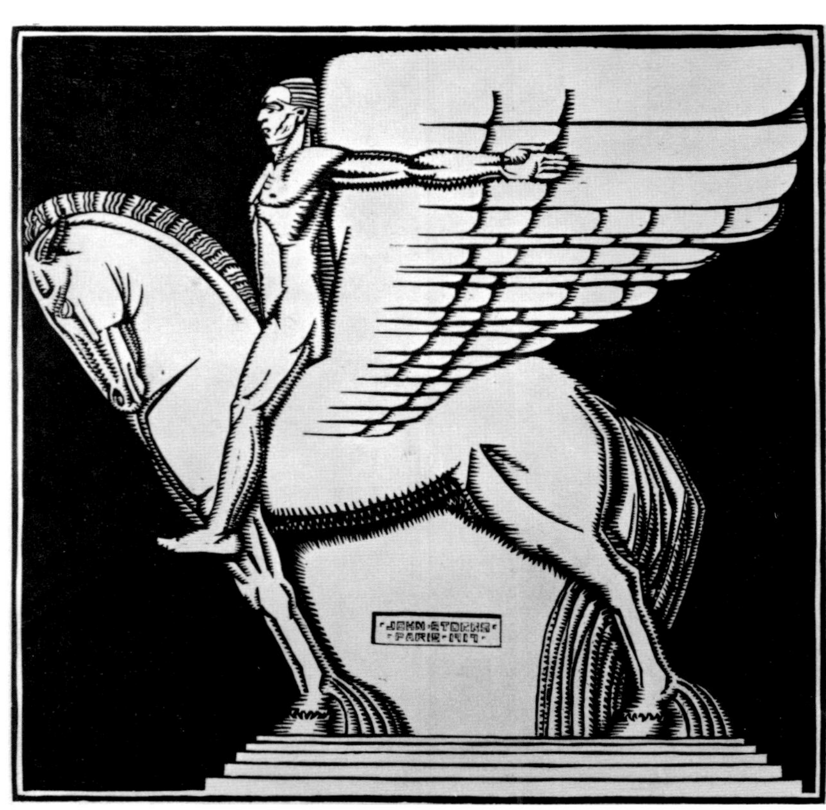

24. *Winged Horse*, c. 1919
Bronze
13¼ x 15 x 2½
(33.7 x 38.1 x 6.4)
The Art Institute of Chicago;
Friends of American Art
Collection

25. *Spirit of Walt Whitman*,
1917
Woodcut:
sheet, 15¾ x 11 (40 x 27.9);
image, 9¹⁄₁₆ x 8³⁄₁₆ (23 x 20.8)
University Art Museum,
The University of New Mexico,
Albuquerque

edition of thirty-seven, this woodcut (Fig. 25) was later used to advertise another Whitman project that Storrs was involved in, a deluxe edition of *Song of Myself* scheduled for publication in 1921 by the Paris publishers Les Muses Français. It was to have included seventeen woodcuts by Storrs,[25] but neither he nor the publisher were able to raise sufficient advance subscriptions, and the project failed.[26]

No doubt related to Storrs' work on the winged horse and rider, the bronze *Horses' Heads* of 1917–19 (Fig. 26) was most likely done with a Walt Whitman monument in mind. *Horses' Heads* carries the stamp of Valsuani, the foundry responsible for casting Storrs' bronzes when he worked in France in the lost wax process. The horses' heads seem based on Greek models of the early Severe style of the first half of the fifth century B.C.[27] However, they have been simplified, stylized, and mechanized in the Art Deco mode so that, like dual pistons, they approximate "horse power."

It is not really clear why Storrs was unable to launch his project for a monumental sculpture to honor Walt Whitman. Yet, never one to give up on an idea easily, he persisted in trying to use the winged horse and rider as the central image in a monumental ensemble that would honor some major figure whom he admired. Thus in the early 1920s, he submitted a proposal for a similar monument to be erected outside the new Field Museum of Natural History in Chicago, which opened to the public in 1923. In 1922, the museum was considering erecting a memorial to Theodore Roosevelt outside the museum by the lakeside. Roosevelt, like Whitman, was one of Storrs' heroes. In

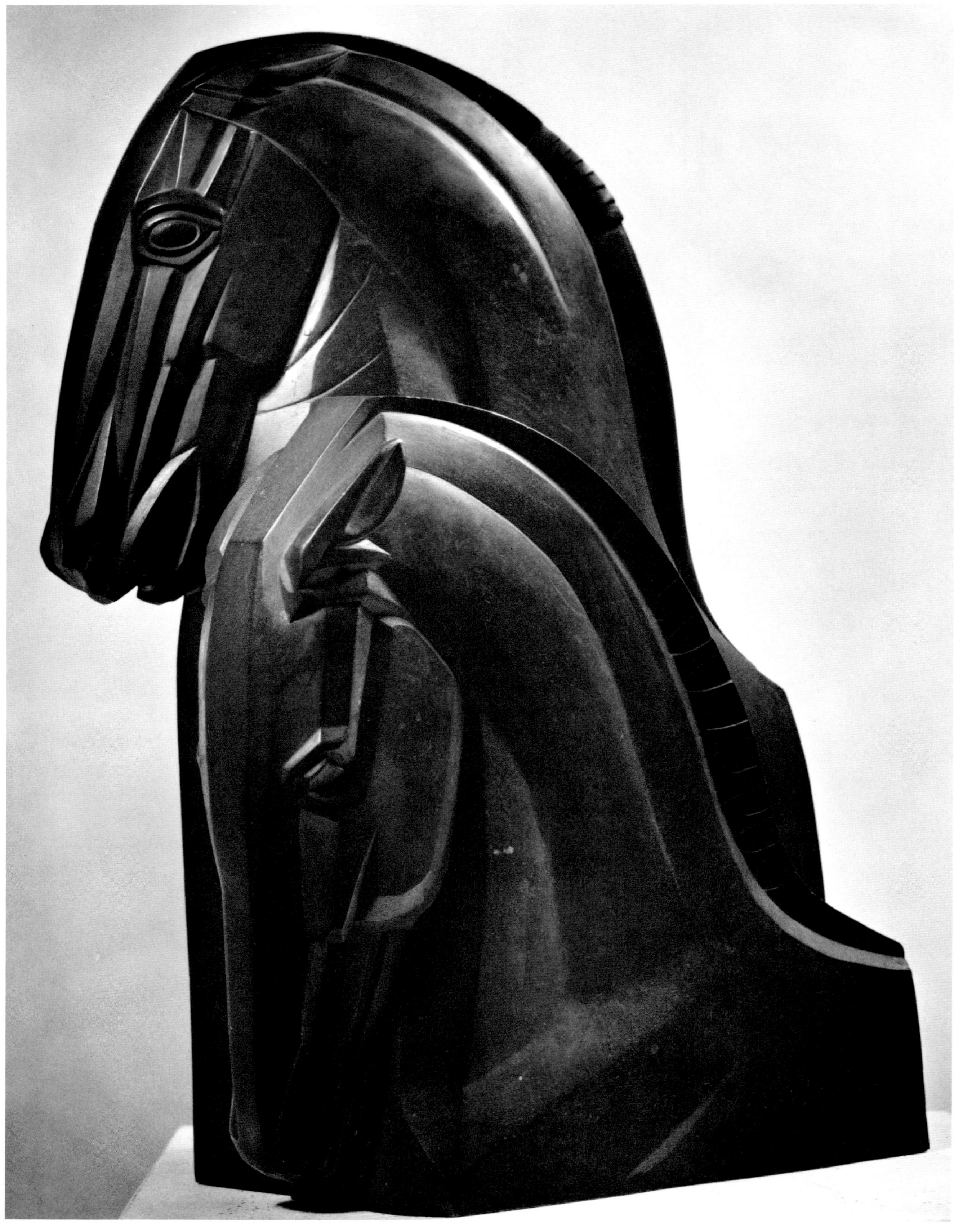

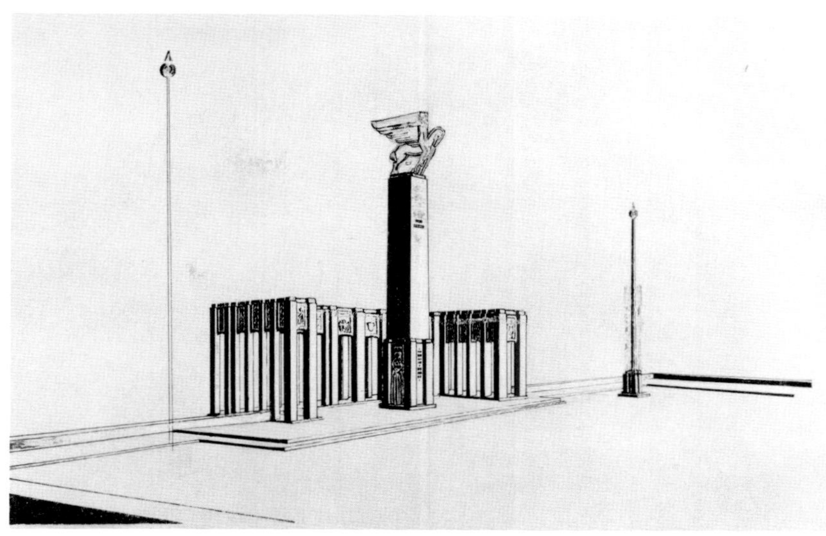

26. *Horses' Heads*, 1917–19
Bronze
13½ x 9 x 4½
(34.3 x 22.9 x 11.4)
The Corcoran Gallery of Art,
Washington, D.C.;
Bequest of George Biddle

27. *Study for a Monument to
Theodore Roosevelt*, c. 1922
Ink and watercolor
9½ x 12 (24.1 x 30.5)
Whitney Museum of
American Art, New York;
Gift of an anonymous donor
76.27

1916, he had written admiring letters to Roosevelt and received replies.[28] Storrs' proposal was for a winged horse and rider placed on a high pedestal, but the committee in charge of the project could not decide between a monument or a colonnade. Storrs wrote to Howard Shaw, the architect in charge of the monument, suggesting that the two ideas be fused—that a winged horse and rider on a shaft be combined with a colonnade. Storrs forwarded several sketches to Shaw in which horse, shaft, and colonnade were combined (Fig. 27). However, this project, too, failed at the level of committee discussions.

One of the most important contemporary sources that influenced Storrs in the creation of his winged figures, birds, and winged animals were Antoine Bourdelle's fresco decorations of similar subjects for the atrium of the Théâtre des Champs-Elysées, a rich thematic and stylistic font for much Art Deco sculpture. Storrs visited the theater at least once, in December 1918, when he "had a good look at the fescos of Bourdell. I felt more than recompensed for the hours of sunshine I was oblidged to sacrifice."[29] Bourdelle had originally intended these works to be bas-reliefs rather than frescoes, but he decided the light was not good for sculpture.[30] Storrs could well have seen Bourdelle's *The Muse and Pegasus* as a fresco in the theater and as a relief in Bourdelle's studio. We also know that Storrs was familiar with Jacob Epstein's 1912 *Tomb of Oscar Wilde* in the Père Lachaise Cemetery, where Storrs' mother was buried.[31] Epstein's primitivizing relief figure, with its face and large headpiece fronting a long winged slab, resulted from his own interest in Egyptian, Assyrian, and Indian art.[32]

In all the themes Storrs dealt with in depth during the war years —the mother and child, men at war, and winged figures—the emotional and spiritual content was built into the subject matter. Storrs avoided the sentimentality often associated with such subjects by using the formal restraints of geometry and by turning to tribal, ancient, and medieval sources, as well as to examples by modern sculptors that confronted such themes with honesty and vigor.

35 Themes of the War

Notes

1. Marc Debrol, *La Route Choisie* (Paris: P. Lethielleux, 1909); one copy is in the estate of Monique Storrs Booz.

2. According to Monique Storrs Booz, this is the single marble by Storrs that we can be certain he carved himself.

3. The insistent geometries, the short cape, flat cap, and also the contrapposto pose in *Howard E. Smith* reappear in Storrs' sculptures of French policemen of the early 1920s (pp. 52–54).

4. Patterson Sims first discussed with me the abstract, geometric elements in Storrs' more conservative works and thus their links to his geometric sculptures. Rodin's marble *Morning* (National Gallery of Art, Washington, D.C.) shows a young girl kneeling, her arms upraised. However, unlike Storrs' *Morning*, the Rodin sculpture is all curves, from the sensuous waved long hair, to a prominently displayed bustline, right down to the swelling block of marble from which she arises.

5. Storrs may also have had a pen-and-ink drawing exhibited in this show; see John Dunlap, sales manager, Panama-Pacific International Exposition 1915, to John Storrs, April 10, 1916, AAA, JSP, 4, Correspondence 1916, where Dunlap writes that he received Storrs' note and will return the pen-and-ink drawing to Storrs and the marble bust care of Mr. Carpenter at the Art Institute (of Chicago). There is no indication in the John Storrs Papers that Storrs helped install or oversee the installation of Rodin's works at this exhibition, a story often repeated but probably apocryphal.

6. Alan G. Wilkinson, "Paris and London: Modigliani, Lipchitz, Epstein, and Gaudier-Brzeska," in William Rubin, ed., *"Primitivism" in 20th Century Art: Affinity of the Tribal and the Modern*, exhibition catalogue, 2 vols. (New York: The Museum of Modern Art, 1984) II, pp. 417–50, makes it clear by drawing from Lipchitz's own writings that Lipchitz began to collect African tribal art in 1909.

7. Storrs had in his collection a number of nineteenth-century Navaho rugs and baskets, probably Mimbres or Papago, and an ivory tusk, possibly African or Eskimo. He also owned a black stone sculpture, a multifigural composition, possibly from the Pacific Northwest, and a number of small objects that appear to be of Mexican Indian origin. Thoroughout his life,

Storrs visited museums where primitive art was exhibited. In 1923, when he (temporarily) decided never to return to Chicago, he wrote to his wife that he only regretted leaving "Mac [his sister Mary] and the children and the American Indian collections in the Field Museum"; undated letter, postmarked Chicago, May 21, 1923, AAA, JSP, 5, John & Marguerite Storrs correspondence, 1923 (2nd folder thus marked). In one of Storrs' last letters to his daughter, 12/9/55, AAA, JSP, 6, Monique Storrs correspondence, he mentions among his possessions of real value "a series of drawings by three Indian chiefs that are *unique* in the history of the Indian wars . . ." and "my collection of Indian *rugs, blankets & objects* in *wood, slate, bone* etc." At that late date, Storrs even arranged to have some of his Indian blankets shipped from Chicago to Marseilles.

8. Entry, 9/8/17, AAA, JSP, 1, Diary 1916, 1918 (diary contains entries from 1916, 1917, and 1918).

9. Partial entry, 9/8/15, AAA, JSP, 1, Diary 1914–1916.

10. For the size of the maquette, see "American Sculptor Chosen to Design French War Medal," *Buffalo Express*, April 26, [1915]; see Chap. I, n. 17, above.

11. Ibid.

12. "Portrait Sculpture by John Storrs," *Vanity Fair*, 16 (March 1921), p. 32, reproduces *Man with the Crutch* and calls it simply *Soldier*. The caption states that the statue was almost two-thirds life-size and was done for the American Hospital at Neuilly. It was not possible to locate this sculpture either at the American Hospital, Neuilly-sur-Seine, or at the former site of the American Hospital, the Lycée Pasteur on the Boulevard Inkermann in Neuilly.

13. A small book kept by John Storrs, "Etching and Poems sent out," AAA, JSP, 9, Financial records and ledgers, notes that a sample proof was sent to Max Eastman on 3/1/18.

14. Storrs' poem "Music" appeared in *The Liberator*, 1 (April 1918), p. 11. His woodcut *Spirit of Walt Whitman* (Fig. 25) was on the front cover of *The Liberator*, 1 (October 1918), while *Winter* was used by the journal to solicit Christmas gift subscriptions for December 1918; one example of the latter follows the letter of Louise

Bryant to John Storrs, December 14, 1918, AAA, JSP, 4, Correspondence 1918. This same woodcut was used to illustrate Émile Verhaeren's poem "Une Heure Mauvaise," *Feuillets d'Art*, 4, pp. 15–16, ill. p. 15; one copy, AAA, JSP, 10, filed separately. Louise Bryant's crucial role in placing Storrs' graphics with *Playboy*, *The Liberator*, and *The Masses* is revealed in her several letters to John and Marguerite Storrs, AAA, JSP, 4, Correspondence 1917 and Correspondence 1918.

15. Draft letter from John Storrs to "dear friends" (Louise Bryant and John Reed), undated, AAA, JSP, 4, Correspondence 1917; this in response to Louise Bryant's letter to John and Marguerite Storrs, September 24, 1917, from Petrograd, Russia, AAA, JSP, 4, Correspondence 1917, in which she proposes the idea of a monument.

16. AAA, JSP, 6, Commission File, Statue de Jeanne d'Arc (Orléans, France).

17. Entry in small blue book, AAA, JSP, 2, Writings (undated).

18. The earliest sculpture thus far located dealing with a winged figure is a plaster relief of a winged man, dated and marked 4/11/13 II, from the estate of Monique Storrs Booz. This coincides with Storrs' listing, AAA, Downtown Gallery Papers, "A Catalogue of the Works of John Storrs, 1915," microfilm no. 70, frames 567–587, of an "Homme Aile" of the same date, with the notation "Two copies in plaster & Terre seche." The dimensions of the existing plaster, 8 x 7½ x 2½ inches, in general coincide with Storrs' given dimensions of "22 x 18" (centimeters).

19. Ibid., Storrs lists "1/8/14. Ange. Terre Seche. Trois copies en platre." This angel, although undated, is stylistically related to the sculpture Storrs created under the influence of Rodin. No dimensions are given for this sculpture in the listing.

20. The Wilbur Wright Monument has been relocated to the front of the Securité Sociale building on the Avenue Léon Bollée in Le Mans. Originally, it was located at the juncture of two roads near the Camp d'Auvours, but in 1979 was displaced by the road administration during road work and lay in a nearby ditch for about a year. It was due to the efforts of Henri Delgove, the last surviving witness to Wilbur Wright's first European trial

flight in 1908, that the monument was saved. The present site would still be a mystery were it not for the gracious assistance of Commandant Provendier, Sergent Jaime Ramsay, and the Second Marine Regiment of the Ninth Marne Division at the Camp d'Auvours.

21. For the program on Whitman that Storrs attended, see "les Fêtes du Peuple," AAA, JSP, 10, Memorabilia. Storrs' early sculpture of Whitman is listed in AAA, Downtown Gallery Papers, "A Catalogue of the Works of John Storrs, 1915," which records, "24/5/14—Study for Head of Whitman. Terre Cuite. 19 c." Thus far the work is unlocated.

22. Draft letter to "My dear Mr. Traubel," undated, AAA, JSP, 4, Fragments of letters. Storrs writes to Traubel that he had had in mind a monument to Whitman since his student days in Philadelphia and that he is writing to Traubel because of the latter's association with Whitman. Traubel was the author of *With Walt Whitman in Camden.*

23. Storrs sometimes did bronzes in varying sizes. A listing of his sculptures, AAA, JSP, 8, Lists of sculptures, drawings, prints & paintings, shows that in the case of the *Winged Horse* (Fig. 24), he set three different prices for what he termed the "original," the "copy," and the "reduction." It should be stressed that all three sizes are what we would call originals, and perhaps Storrs should have used the term "initial" to indicate the first effort at casting. Storrs does seem to have made *Winged Horse* in all three sizes, for the version in the collection of the Art Institute of Chicago is 13¾ inches high; a plaster version 12½ inches high is in the Robert Schoelkopf Gallery, New York (it was probably cast in bronze but the bronze of this size has not been located); and another bronze (for which there exists more than one cast in this size) measures 11½ inches high and is in a private collection.

24. AAA, JSP, 1, Diary 1929, a small book of sayings and poems that actually dates from 1918–20. This particular quote from Whitman's poem is undated. See also a shortened version of this same quotation in AAA, JSP, 1, Biography & Chronology, in an unsigned letter to "Dear Sir," December 20, 1921. This letter was probably written by Marguerite Storrs and has corrections in John Storrs' handwriting. It appears to be a reply to an inquiry concerning Storrs' *Winged Horse* (Fig. 24). The letter states that the sculpture could be made available in the same size, in a one-third smaller size, and in bronze or terra-cotta.

25. Two woodcuts that can be identified as having been created for this ill-fated edition are *Reclining Figure Under a Tree*, perhaps representing the poet as dreamer, and *Family*, whose trinity reflects Storrs' own family. These woodcuts are reproduced without titles but identified as created for "a monumental edition of Whitman's poems, shortly to be published in Paris by a French publisher" in Charles Belmont Davis, "The Roulette Wheel of Literature," *Vanity Fair*, 16 (April 1921), p. 61.

26. A copy of the 1921 brochure advertising the deluxe edition of *Song of Myself* under the imprimatur of Les Muses Français, Paris, is in AAA, JSP, 9, filed separately. The brochure contains a subscription blank that says subscriptions in America may be sent to Egmont H. Arens, The Washington Square Bookshop, 27 West 8th Street, New York City. It cannot be ascertained why sufficient advance subscriptions could not be obtained in France, but Egmont Arens, in an undated letter to John Storrs, AAA, JSP, 4, Correspondence 1920, writes that he thinks it unwise to count on selling more than one hundred copies in America because "Americans buy what it is fashionable to buy, and the fashion for special de lux editions has not yet been set. The collectors of Whitmania, and those who use individual discrimination in the selection of their libraries form a comparatively small group."

27. Storrs cast one of the two horses' heads individually, and this single bronze horse's head is in a private collection. These heads are reminiscent of the horses' heads from the chariot team of Oenomaus from the east pediment of the Temple of Zeus at Olympia; see Bernard Ashmole, *Architect & Sculptor in Classical Greece* (New York: New York University Press, 1972), p. 41, ill. 45.

28. The correspondence between John Storrs and Theodore Roosevelt is in AAA, JSP, 4, Correspondence 1916. Chiefly, these letters reveal Storrs' admiration for Roosevelt and Roosevelt's polite replies.

29. Draft letter from John Storrs to his wife, undated, postmarked Paris, 16 (or 18)/12/18, AAA, JSP, 5, John & Marguerite Storrs correspondence, 1912–1919.

30. With thanks to Rhodia Dufet Bourdelle for her time and for clarifying her father's work on these frescoes; also for recommending a most useful book, Denis Basdevant, *Bourdelle et le Théâtre des Champs-Elysées* (Paris: Chêne Hachette, 1982).

31. Draft letter in Storrs' handwriting to "Dear Mr. Pond" (Ezra Pound), AAA, JSP. As of 1983, this material had recently been given to the Archives of American Art by Monique Storrs Booz and was temporarily catalogued as "Correspondence—undated —1951." The context of the letter dates it around 1918; it reads in part, "Epstein is another man who is *getting away*—I know his monument to Wile—I like it *direction* but not altogether the result—its archectural tritment could not be better—But I have had no opportunity whatever to see any of his other things. His mother & child—sun god—every thing in fact—I desire very much to know some day—But if it is possible to procure photos of all these works—I would be most interrsted."

32. For Epstein, see Wilkinson, "Paris and London: Modigliani, Lipchitz, Epstein, and Gaudier-Brzeska," in *"Primitivism" in 20th Century Art*, II, pp. 417–50.

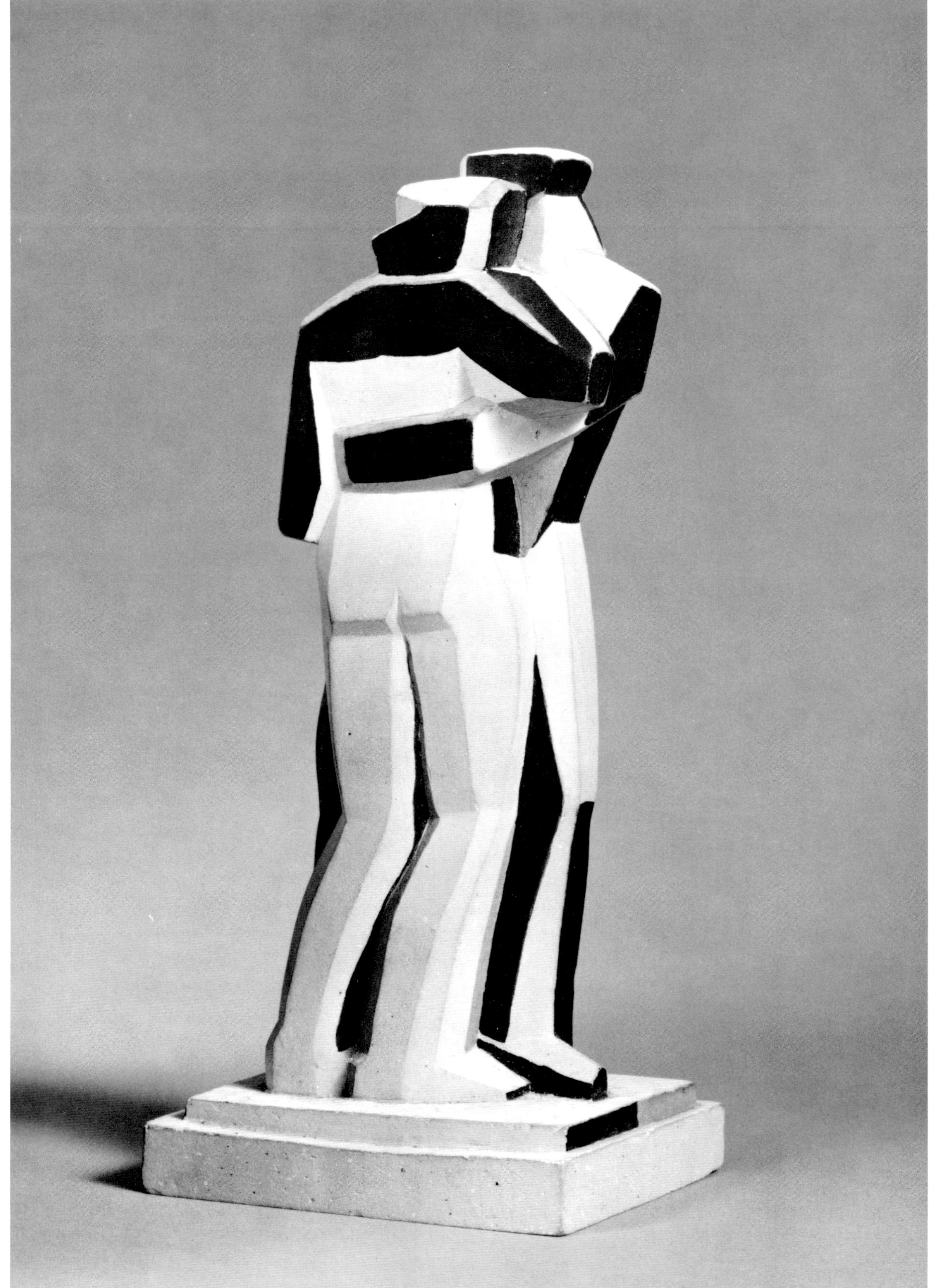

28. *Dance (Dancers)*, 1918
Polychromed terra-cotta
9 x 2⅞ x 3 (22.9 x 7.3 x 7.6)
Estate of Monique Storrs Booz;
courtesy of Robert Schoelkopf
Gallery, Ltd., New York

Figurative Sculpture 1917–1920

John Storrs' first one-artist show opened at the Folsom Galleries in New York in December 1920. In addition to several early Rodinesque pieces and examples of the war years themes, the exhibition presented some newer sculptures in which Storrs sought to express aspects of modern life, often working with complex two- and three-figure compositions.[1]

The 1918 *Dance (Dancers)* is a direct reflection of the jazz age (Fig. 28). A polychromed terra-cotta sculpture, its interlocking pair of closely embracing dancers is full of vitality. The color planes—painted in highly saturated hues of green, orange, and black—are sharply delineated, rhythmic, and syncopated. As in all of Storrs' polychromed sculptures, solid areas of color are used to define planes rather than to simulate reality. To trap and reflect light, Storrs often opposed black areas with unpainted areas of terra-cotta. With its coloristic rhythm of planes, *Dance* encapsulates the jazz age mania for all types of social dancing from the tango to the Charleston.

In *Three Figures (Bathers)* (Fig. 29), the arched shape of the three intertwined nudes suggests swimmers in the waves—and swimming was becoming popular in the 1920s as an accompaniment to sunbathing on the Riviera. The polychromed marble *Pietà* (Fig. 30), although not in the Folsom show, also employs an arched shape and interconnected bodies. Here Storrs turned to a sadder aspect of modern life, the sense of loss that defined the years immediately following the war. Within the generalized arch, the large, triangular, kneeling figure of Mary supports the smaller nude body of Christ, which curves backwards over her draped body. This disparity between the relatively small body of Christ and the large one of Mary may reflect Storrs' knowledge of late medieval and early Renaissance Pietàs, where the adult body of Christ was reduced to fit on the Virgin's lap.

The Folsom Galleries show also featured woodcuts, one of which Storrs designed as a cover for the exhibition catalogue (Fig. 34). The man's head appears to be a variant of Storrs' renderings of soldiers (Fig. 20, also in the Folsom exhibition). Among the other woodcuts, *Romantic Night (Eagle)* (Fig. 31) reflects Storrs' contemporaneous interest in winged figures, here fused with the suggestion of nocturnal planetary motifs. *The Spirit of the Night* (Fig. 32) reveals Storrs' familiarity with the woodcuts of Nolde, Heckel, and Kirschner, as well as other artists around the Blaue Reiter group in Germany.[2] Yet, more important, he was looking directly at some of the same sources that the German Expressionists studied—the woodcuts of the Orient and

29. *Three Figures (Bathers),*
c. 1918
Bronze
Whereabouts unknown

30. *Pietà,* c. 1919
Polychromed marble
11 x 9¾ x 5¼
(27.9 x 24.8 x 13.3)
Estate of Monique Storrs Booz;
courtesy of Robert Schoelkopf
Gallery, Ltd., New York

opposite (clockwise):

31. *Romantic Night (Eagle),*
1916
Woodcut:
sheet, 9¾ x 7⅞ (24.8 x 20);
image, 4 x 4 (10.2 x 10.2)
Whitney Museum of
American Art, New York;
Purchase, with funds from the
John I.H. Baur Purchase Fund
82.33

32. *The Spirit of the Night,*
c. 1917
Woodcut:
sheet, 11⅜ x 8⅛ (28.9 x 20.6);
image, 6½ x 6⁷⁄₁₆ (16.5 x 16.4)
Whitney Museum of
American Art, New York;
Gift of the Robert Schoelkopf
Gallery, Ltd.   80.23

33. Paul Gauguin
Nave Nave Fenua, c. 1893–95
Woodcut
14 x 8 (35.6 x 20.3)
The Art Institute of Chicago;
The Clarence Buckingham
Collection

34. Cover of Folsom Galleries
Exhibition Catalogue, 1920
Woodcut:
sheet, 8⅛ x 8⅛ (20.6 x 20.6);
image, 4⅜ x 4⅜ (11.1 x 11.1)
John Storrs Papers,
Archives of American Art,
Smithsonian Institution,
Washington, D.C.;
Gift of Monique Storrs Booz

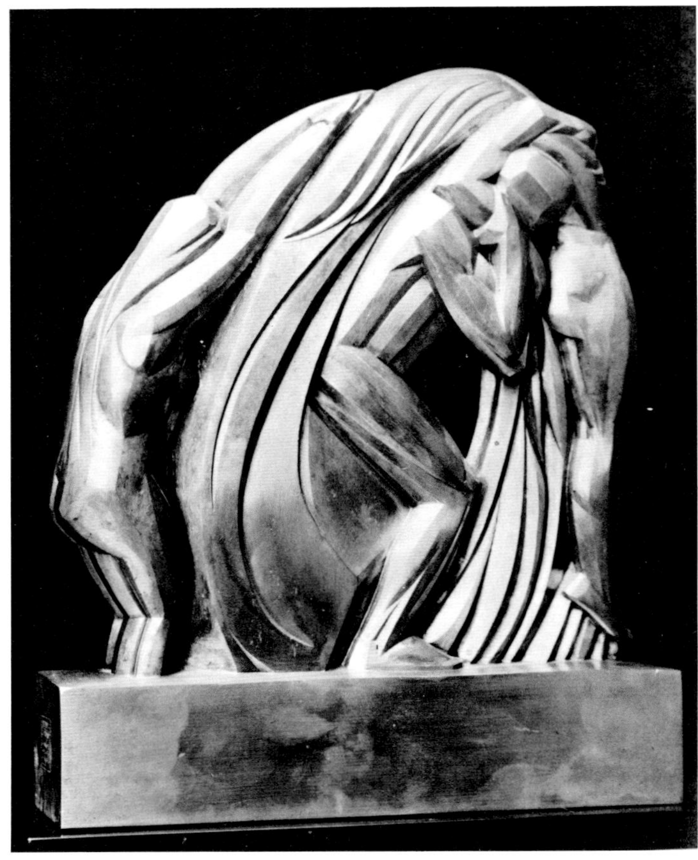

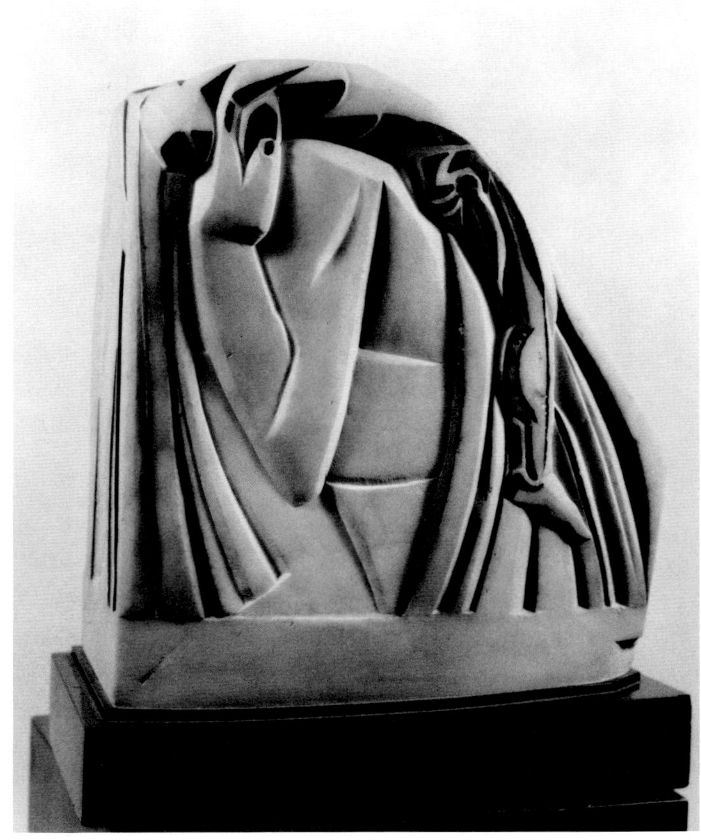

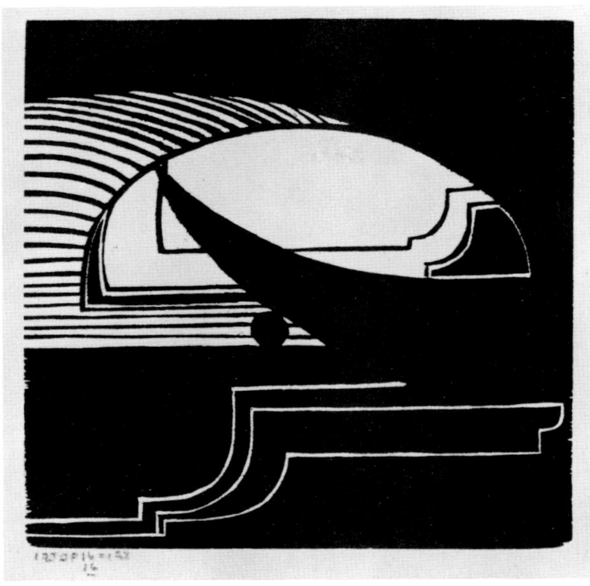

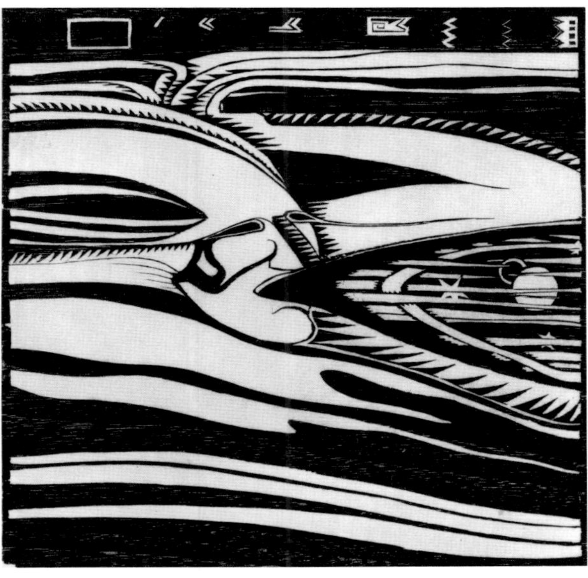

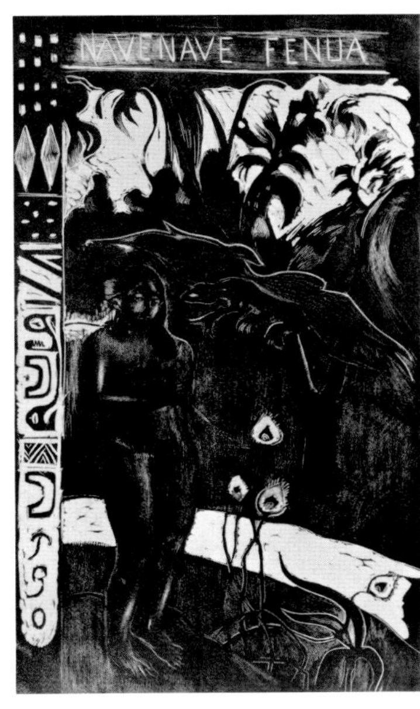

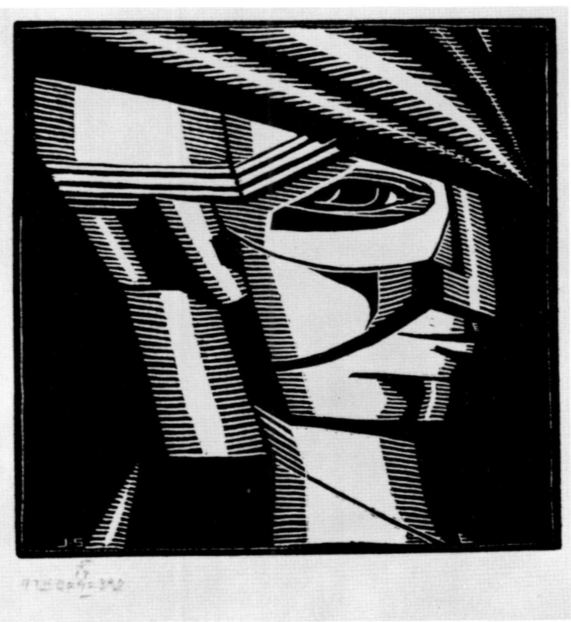

of Gauguin. If we compare Gauguin's *Nave Nave Fenua* (Fig. 33) of
c. 1893–95 with Storrs' *The Spirit of the Night*, the Gauguin influence
becomes apparent in the band of glyphics, placed vertically in the
Gauguin print and horizontally in the Storrs woodcut. In fact, one of
Storrs' scrapbooks contains a reproduction of *Nave Nave Fenua*.

When the Folsom show moved on to the Arts Club of Chicago,
Storrs felt it looked better than it had in New York. Nevertheless,
sales were poor both in New York and Chicago and although the show
attracted considerable critical attention, it was a financial failure.[3]

41 Abstraction and Figuration

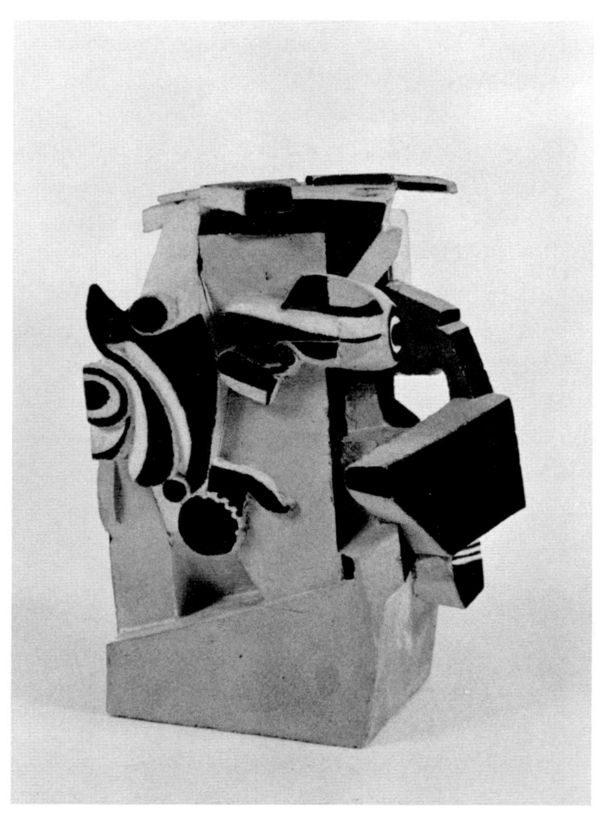

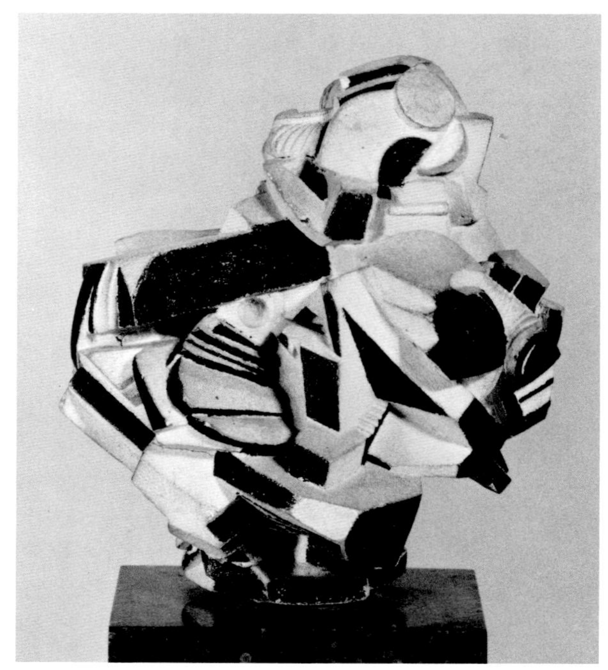

35. *Abstraction*, 1919
Painted terra-cotta
4¾ x 2¾ x 2 (12.1 x 7 x 5.1)
Estate of Monique Storrs Booz;
courtesy of Robert Schoelkopf
Gallery, Ltd., New York

36. *Untitled* (*The Dancer*),
c. 1918
Polychromed terra-cotta
4¾ x 4 x 4 (12.1 x 10.2 x 10.2)
Yale University Art Gallery,
New Haven, Connecticut;
Bequest of Katherine S. Dreier to
the Collection Société Anonyme

37. *Untitled*, 1920–51
Polychromed terra-cotta
3 x 4⅜ x 1¾ (7.6 x 11.1 x 4.4)
Estate of Monique Storrs Booz;
courtesy of Robert Schoelkopf
Gallery, Ltd., New York

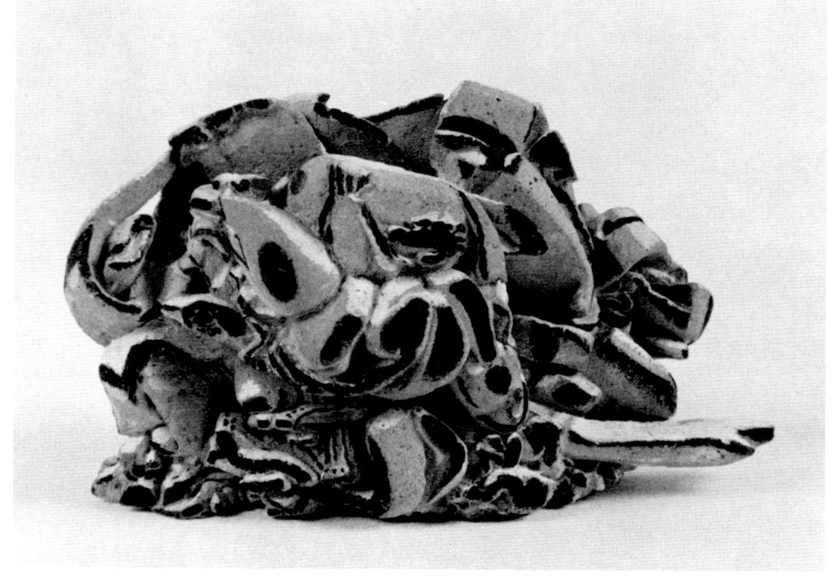

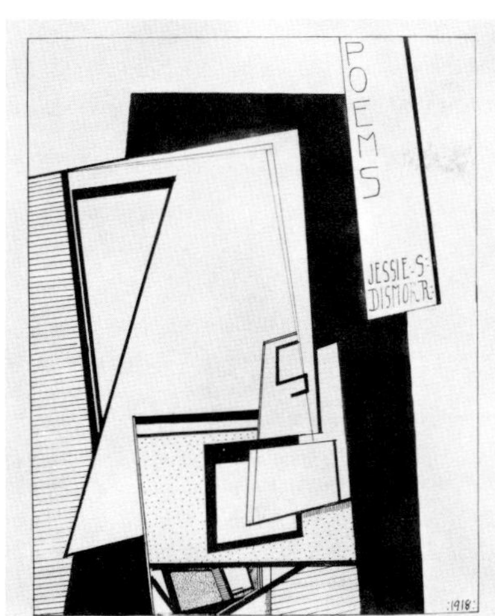

38. Jessie Dismorr
Cover design for *Poems*, 1918
Ink on paper
10¾ x 8 (27.3 x 20.3)
John Storrs Papers,
Archives of American Art,
Smithsonian Institution,
Washington, D.C.;
Gift of Monique Storrs Booz

Early Non-Objective Sculpture 1917–1920

Storrs left out of the Folsom Galleries exhibition the advanced non-objective sculpture he had produced from about 1917 to 1919—terra-cotta and stone pieces in which there was no reference to human or animal form. He had been experimenting with small painted terra-cottas, inlaid stone relief panels, and inlaid sculpture in the round. The terra-cotta pieces reveal the combined influences of Cubism, Futurism, and, especially, Vorticism. *Abstraction* (Fig. 35) combines the calm center and concentrated effort to express energy that were so much a part of the Vorticist sensibility. Conceived around the structure of a cube, *Abstraction* gains its energy from the interplay of geometric forms cut in and out of the surfaces. Rectangles, circles, triangles, and rhomboids are emphasized by the black and white paint. The sense of movement that the piece projects comes not from an actual torsion of the cube, but from the play of light and shadow, chiefly produced by the black and white contrasts, and from the shifts in geometric patterning. Only when the piece is viewed from the corners can the jarring, shifting, rapidly advancing forms be truly experienced.

Closely related to *Abstraction* is an untitled terra-cotta sculpture known as *The Dancer* (Fig. 36). Polychromed in light green and black, it also uses playful geometric forms. But unlike *Abstraction*, the structure has been twisted on its axis, thus bringing it closer to Boccioni's *Development of a Bottle in Space*, which Storrs would undoubtedly have seen at the Panama-Pacific International Exposition. Yet maintaining an inner equipoise within the piece itself was important to Storrs, for he described *The Dancer* as "a small abstract form in pottery, which balances."[4] The title was given to the sculpture by its owner, Katherine Dreier, who loved it and claimed that she always kept it close to her in her library or studio.[5] In later years, Storrs called the piece "my dancing terra cotta of many colors—as far as I know the first 'mobile' in three dimensional forms."[6]

A third, untitled terra-cotta in this group (Fig. 37) is dated on the piece itself 1920–51. Polychromed in yellow, black, green, and red, it defies stylistic analysis because Storrs worked and reworked it for thirty years. Nevertheless, it forms an interesting companion to *The Dancer* and *Abstraction*. If *The Dancer* suggests the feeling of centrifugally whirling speed, staccato rhythms, fast starts, stops, and the spinning of machine gears, then, by contrast, the 1920–51 piece has been softened into a surreal mechanism that appears to have ground to a halt.

The artist who did more to introduce John Storrs to the concepts of Vorticism than anyone else was the Vorticist painter Jessie Dismorr. In 1918, Dismorr sent John and Marguerite Storrs a book of her poems with a cover that she had designed and painted in ink (Fig. 38). This cover, with its abrupt shifts in geometric patterning, sharp tonal contrasts, and actual layering of space—the front page is cut out to reveal a pattern on the second page—is stylistically connected with Storrs' terra-cotta pieces such as *Abstraction* or *The Dancer*.

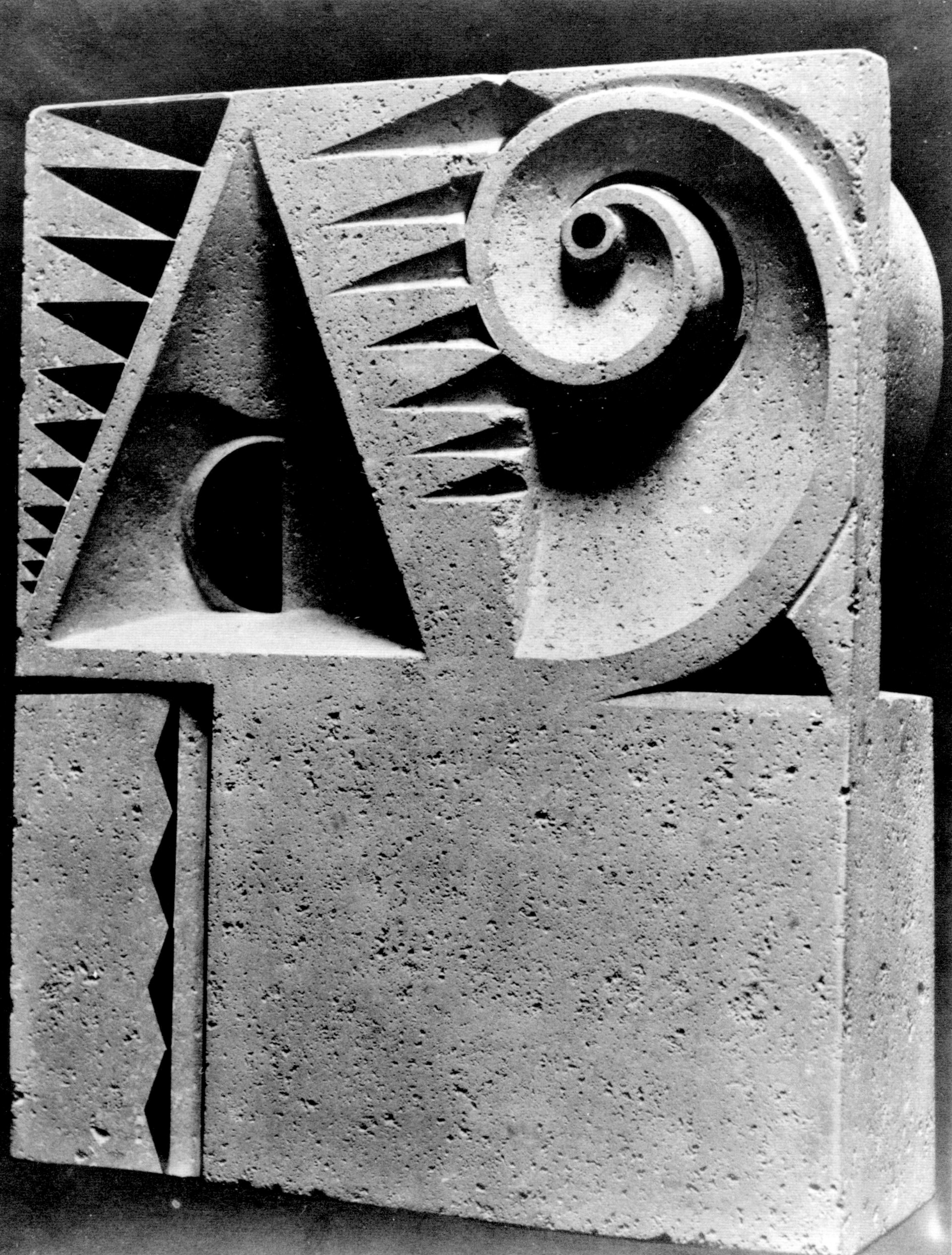

Among the Vorticist sculptors, Storrs most admired the work of Henri Gaudier-Brzeska, who had been born in St.-Jean-de-Braye, near Orléans, where Storrs spent much of the war. After Storrs read Ezra Pound's *Gaudier-Brzeska*, he wrote to the author, probably in 1917, asking if Pound could help him obtain another photograph of Gaudier's *Birds Erect*, published in that commemorative volume. In a draft letter that remains from this correspondence, Storrs mentions that he had seen nothing of Gaudier's original works, but "have *heard* enough to relize that he was a fresh & vital influence in the world of form."[7]

While the non-objective terra-cottas were inspired by Vorticism, Storrs' inlaid relief panels and freestanding inlaid sculptures of this period (Figs. 39–42, 44) stress the broader, smoother planes of Synthetic Cubism. In these stone sculptures, Storrs sometimes inlaid with black marble or mirror glass and sometimes applied black enamel to simulate inlaying.

The stone sculptures with inlay all employ geometric, patterned motifs that derive from primitive art and, most specifically, from American Indian art. Thus they use a repertory of patterns frequently seen in Art Deco designs of the period. The entire Cubist movement, of course, affected Art Deco design; one aspect of its influence was the adoption of flat, planar patterns. The Art Deco shell motif, for example, was customarily a flat spiral rather than the full, splayed, Rococo shell. And like so many Art Deco artists and designers, Storrs also incorporated stylized motifs derived from nature: planets, sunbursts, rays of moonlight, and stylized shell and cloud forms.[8]

The process of inlaying was itself a penchant of Art Deco designers, who used it for everything from bookends to cigarette boxes; the lavish use of marble and mirrors was synonymous with the period. Storrs certainly admired the furniture designs of Émile-Jacques Ruhlmann, the French Art Deco decorator who was known for his use of exotic materials and rich inlays, for the firm of Ruhlmann et Laurent had borrowed Storrs' sculptures (probably for use in their display rooms) and made inquiries concerning others.[9] Also, Victorian homes, like Storrs' boyhood home on Wentworth Avenue in Chicago, used various types of inlaying. Storrs recalled that the entrance hall of this home exuded an exoticism like the Alhambra and that it had a fireplace inlaid with mirror glass and tile.[10]

A stone piece with black enamel (Fig. 39) that was originally owned by William C. Bullitt, Louise Bryant's second husband and later ambassador to Russia, combines semicircles and a spiral shell motif with saw-toothed edges like the patterns in Navaho rugs.[11] The combination of triangular shapes, serrated edges, and circular forms strongly suggests the patterns found in American Indian Mimbres pottery.

Another stone sculpture, directly related to the Bullitt abstraction, is *Abstract Forms No. 2* (Fig. 40). Although not inlaid, its indentations suggest the process. It is conceived roughly in terms of a block; in fact, the sculpture consists largely of a simple block without decoration

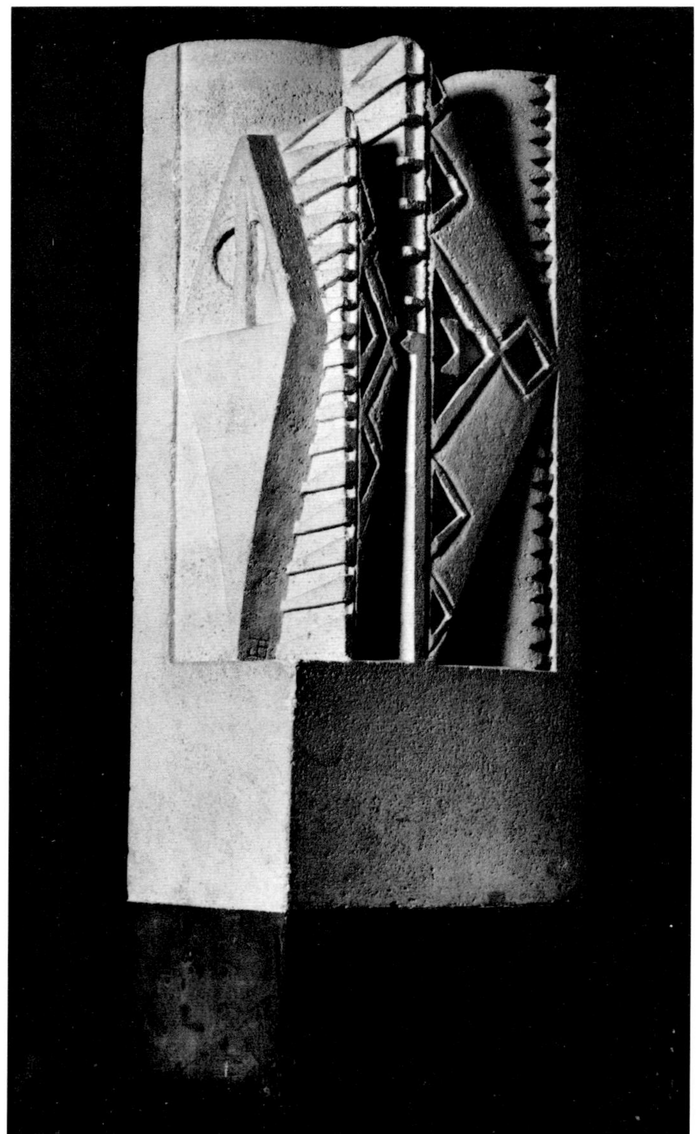

or perforation. The upper portion, however, presents an intricate complex of angles and facets. The indentations and geometric protrusions allow light to flicker over the architecture of the sculpture. It was in fact at this point in Storrs' career that primitivizing and nature motifs merged with architectural elements to establish his definitive vocabulary of forms.

More obviously architectural is *Stone Panel with Black Marble Inlay* (Fig. 41), for it suggests the shadows trapped in arches or doorways. In the uppermost portion are planets, perhaps a crescent moon, or a portion of the sun coming through clouds, with stylized rays of the sun or moon and a diamond-shaped shooting comet.[12] A similar comet shape is the focal point of *Abstract Forms No. 1* (Fig. 42). Storrs continued to be fascinated by towers, stepped shapes, windows (or other apertures), and arches. A postcard view that he saved of the Italian hill town of San Gimignano (Fig. 43) underscores his ongoing

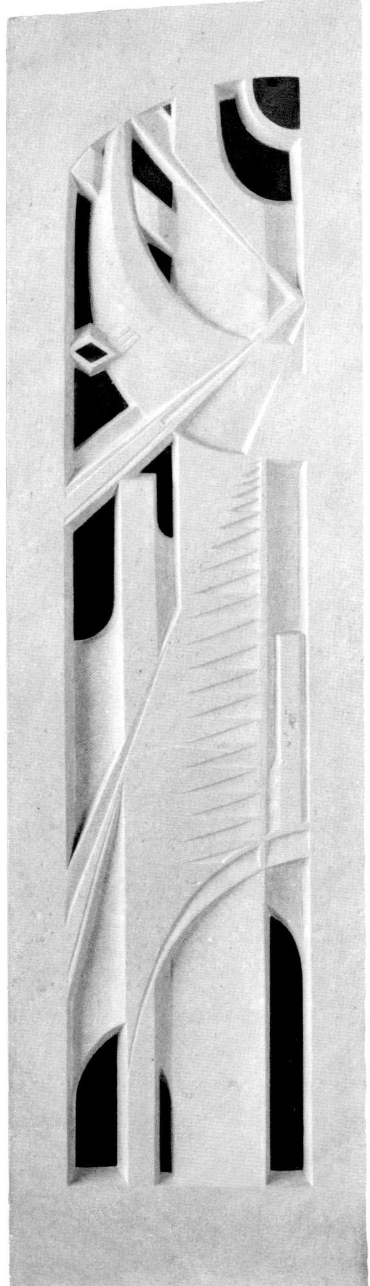

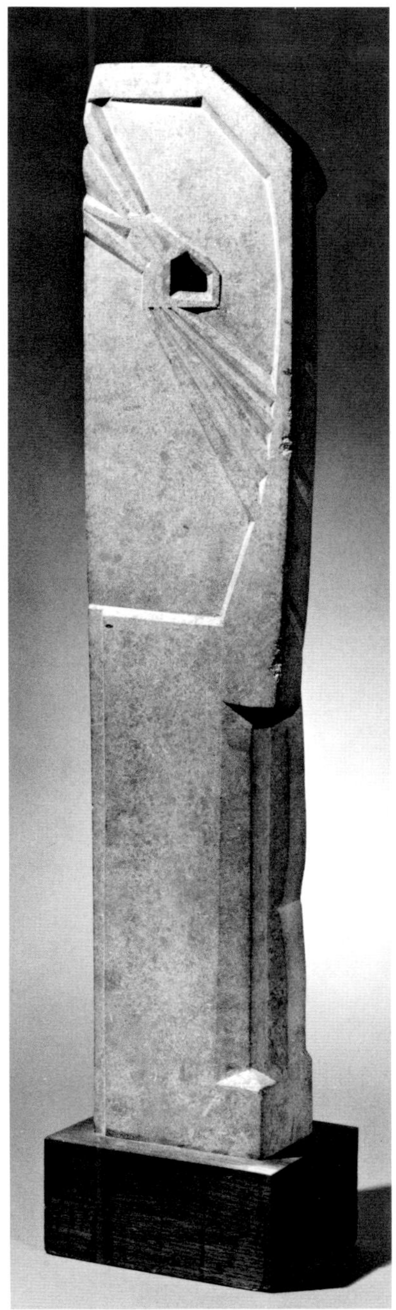

attraction to such architectural units and views—an attraction particularly evident in *Panel with Mirror Insets* (Fig. 44) of c. 1920. But this work can also be seen as a response to the Cubist confounding of reflection and object, a deliberate punning on what is real and what is illusion.[13] Art Deco designers and decorators lavishly used mirrored interiors in an attempt to create the same effect. In its primitivizing motifs and inlaying, *Panel with Mirror Insets* relates to Storrs' inlaid stone sculptures of 1917–19. Here, inlaying and polychroming are used to achieve contrasts of light and dark and to create the shifting planes found in Analytic and Synthetic Cubist paintings.

47 Abstraction and Figuration

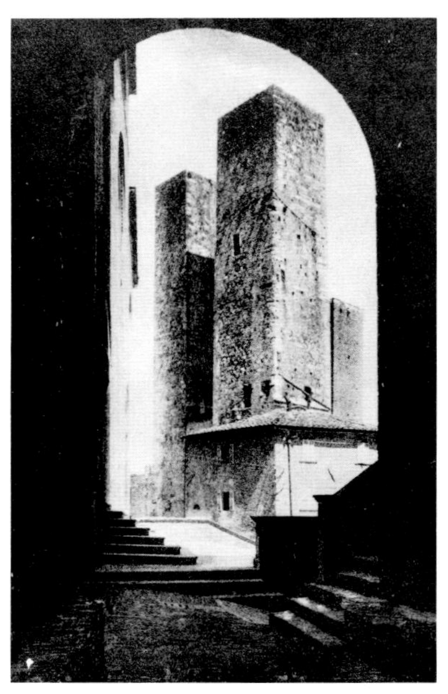

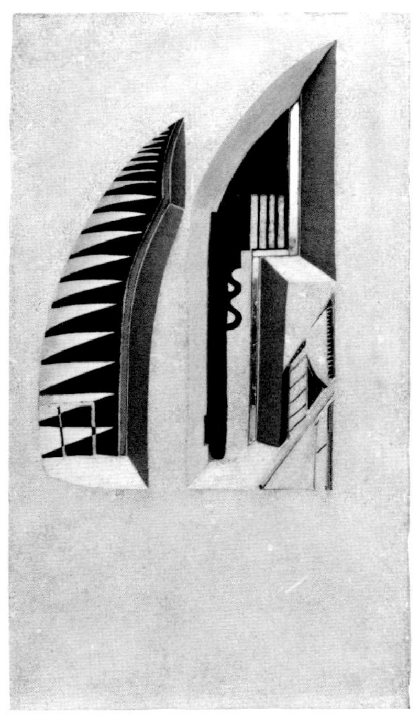

44. *Panel with Mirror Insets*, c. 1920
Polychromed stone and mirror glass
26½ x 14⅛ x 2⅞
(67.3 x 35.9 x 7.3)
Museum of Art, Carnegie
Institute, Pittsburgh; Gift of
Dr. and Mrs. Sidney S. Kaufman,
in memory of Mitchell Kaufman

At the beginning of the 1920s, Storrs' personal life was in an upheaval. His father died in 1920 and the will stipulated that Storrs spend a certain amount of time each year in the United States or give up the full income from a trust fund. This was interpreted to mean that Storrs would have to spend eight months each year in America.[14] He fought the terms of his father's will unsuccessfully throughout his lifetime. D.W. Storrs probably feared that his son would become an expatriate. Indeed, John Storrs did have dual loyalties, for in 1923 he wrote to his wife from New York, "I love America and all that—love it like one ordnairly loves one's mother—But France is my mistress & I am a lover of hers—a lover willing to sacrifice every thing to live in her heart—to rest his head in her peaceful lap of culture & age old beauty. It is not shame that I have for America but pitty—mixed with a sort of hopefulness."[15] Unwilling to give up his life or career in France, in 1921 Storrs purchased the fifteenth-century Château de Chantecaille in Mer, near Orléans. He also maintained a Paris studio on the rue du Cherche-Midi.

Architectonic Sculpture 1920–1923

Storrs' 1923 one-artist exhibition at the Société Anonyme in New York (which then traveled to the Arts Club of Chicago) established him as a member of the international avant-garde. In addition to drawings, the show contained twenty-one sculptures, and those executed after 1920 show Storrs moving more and more in the direction of architectonic sculpture.[16] Also, as he grew closer to the Société Anonyme circle, he became increasingly immersed in the Dada spirit of the "geste"—the visual pun, rooted in the desire to shock, which transposed one form into another. Storrs had always reveled in jokes and puns, visual and verbal. Literary punning reached a level of incredible sophistication with the publication of *Ulysses*, and Storrs, in Paris in 1922, "went to Shakesper shop and got my copy of U. by Joyce."[17] Thus why not create twin columns that were simultaneously a male-female couple? Why couldn't a tower become a racing car?

Action, Inaction, and Reaction (Figs. 45a, 45b), exhibited at the Société Anonyme show, reveals that even before 1920 Storrs was moving toward architectonic sculpture. A stone work with areas of painted black enamel, its formal vocabulary relates to his non-objective inlaid panels and sculptures of 1917–19. In structure, it combines three blocky, architectonic figures, as threatening in their totemic frontality and fierce, primitive solidity as African effigies.

More architectonic in its relative paucity of curves, and clearly involved with visual puns, is *Untitled* of c. 1922 (Fig. 46), a terracotta with black and gray paint. It can be read as a double column, or two flat buildings, or "male" and "female" columns nestling together —the "female" column is more open and vulnerable, the "male" form flatter and more spatially assertive. There is a formal and iconographic relationship between Storrs' *Untitled* and Jacques Lipchitz's

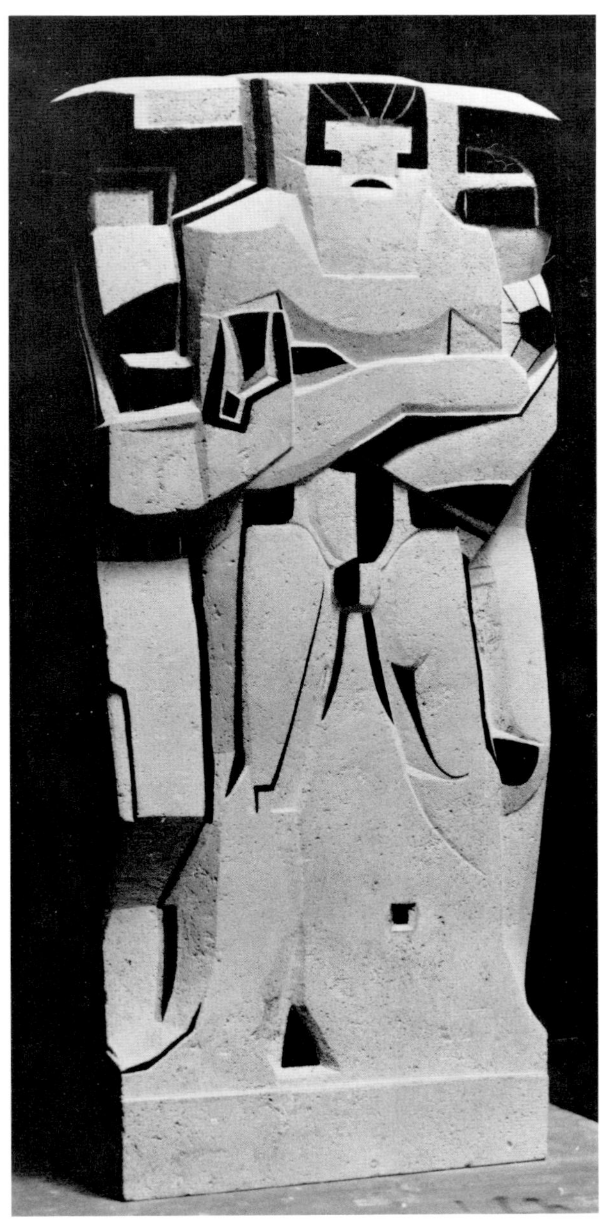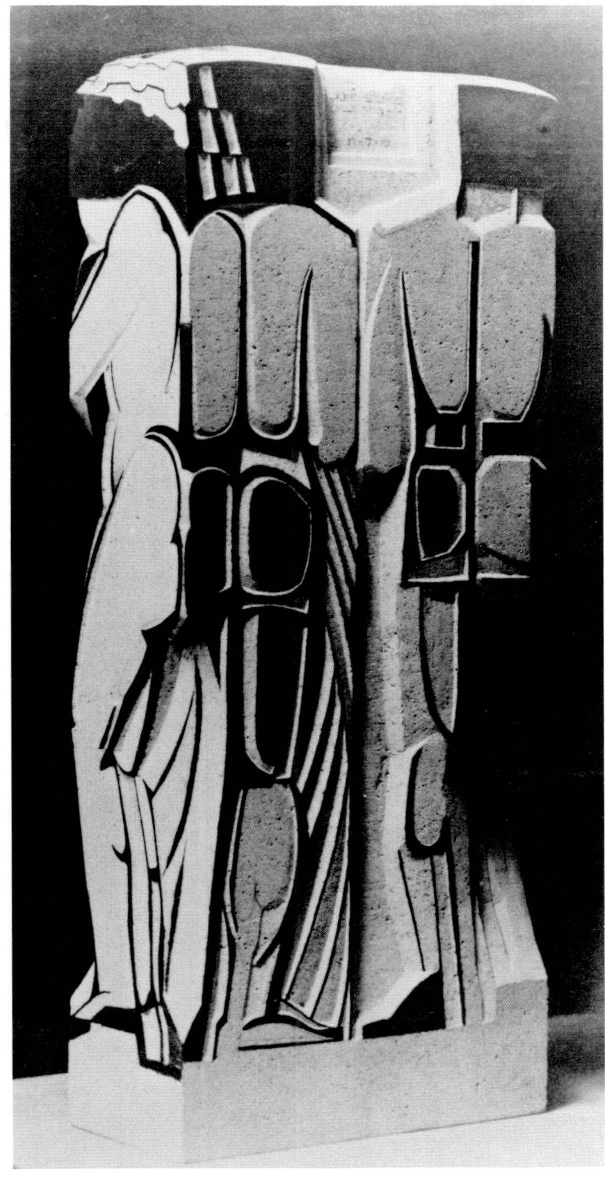

Man with Mandolin. In 1922, Storrs had taken Katherine Dreier to Lipchitz's studio, where Mrs. Dreier purchased Lipchitz's stone sculpture (Fig. 47), now part of the Société Anonyme collection at the Yale University Art Gallery. Like Storrs' double column work, Lipchitz's *Man with Mandolin* has a basis in figuration but makes architectural elements equally evident through blocky, towerlike forms.

That Storrs was moving specifically in the direction of architectonic sculpture is revealed in the bronze *Auto Tower (Industrial Forms)* (Fig. 48), the plaster model for which was probably exhibited in the Société Anonyme show. Storrs called this sculpture his "auto tower," but it is actually a triple pun. To a basic tower form, he added the sleek lines, wheels, and chassis of a touring car—apparent when the piece is turned horizontally. In addition, an ink drawing

49   Abstraction and Figuration

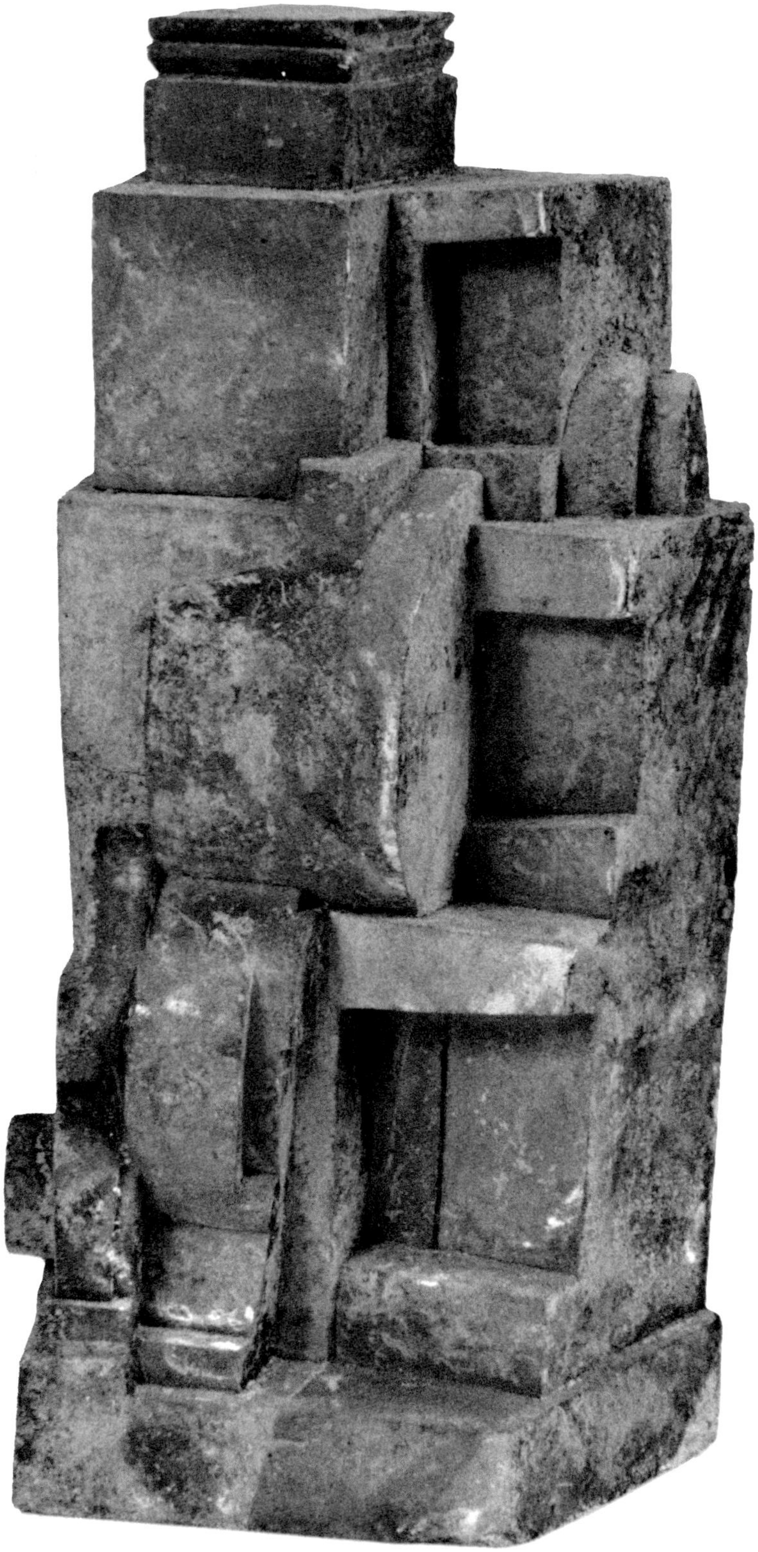

46. *Untitled*, c. 1922
Painted terra-cotta
8 x 3⅛ x 3 (20.3 x 7.9 x 7.6)
Estate of Monique Storrs Booz;
courtesy of Robert Schoelkopf
Gallery, Ltd., New York

47. Jacques Lipchitz
Man with Mandolin, 1916–17
Stone
29¹⁵⁄₁₆ x 10⅝ x 10¼
(76 x 27 x 26)
Yale University Art Gallery,
New Haven, Connecticut;
Gift of Collection
Société Anonyme

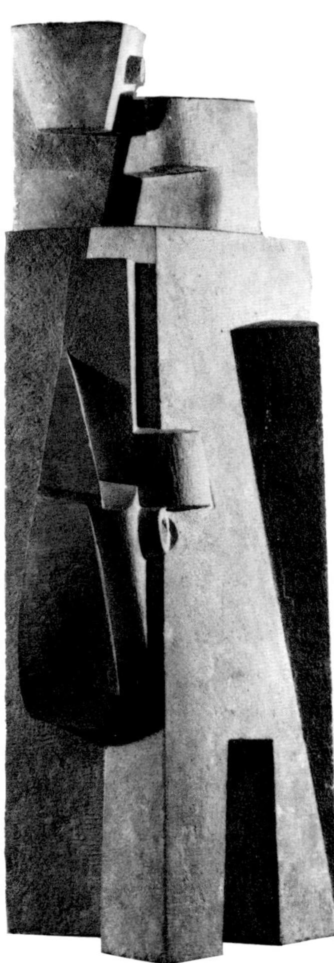

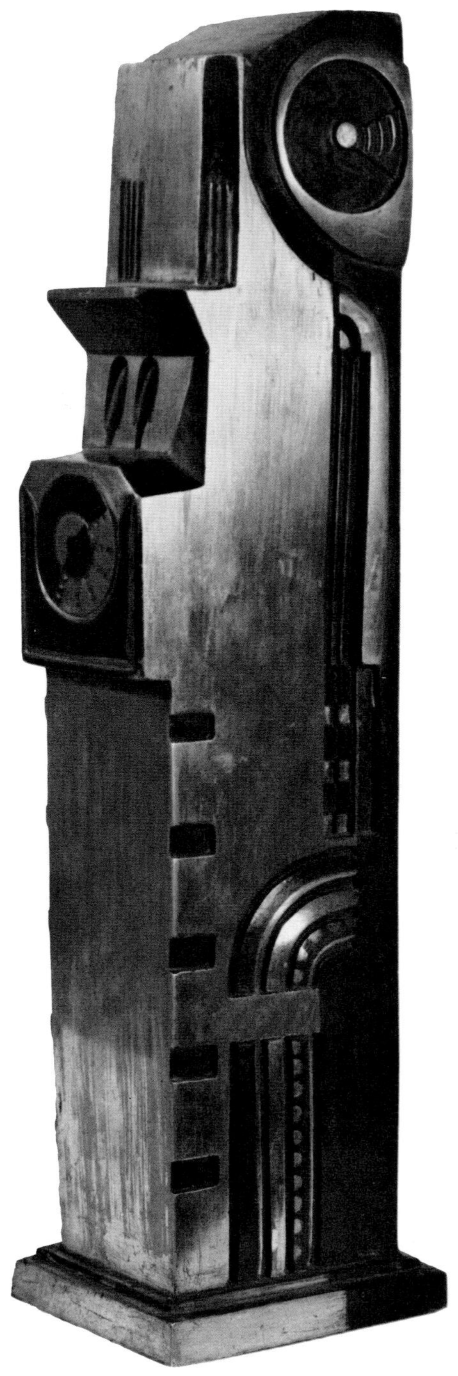

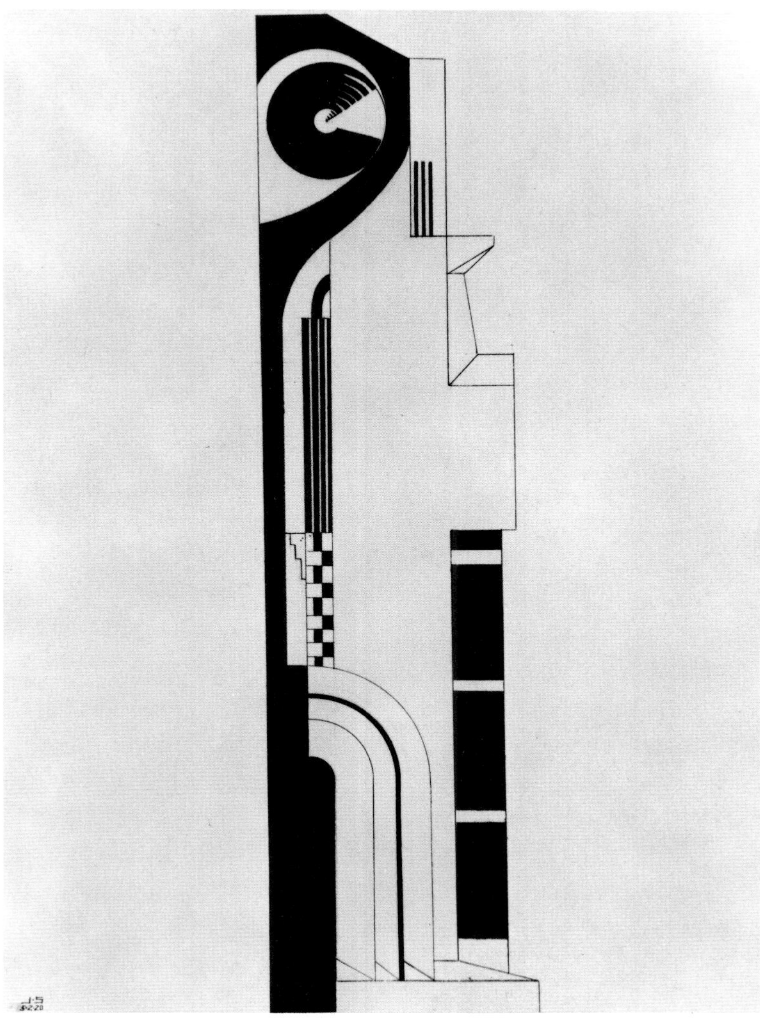

48. *Auto Tower* (*Industrial Forms*), c. 1922
Bronze with brass plating and enamel
12⅝ x 3¹⁄₁₆ x 2¹¹⁄₁₆
(32.1 x 7.8 x 6.8)
Whereabouts unknown

49. *Study for Auto Tower* (*Industrial Forms*), 1920
Pencil and ink on paper
12⅛ x 9 (30.8 x 22.9)
Collection of Mr. and Mrs. Alvin S. Lane

of the sculpture (Fig. 49) shows that Storrs also intended the work to be viewed as the profile of a figure or a totemic personage. Such inversions, reversals, and simultaneities of forms are frequent in Storrs' oeuvre.

Auto Tower also marks Storrs' continuing interest in the machine, a taste shared by Picabia, Duchamp, Man Ray, Morton Schamberg, and others connected with Dada, Surrealism, and the Société Anonyme. All types of machinery captured Storrs' imagination—in Paris in 1922 he "went to the Salon Farming Machines—very interesting!"[18] *Auto Tower* encapsulates the decade's fascination with advanced technology

51   Abstraction and Figuration

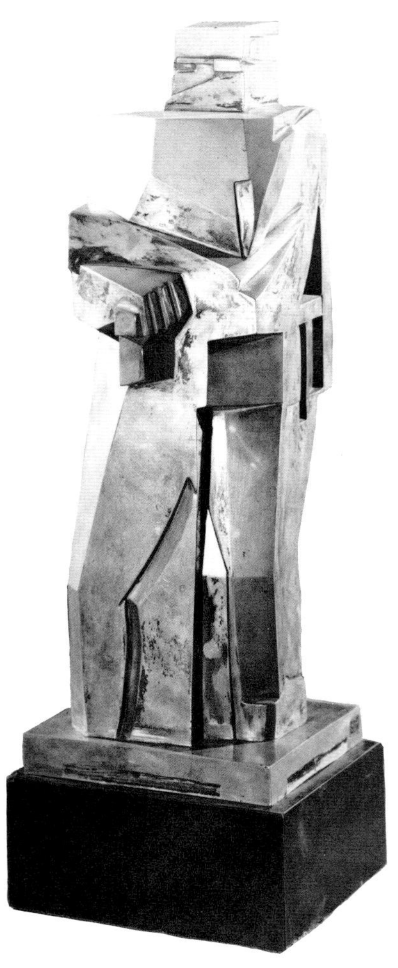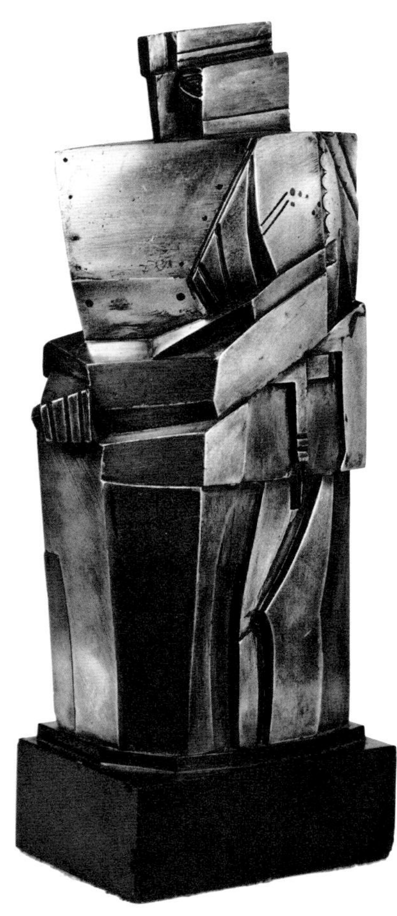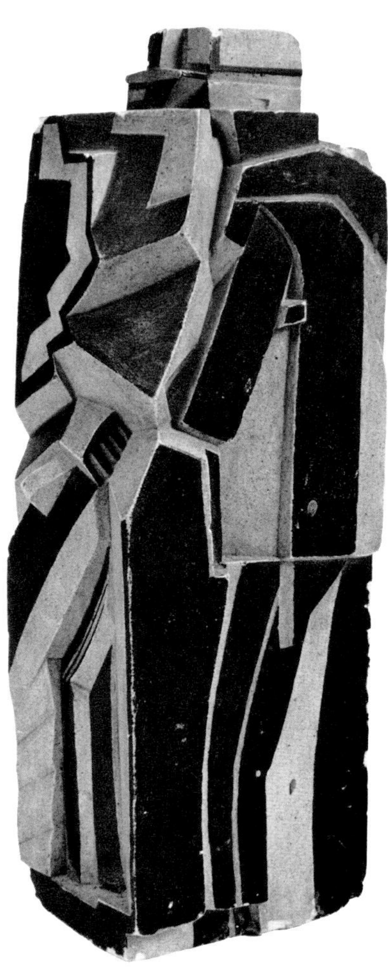

50. *Le Sergent de Ville*
(*Gendarme*), c. 1920
Bronze with silver gilt
13¼ x 5¼ x 5¼
(33.7 x 13.3 x 13.3)
The Corcoran Gallery of Art,
Washington, D.C.;
W.A. Clark Fund

51. *Le Sergent de Ville*
(*Gendarme*), c. 1920
Bronze with silver gilt
9 x 2¼ x 3⅝ (22.9 x 5.7 x 9.2)
Collection of Mr. and Mrs.
George Blow

52. *Le Sergent de Ville*
(*Gendarme*), 1919
Painted terra-cotta
9¼ x 2⅛ x 3¼ (23.5 x 5.4 x 8.3)
Estate of Monique Storrs Booz;
courtesy of Robert Schoelkopf
Gallery Ltd., New York

in building and machinery. More cars were coming on the market at lower prices, and the rage for the automobile as a sophisticated image of modernity, stylishness, speed, liberation, and power was romanticized in the many travel posters of this period.[19] Although not mechanical himself, Storrs loved cars; he bought a Delage in 1926 and owned at various times a Cadillac, a Stutz, and several Rolls Royces.[20]

Among the more definitively figural works in the Société Anonyme exhibition, some are so markedly architectonic that we could call them figure-columns or architectural figures. One such sculpture was listed in the Chicago catalogue as "Policeman (bronze, silver plated)."[21] Two extant bronze figures that fit this description are both entitled *Le Sergent de Ville* (*Gendarme*) (Figs. 50, 51). Storrs also created several versions of his policeman figure in terra-cotta, plaster, and stone; one example is a terra-cotta with black paint, dated 1919 (Fig. 52). In these various interpretations of French policemen, Storrs presents a protection symbol, every bit as powerful and concerned with rank as that of a primitive medicine man. Yet he treated this authority figure with a sense of humor, for the gendarme figures, perhaps because of their imposing, rigid stances, seem self-important and slightly pompous.

53. *The Abbot*, 1920
Bronze
17⅛ x 8¼ x 12⅝
(43.5 x 21 x 32.1)
The Hirshhorn Museum and
Sculpture Garden, Smithsonian
Institution, Washington, D.C.;
Gift of Joseph H. Hirshhorn

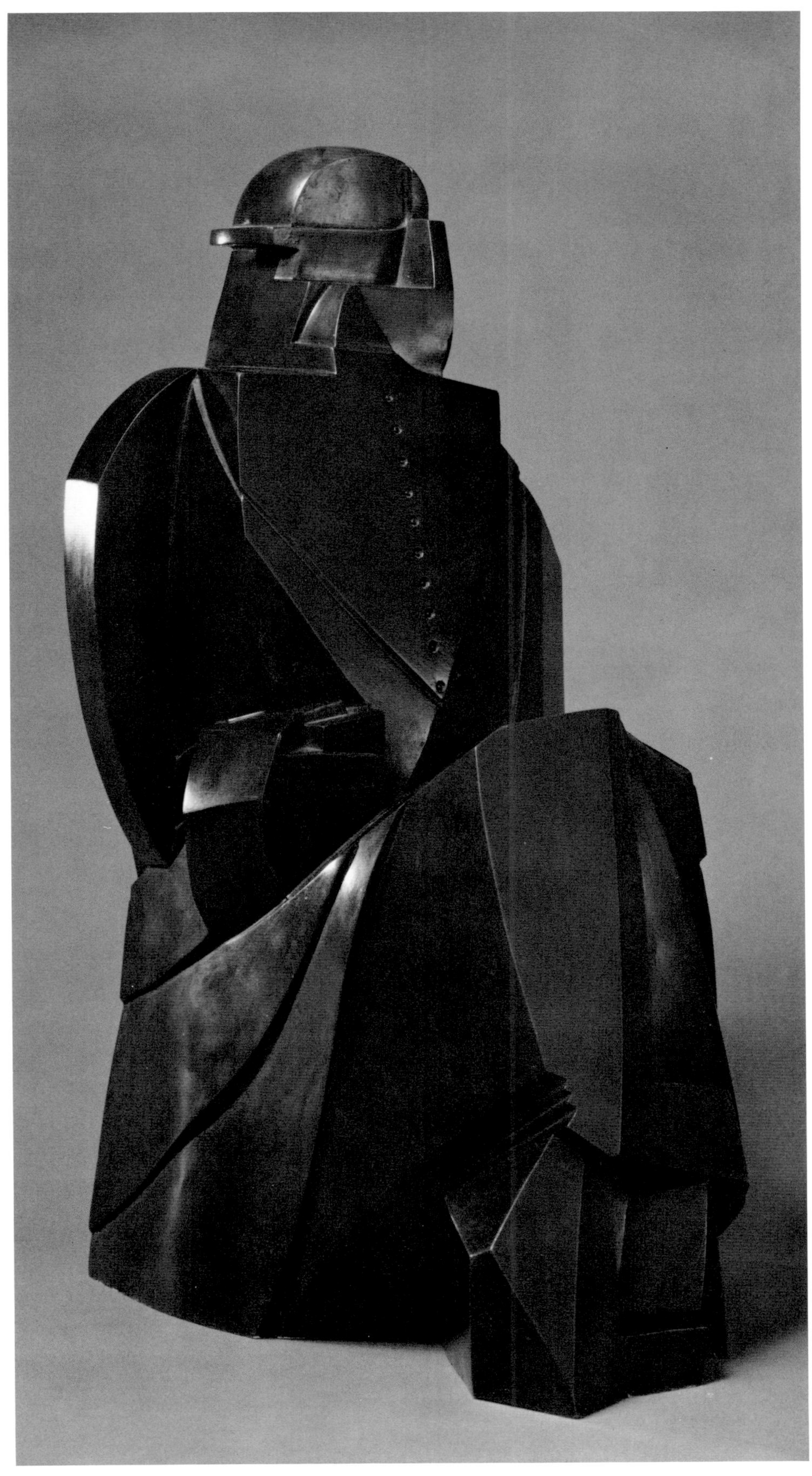

A piece so closely related to the standing *Le Sergent de Ville*
sculptures that it once carried the title of *Gendarme Seated* is a 1920
bronze, now more accurately titled *The Abbot* (Fig. 53), since the figure wears a French cleric's soutane and round hat. Having experimented with standing architectonic figures, Storrs probably wished
to see if he could create a similar effect with a seated figure. However, *The Abbot*, because of the combination of stepped, planar shapes,
sharp angles, craggy forms, and the rounded cap that also suggests
a dome, seems not so much a columnar figure as an entire architectural landscape. If we play down such figurative details as the buttons
on the soutane, the suggestion of feet, or the brim of the hat, and
seek a more generalized abstraction, *The Abbot* could simultaneously
be a grouping of geometrized triangular, flat, rectangular, and
rounded building forms.

As with the Folsom Galleries show of three years earlier, the Société
Anonyme exhibition received a great deal of critical attention. In one
review, Storrs work was described as "the most complete and consis-
tent sculptural embodiment of the abstract by an American artist."[22]
Unfortunately, as had also been the case with the earlier show, no
financial success attended either the New York or Chicago exhibitions
and Storrs was discouraged. He wrote to his wife from Chicago:

*The show closes tomorrow and I havent sold a cents worth—no one even
showed the slightest interest in wanting to posses any of the things except
Alice Roulleir and Jim. The Arts Club has no money (having just
bought a Rodain for 2500—) and the Art Ins—wouldn't take one of
them as a gift! I've done everything that I could possibly do to sell or
to get work. I've exposed my work and myself to the vulgar gaze of
this vulgar town until I feel as if I were walking around without any
clothes on—may God forgive me if I ever show as much as my face
here again—. . . .*[23]

Notes

1. The Folsom Galleries show traveled
to the Arts Club of Chicago. Paul T.
Gilbert, "Fortune or No, Storrs Will
Go Back to France." *Chicago Evening
Post*, January 20, 1921, AAA, JSP, 10,
Clippings (2nd folder thus marked),
summarized the works on exhibition:
"His exhibit at the Arts club, which
opens tomorrow, includes a portrait of
his mother in marble, Horses' Heads,
the Winged Horse, the Bather, the
Modern Madonna, and other figures
in hand-finished bronze, and a group
of small figures and busts in terra
cotta. His treatment, as he calls it, is
architectural. He is in hopes of making
these figures in heroic size for building ornamentation."

2. Although there is no listing of
woodcuts for the Folsom Galleries
show, *The Spirit of the Night* is reproduced in Henry McBride's review,
"Modern Art," *The Dial*, 70 (February 1921), pp. 234–36.

3. The only certain sales in sculpture
from the New York and Chicago
shows were a *Winged Horse*, sold to
The Art Institute of Chicago, and a
terra-cotta head purchased by Alice
Roullier; see John Storrs to Marguerite
Storrs, January 23, 1921, postmarked
Chicago, AAA, JSP, 5, John & Marguerite Storrs correspondence 1921–1922.

4. Written on a receipt of November 20, 1922; quoted in Robert L.

Herbert, Eleanor S. Apter, and Elise K. Kenney, eds., *The Société Anonyme and the Dreier Bequest at Yale University: A Catalogue Raisonné* (New Haven, Connecticut: Yale University Press, 1984), p. 641. This definitive catalogue raisonné contains much useful information on Storrs' works in the Yale University Art Gallery collection as well as an informative listing, p. 777, of Storrs' 1923 Société Anonyme exhibition.

5. Katherine Dreier to John Storrs, May 9, 1949, Société Anonyme Archive, Collection of American Literature, Beinecke Rare Book and Manuscript Library, Yale University, New Haven, Connecticut. Dreier's affection for the piece is also cited in *The Société Anonyme and the Dreier Bequest at Yale University*, p. 641.

6. John Storrs to Katherine Dreier, May 15, 1949, Société Anonyme Archive. That Storrs called this a "mobile" suggests that the piece may actually have rocked on its original base; this might help justify Dreier's title of *The Dancer*.

7. John Storrs' draft letter to Ezra Pound, undated; see Chap. II, n. 31, above.

8. Connections between American Indian Art and Art Deco motifs are succinctly discussed by Bevis Hillier, "Influence of American Indian Art," in *Art Deco* (London: Studio Vista/ Dutton Pictureback, 1968), pp. 40–50, and again in *The World of Art Deco*, exhibition catalogue, The Minneapolis Institute of Arts (New York: E. P. Dutton, 1971), p. 26. In both books Hillier considers American Indian art and culture as being that of Old and New Mexico, of Brazil, and of North America.

9. A letter from the firm of Ruhlmann et Laurent to Storrs, December 15, 1919, AAA, JSP, 4, Correspondence 1919, inquires about the price of ". . . un de vos bronzes doré representant deux têtes de chevaux." In another letter to Storrs, January 29, 1920, AAA, JSP, 4, Correspondence 1920, the firm asks to have three works loaned to them: "No. 1— Femme accroupie, No. 2—Les deux soeurs, No. 8—Tête d'enfant."

10. Storrs' recollections of his early homes are in AAA, JSP, 2, Writings, 1942, "The Scribble-in Book," pp. 100–01.

11. Much of the dating of Storrs' Vorticist influenced terra-cotta abstrac- tions and his inlaid sculptures is based on his letter to Katherine Dreier, May 15, 1949, Société Anonyme Archive, in which he writes about *The Dancer* (Fig. 36) and other pieces, "You acquired it, as I remember, about 1922 or 23, and it possibly dates from 1917 or 18, when I was first experimenting in polychrome abstract and semi-abstract forms. If either you or Yale have any intention, or are interested in adding to the collection other pieces of that period, I still have here two or three of my most impor- tant pieces dating from 1917 to 19. At that time, for example, I did three large abstact pieces in stone with black marble inlays—one of which belongs to William C. Bullett, the remaining two being here, and all three—as I remember, were shown at the Société Anonyme."

Patterson Sims, who examined the Bullitt sculpture, noted a date of 1924 on the base, which conflicts with Storrs' own recollection. However, it is possible that Storrs gave the work as a gift to the Bullitts, who were married in December 1923. Hence the date might represent the date of the gift. Stylistically, the piece would appear to be c. 1917–19.

12. The identification of this form as a comet shape is based on the meteor shape Storrs used in a political draw- ing, reproduced in Garnett McCoy, "An Archivist's Choice: Ten of the Best," *Archives of American Art Journal*, 19 (1979), p. 15.

13. Abraham A. Davidson first made the astute connection between Storrs' *Panel with Mirror Insets* and issues of Synthetic Cubism in "John Storrs, Early Sculptor of the Machine Age," *Artforum*, 13 (November 1974), pp. 41–45. Storrs' *Panel with Mirror Insets* may date as early as 1917–19, but there is no documentation since the materials are polychromed stone and mirror glass rather than stone and inlaid black marble; see above, n. 11. However, it seems to be the piece discussed by Henry McBride in his review of the 1923 Société Anonyme show, "Abstract Sculpture by John Storrs," *New York Herald*, March 4, 1923, section 7, p. 7, as "a carved and colored stone with insets of mirror by way of further enrichment. It has a somewhat cold suggestion of Indian ornament about it at first glance, due to the employment of zig-zags that suggest the feathered headdress."

14. Gilbert, "Fortune or No, Storrs Will Go Back to France."

15. John Storrs to Marguerite Storrs, January 23, 1923, AAA, JSP, 5, John & Marguerite Storrs correspondence, 1923.

16. The version at the Arts Club of Chicago (April 13–24, 1923) was essentially identical to that in New York. The brochure for the show, *Exhibition of Sculpture by John Storrs*, has a listing of twenty-one sculptures. Nevertheless, it is difficult to identify the exact sculptures shown, e. g., nos. 6, 7, and 8 are listed as "Small terra cotta," "Small terra cotta," and "Small bronze." That the shows were similar is assumed from Katherine Dreier's letter to John Storrs, April 6, 1923, AAA, JSP, 4, Correspondence 1923, in which she writes, "Every- thing was sent, except the little piece purchased by me." That piece is no doubt *Untitled (The Dancer)*, Fig. 42, now in the collection of the Yale University Art Gallery.

17. Entry, March 27, 1922, AAA, JSP, 1, Diary 1922.

18. Entry, January 31, 1922, AAA, JSP, 1, Diary 1922.

19. See Bevis Hillier, *Travel Posters* (Oxford: Phaidon Press and New York: E. P. Dutton, 1976), unpag- inated; especially the text and posters 40 and 77, with Hillier's comments.

20. From conversations with Monique Storrs Booz. That Storrs frequently wedded machine images to architec- tural forms is also revealed in his 1920 ink drawing *Machine Form* (Yale University Art Gallery), purchased by Katherine Dreier in 1923 at the time of Storrs' show; see *The Société Anonyme and the Dreier Bequest at Yale University*, pp. 641–42.

21. Arts Club of Chicago, *Exhibition of Sculpture by John Storrs*, no. 9.

22. R. F., "New York Art News: "John Storrs' Sculpture," *The Chris- tian Science Monitor*, March 8, 1923, p. 6.

23. April 25, 1923, AAA, JSP, 5, John & Marguerite Storrs correspondence, 1923 (2nd folder thus marked). Alice Roullier was the guiding force of the Arts Club of Chicago at that time. "Jim" was James Harrington, Storrs' first cousin.

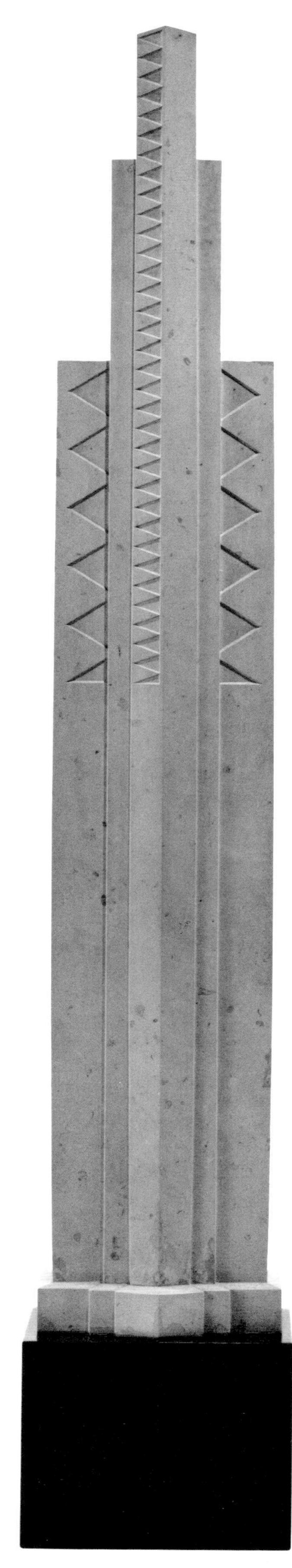

IV. Architectural Forms in Sculpture 1922–1928

54. *Forms in Space No. 1,*
c. 1924
Marble
76¾ x 12⅝ x 8⅝
(194.9 x 32.1 x 21.9)
Whitney Museum of
American Art, New York;
50th Anniversary Gift of
Mr. and Mrs. B.H. Friedman
in honor of Gertrude Vanderbilt
Whitney, Flora Whitney Miller,
and Flora Miller Biddle   84.37

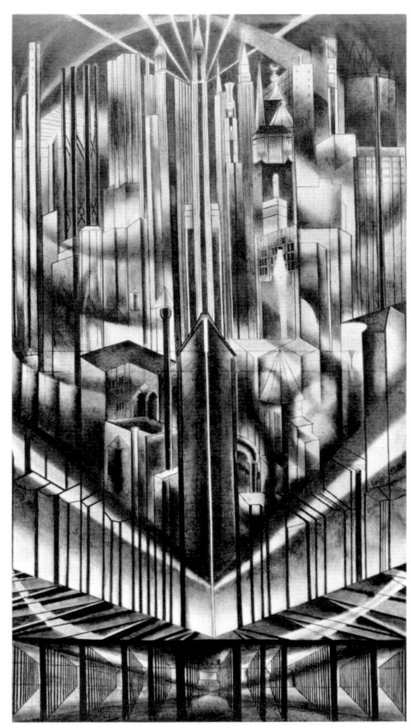

55. Joseph Stella
*The Voice of the City of
New York Interpreted:
The Skyscrapers (The Prow),*
1920–22
Oil and tempera on canvas
99¾ x 54 (253.4 x 137.2)
The Newark Museum,
New Jersey; Purchase,
Felix Fuld Bequest

At the time of the Société Anonyme exhibition, Storrs came under another influence, one that would soon impel him toward sculpture that was purely architectural and increasingly differentiated from his figurative work. A Joseph Stella show had just closed at the Société and, upon arriving in New York, Storrs went immediately to see Stella's work. So impressed was Storrs that he insisted that Stella's five panels entitled *The Voice of the City of New York Interpreted* (Fig. 55) accompany his own sculpture when the Société exhibition traveled to Chicago.[1] What Storrs found in Stella's panels was a poetic conception of urban America that matched his own. He had recently urged artists to create "an expression of today" as complete in its way as the "gigantic commercial or financial structures."

Let the artists create for . . . public buildings and homes forms that will express that strength and will to power, that poise and simplicity that one begins to see in . . . factories, rolling-mills, elevators and bridges.[2]

Storrs also seems to have found in Stella's paintings the formal means to effect this goal. Stella's skyscrapers, towers, and smokestacks were devoid of all but the most significant detail. The shafts of the skyscrapers appeared to be shining and full of light. The planes of the arched bridges, buildings, and roads overlapped and were angled, yet the basic structure of the paintings was vertical and horizontal. For Storrs, it must have seemed as if Stella had truly caught the dynamics and rhythms of a big city. In Stella's *New York Interpreted* panels, Storrs saw idealized building forms that inspired him to strive for a similar self-contained energy and symbolism in his own architectural sculptures.

At some point prior to 1925, Storrs advanced to radical planar and geometric simplicity in his sculpture as he sought a highly distilled unity and balance—the same sense of stability, combined with urban dynamism, that Storrs had discovered in Stella's paintings. He began to produce a new series of non-objective sculptures, works that had little basis in figuration, but in architecture itself.

In addition to Stella's work, there were architectural influences that began to come together around 1923 to produce these new, non-objective sculptures. Of course, Storrs had always been enthusiastic about all types of architecture. His scrapbooks are filled with photographs and postcards of architectural monuments that he saw in his travels: Hagia Sophia in Istanbul, the pyramids in Egypt, the Alhambra in Spain, and Gothic churches in France. He executed drawings of visionary architecture that seem based on a fusion of ancient models—

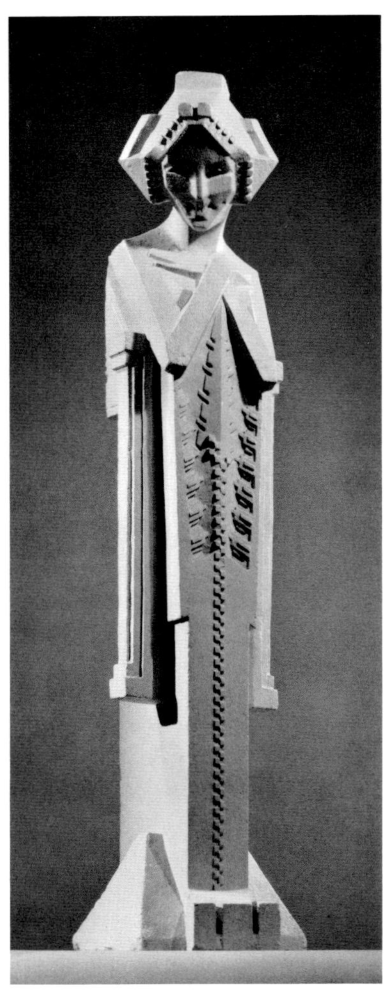

56. Alfonso Iannelli
Sprite, for Midway Gardens,
Chicago, 1914
Painted cement
65 x 14 x 12
(165.1 x 35.6 x 30.5)
The Metropolitan Museum of
Art, New York; Gift of
Mrs. John Steele

57. Richard Bock
Interior relief for the Larkin
Company Administration Building,
Buffalo, New York, 1904
Destroyed

58. Richard Bock
Model for pier capitals,
Midway Gardens, Chicago, 1914
Destroyed

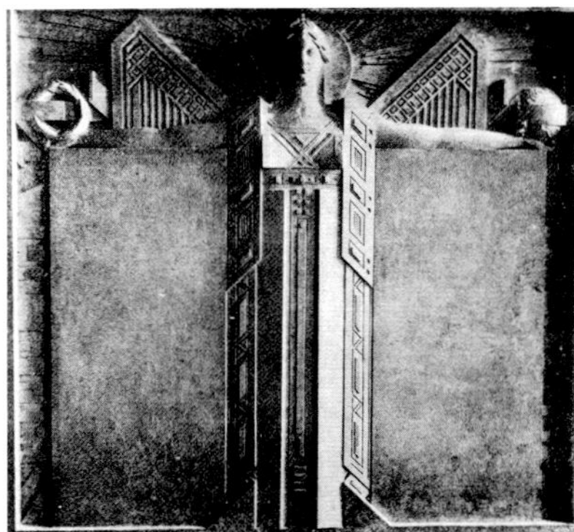

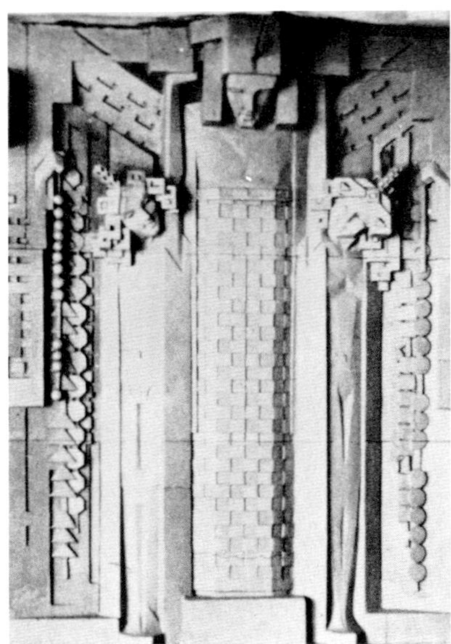

Greek, Assyrian, and Egyptian.[3] Moreover, he created plaster models of invented monuments, some of them still extant.

During the early 1920s, Storrs' ideas about how sculpture should be used in conjunction with architecture were coming into sharp focus. Around 1922, he wrote about his *Winged Horse* monument to the conservative architect Howard Shaw. A draft copy of the letter contains the following excised passage:

It has always been one of my great desires to find an architect in America with whom I could work in the making of things for America that are niether Greek nor Gothic—purely forms & combinations of forms. Merely something that throw [through] modern mediums is expressive of forms & combinations of forms which are the natural out growth of the real & the lasting in our life of today.[4]

The idea of using "purely forms & combinations of forms" was not unique to Storrs. It was also embraced by Frank Lloyd Wright: "I meant to get back to first principles—pure form in everything. . . . "[5]

Wright and Storrs were contemporaries, and the architect's buildings—or those designed under his influence—punctuated Storrs' native Chicago and its environs. Moreover, the two men shared certain tastes and interests. Both were attracted to the more geometric aspects of the Arts and Crafts movement and the Vienna Secession; both admired and collected Japanese prints; and both used the American Indian motifs that were an inherent part of the Art Deco style.[6]

Storrs' own sculpture had already responded to certain forms of architectural sculpture produced in Wright's milieu. In addition to the punning columnar sculptures (Figs. 46, 48), Storrs had always been interested in what might be called the "expressive column," that is, the column combined with a head or figure of symbolic content. In Storrs' time, the concept of a figure-capped column or pilaster

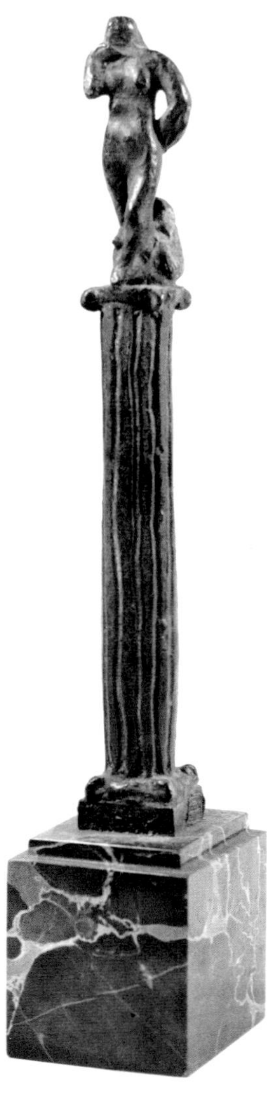

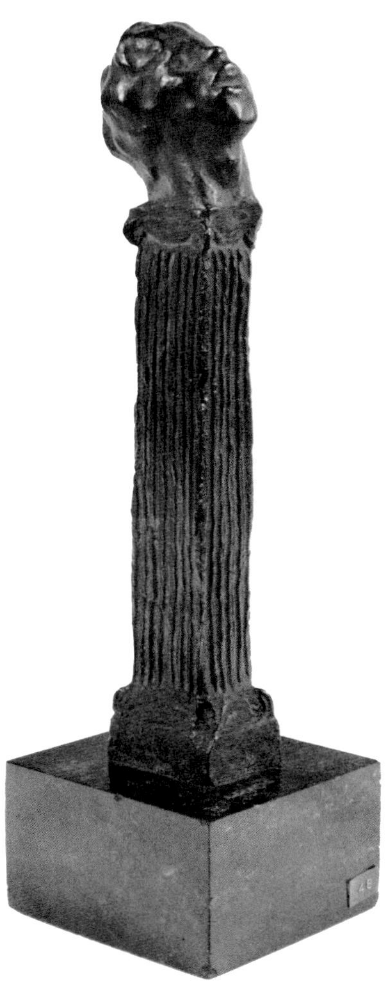

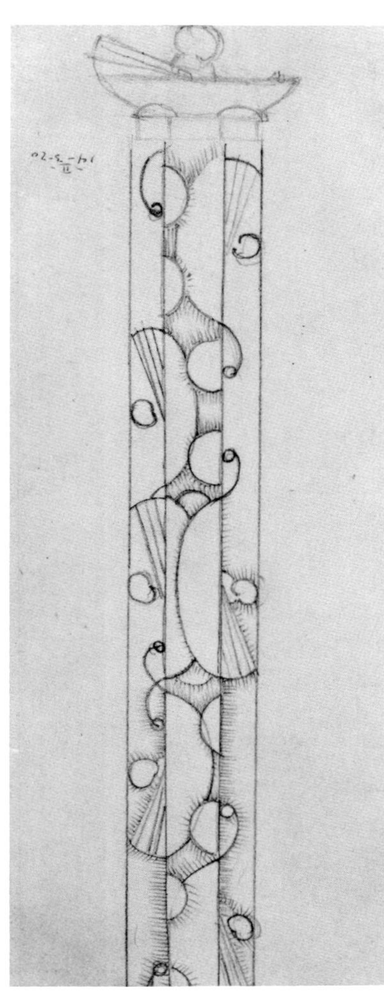

59. *Dancing Woman on a Column*, 1914
Bronze
10 x 1¼ x 1¼ (25.4 x 3.2 x 3.2)
Estate of Monique Storrs Booz;
courtesy of Robert Schoelkopf
Gallery, Ltd., New York

60. *Head on Column*, 1913
Bronze
9⅛ x 1⅝ x 2¼ (23.2 x 4.1 x 5.6)
Estate of Monique Storrs Booz;
courtesy of Robert Schoelkopf
Gallery, Ltd., New York

61. *Study for a Monumental
Sculpture of the Artist's Daughter in
a Baby Carriage*, 1920 (detail)
Pencil on paper
14 x 17 (35.6 x 43.2)
Estate of Monique Storrs Booz;
courtesy of Robert Schoelkopf
Gallery, Ltd., New York

had appeared in Richard Bock's 1904 relief for Wright's Larkin Building in Buffalo (Fig. 57) and in Bock's model for a pier sculpture for Wright's Midway Gardens in 1914 (Fig. 58). When Storrs and his wife traveled with D.W. Storrs in 1915, they could scarcely have missed seeing the Midway Gardens in Chicago, then an active area for pleasure and dining. Also at the Midway Gardens—strategically located throughout the complex—were Alfonso Iannelli's columnar *Sprite* figures (Fig. 56). Storrs' 1914 bronze with a female nude dancing atop a column (Fig. 59) may represent Dance,[7] while a bronze of 1913 that shows a single male head atop another column (Fig. 60) may represent Music.[8] A 1920 sketch of his daughter in a baby carriage placed atop a column (Fig. 61) reveals the monumental scale on which Storrs thought.

While Storrs' columnar figures may be described as architectonic, these later columnar conceits more closely approach pure architecture; there is little integration or double-functioning of figurative and architectural motifs, and the simple columnar form predominates.

When Storrs created earlier inlaid panels and blocklike sculptures

59 **Architectural Forms in Sculpture**

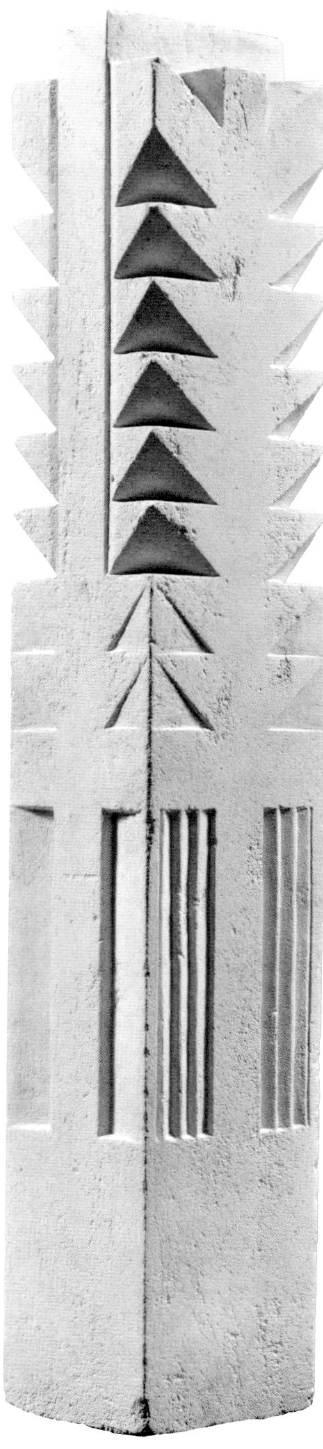

62. *Architectural Form*, c. 1923
Stone
19¾ x 3¼ x 3 (50.2 x 8.3 x 7.6)
Estate of Monique Storrs Booz;
courtesy of Robert Schoelkopf
Gallery, Ltd., New York

such as *Abstract Forms No. 2* (Fig. 40), he was already influenced by Wright in the use of similar geometric motifs, parallel forms, and forms cut in and out of surfaces at different levels. These earlier inlaid works, however, were highly dependent on black and white contrasts (and sometimes the use of color), shifting light effects, and patterning. Storrs' columnar pieces show far greater simplification of form and focus on shape and silhouette. And in this group of non-figurative architectural sculptures, he once again turns to the work coming out of Wright's shop. It is surely no coincidence that it was precisely at this time that Storrs was meeting the cast of characters around Wright (he did not meet Wright himself until the late 1920s or early 1930s).

The first person in the Wrightian orbit that Storrs encountered was Viscount Inouye, who had been the Japanese ambassador to England, and for whom Wright had designed a house in Tokyo in 1918—the same year Storrs began working in Paris on a plaster bust of Inouye; the viscount received his silvered bronze bust in 1922.[9] A year later, at Storrs' 1923 exhibition at the Arts Club of Chicago, he met the architect Barry Byrne, a former assistant to Frank Lloyd Wright who had formed his own architectural firm in Chicago.[10] Through Byrne, Storrs also became acquainted with Alfonso Iannelli, the sculptor who had worked closely with Wright on the Midway Gardens. Both Byrne and Iannelli were impressed with Storrs' sculpture and they promised to give him work on their next large project.[11] They also visited Storrs in Paris in the summer of 1924 and at that time purchased sculpture from him.[12]

Column-Towers

What we see in Storrs' column-tower sculptures that reflects Wright and the sculptors who worked with him is not an imitation of Wright but a Wrightian nuance. The pier elements in Wright's Unity Temple in Oak Park, Illinois, completed in 1908 (Fig. 63), have the kind of planar vertical support and parallelisms of form and line that Storrs would favor in his column-tower sculptures. Storrs also took a Wrightian approach in proportions and in his vocabulary of geometric motifs, including the chevron pattern.[13] Richard Bock's model for an ornamental relief made for Wright's Larkin Building of 1904 (Fig. 64) uses the same motif—as does Storrs' *Architectural Form* of c. 1923 (Fig. 62). Because the carved pattern on *Architectural Form* terminates in a cross at the very bottom, Storrs' sculpture becomes simultaneously a Christian as well as a primitivizing totem.

Study in Form (*Architectural Form*) (Fig. 66), a cast stone columnar tower of poise and extreme simplicity, recalls the square columns of Wright's Larkin Building (Fig. 65). Both Storrs and Wright employed cut-in parallel shapes contrasting with an expanse of sleek, smooth, unadorned surfaces. If we imagine Storrs' sculpture on a monumental scale, the comparison becomes even more striking.[14]

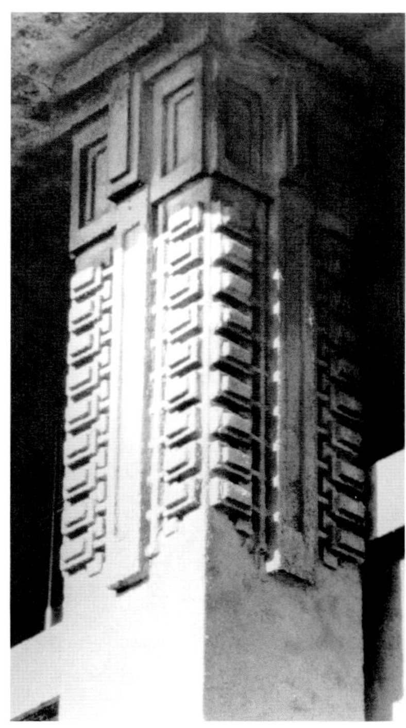

63. Frank Lloyd Wright, architect
Pier elements of Unity Temple,
Oak Park, Illinois, 1908

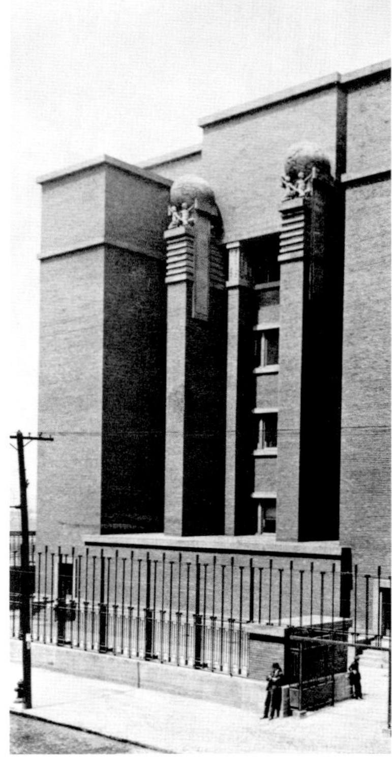

65. Frank Lloyd Wright,
architect
Larkin Company Administration
Building, Buffalo, New York, 1904

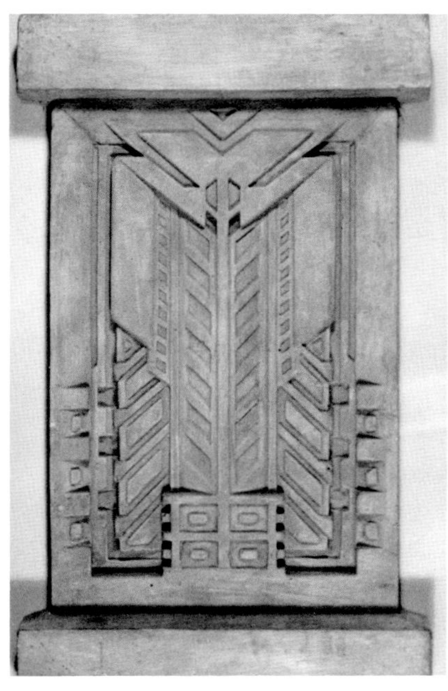

64. Richard Bock
Model for side pier reliefs,
Larkin Company Administration
Building, Buffalo, New York, 1904
Plaster
17¾ x 11⅜ x 1⅜ (45.1 x 28.9 x 3.5)
The Richard W. Bock Sculpture
Collection, Greenville College,
Greenville, Illinois

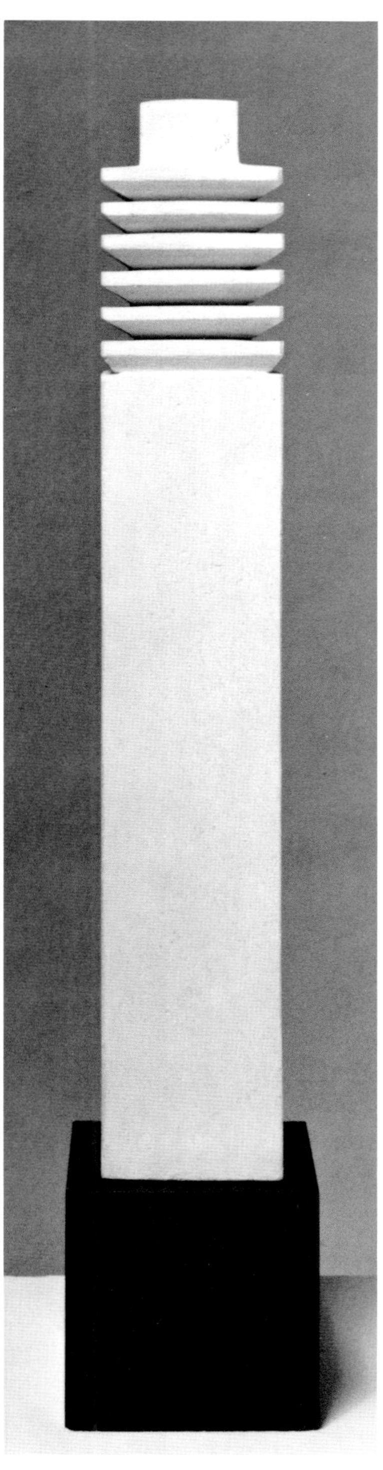

66. *Study in Form*
(*Architectural Form*), c. 1923
Stone
19½ x 3⅛ x 3¼
(49.5 x 7.9 x 8.3)
San Francisco Museum of
Modern Art; Purchased through
a gift of Julian and Jean Aberbach

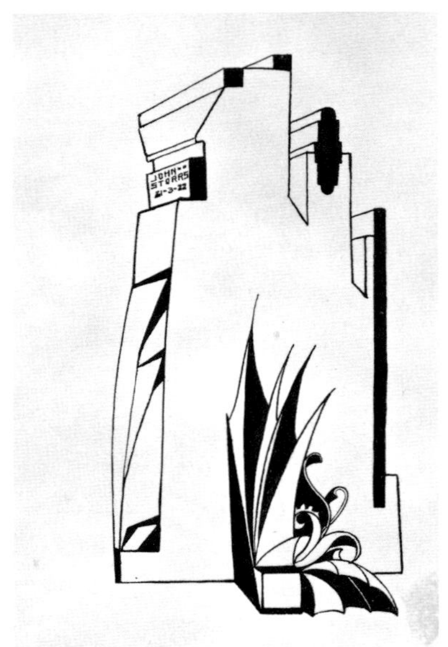

67. *Study for a
Metal Sculpture*, 1922
Ink on paper
6¹³⁄₁₆ x 4⁵⁄₁₆ (17.3 x 11)
Yale University Art Gallery,
New Haven, Connecticut;
Anonymous gift

68. *Study in Form No. 2*,
c. 1923
Stone
19 x 3¼ x 3¼ (48.3 x 8.3 x 8.3)
Collection of Abby and
B.H. Friedman

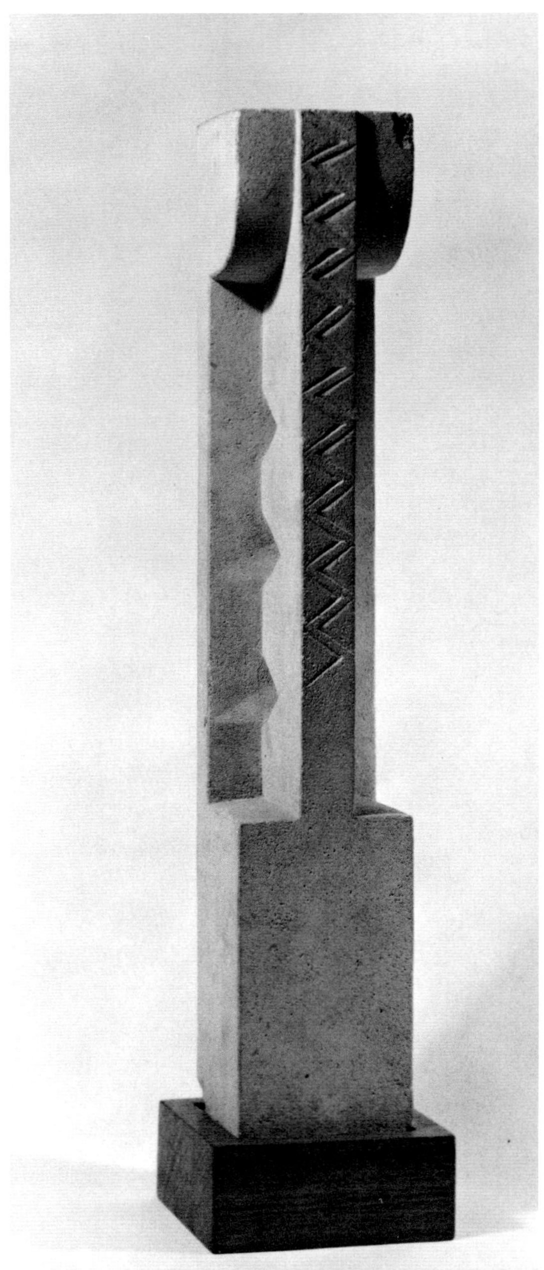

Study in Form No. 2 (Fig. 68) combines a zigzag and a curved
motif to suggest a caryatid column. Triangular apertures cut through
at the sides echo the zigzag motif and give an added dimension of space
and light. This echoing of solid and void, the viewing of positive and
negative space as two sides of the same coin, is a fundamental Wrightian concept. Both Wright and Storrs also perceived architecture as
organic; many of Wright's decorative motifs derived from flower,
plant, and tree forms. Storrs made such organic-architectural-sculp-
tural connections when he wrote in his diary and sketchbook: "Architecture is the plant and sculpture is the blossom as the sea has waves
and the sky has clouds."[15] In a 1922 ink drawing (Fig. 67), Storrs

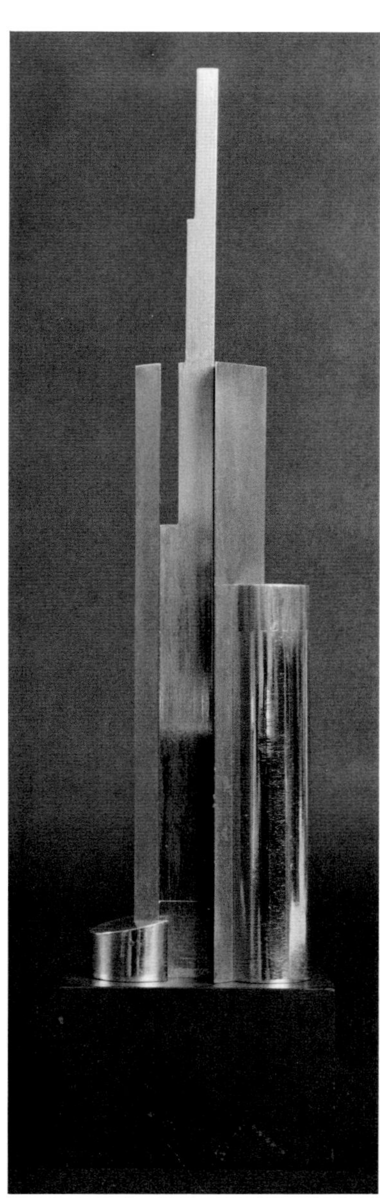

69. *Study in Pure Form*
(*Forms in Space No. 4*), c. 1924
Steel, copper, and brass
12¼ x 3 x 1½ (31.1 x 7.6 x 3.8)
Munson-Williams-Proctor
Institute Museum of Art,
Utica, New York

juxtaposes plant and architectural forms and tries to make visual coordinates between them. He makes the architectural structure organic, even humanoid, while hardening the plant form to make it equivalent in weight and crispness to the architectural form. By extension, such column-towers as Storrs' *Study in Form No. 1* (Fig. 70) and *Study in Form No. 4* (Fig. 71) seem based not solely on pure geometry but suggest aspects of organic growth.

The shape of Storrs' monumental marble *Study in Architectural Forms* (Fig. 75) is unusual among his architectural sculptures. Not quite a column-tower, nor a building cluster, nor a skyscraper, it is nevertheless so Wrightian in feeling with its superimposed and cut-out zigzag forms that it could easily have served as a sculptural architectural element for Wright's Midway Gardens or Imperial Hotel.

The recently rediscovered *Architectural Forms No. 3* is geometrically constructed.[16] One side of the sculpture looks like a futuristic skyscraper (Fig. 72a), while another has a cut-in aperture in the form of an arch (Fig. 72b). Such a highly original work reveals Storrs' constantly developing vocabulary of personalized architectural forms, for here he has combined a most ancient architectural shape, the arch, with a visionary skyscraper of his own design. Conceptually, he seems to have wanted to encapsulate within a single sculpture a broad span of architectural history. In such an inspired piece, any specific Wrightian connection is tenuous. In some of Storrs' best sculptures, he superseded Wrightian influence.

Skyscraper Cities

Storrs' originality is apparent in the novel sculptures he was creating by 1924 in metal, which look like building clusters or miniature skyscraper cities. Based on wood models and drawings, they were fabricated under Storrs' supervision from aluminum, brass, copper, and steel. These building clusters were Storrs' idealized cities. By the mid-1920s, he expressed the opinion that "architecture proper had not caught up with sculpture either in ideals or execution." Although he felt that architecture was the plant and sculpture its blossom, it seemed to him that sculptors were "in danger of having to spend their lives making bibelots for the mantlepiece or contriving museum exhibits."[17] Storrs set about to reunite architecture and sculpture in his own body of work. His building clusters or skyscraper cities were immaculately crafted, exquisitely proportioned, and the natural colors of the metals provided contrasts in tone and hue. In his idealized cities, he could control the spatial elements in a manner not feasible for an architect designing a single building amid a complex of existing structures.

Study in Pure Form (*Forms in Space No. 4*) (Fig. 69) was a pioneering effort by Storrs to create what today are termed "multiples."[18] Fabricated of combined units of steel, copper, and brass, the sculpture resembles a cluster of buildings that create a silhouette of staggered

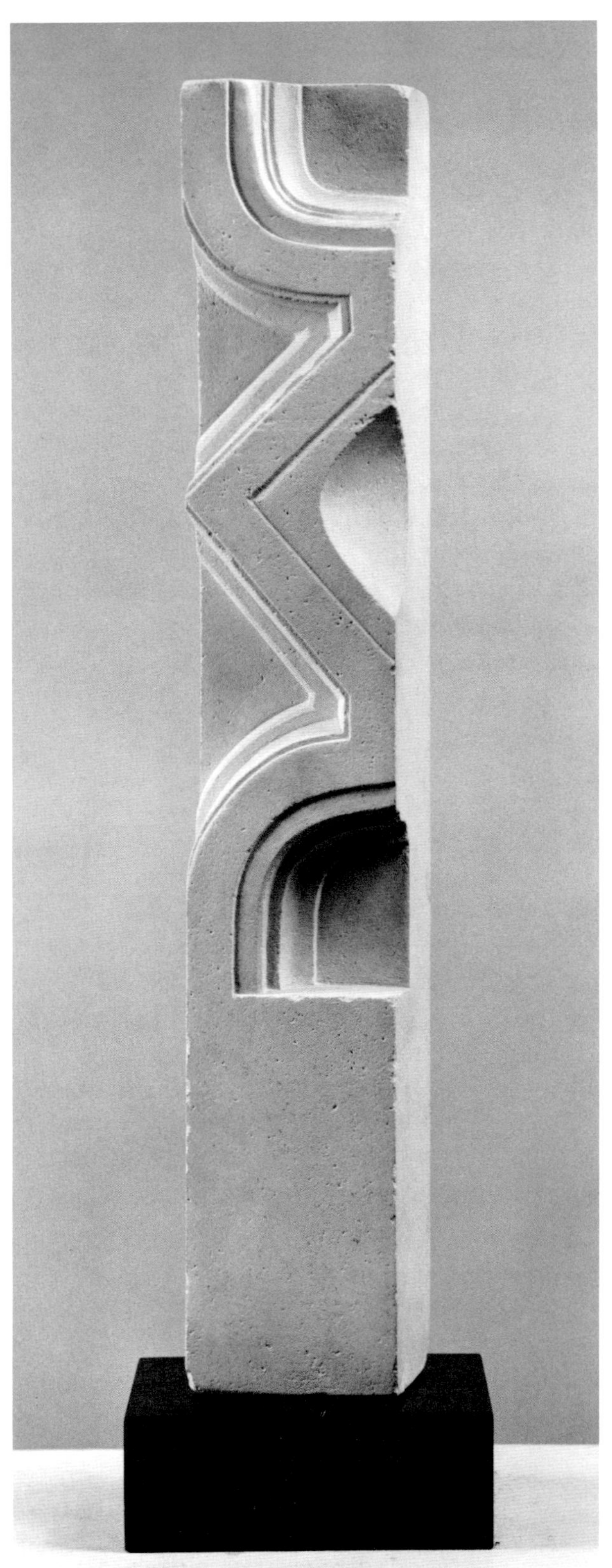

70. *Study in Form No. 1*,
c. 1923
Stone
19¾ x 3¼ x 3⅛ (50.2 x 8.3 x 7.9)
Estate of Monique Storrs Booz;
courtesy of Robert Schoelkopf
Gallery, Ltd., New York

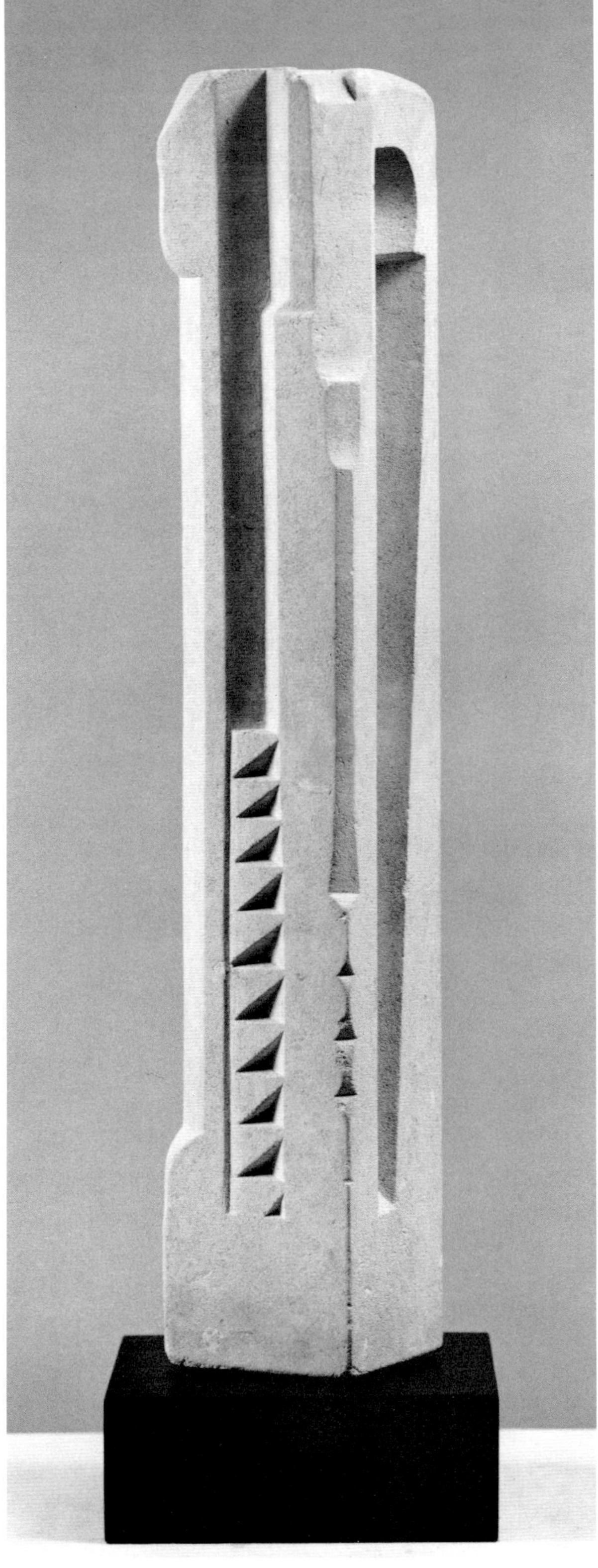

71. *Study in Form No. 4*,
c. 1923
Stone
18⅜ x 3⅛ x 3 (46.7 x 7.9 x 7.6)
Estate of Monique Storrs Booz;
courtesy of Robert Schoelkopf
Gallery, Ltd., New York

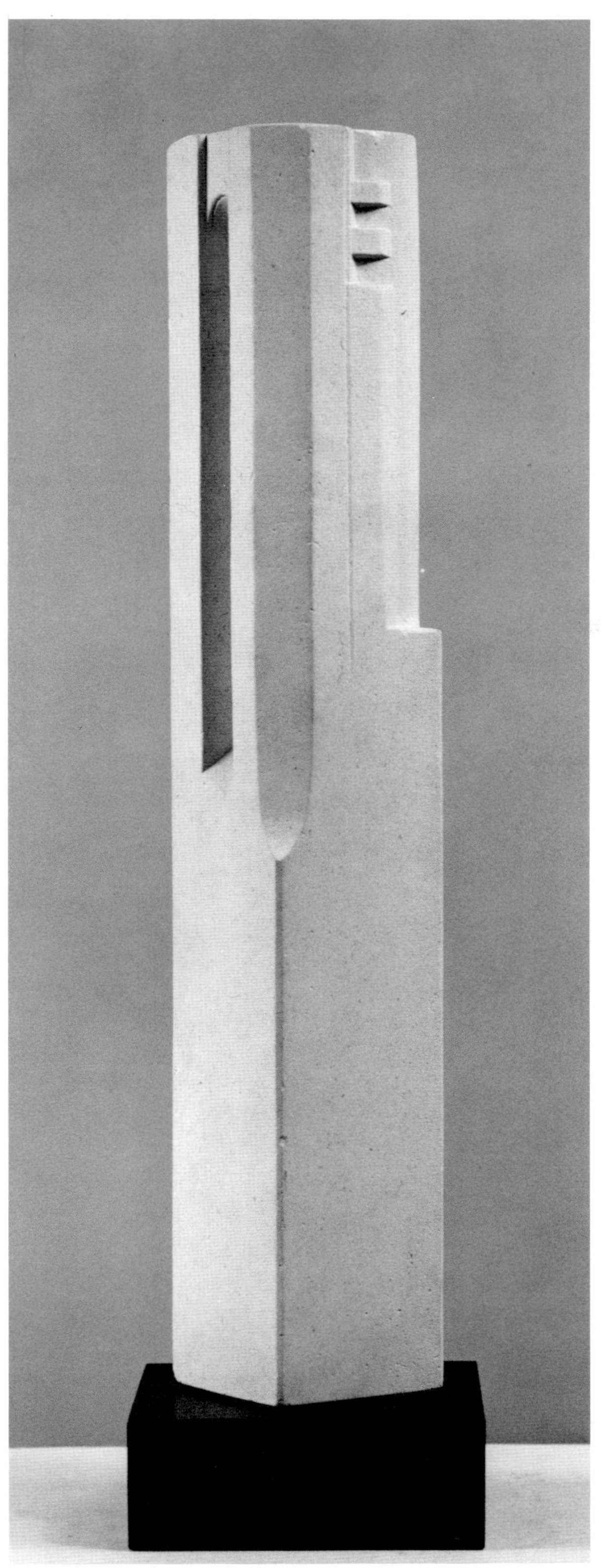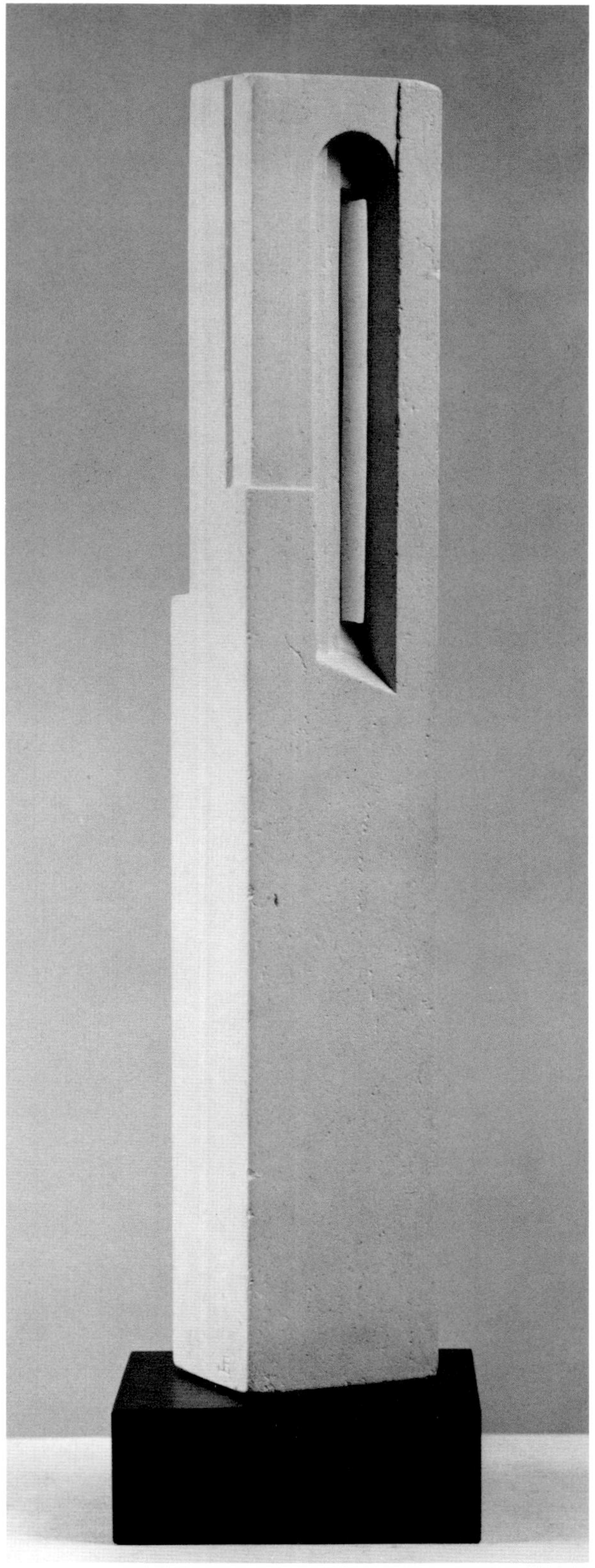

72a, 72b. *Architectural Form*
No. 3, c. 1923
Stone
19¾ x 3¼ x 3¼ (49.5 x 8.3 x 8.3)
Collection of Mr. and Mrs.
Meyer Potamkin

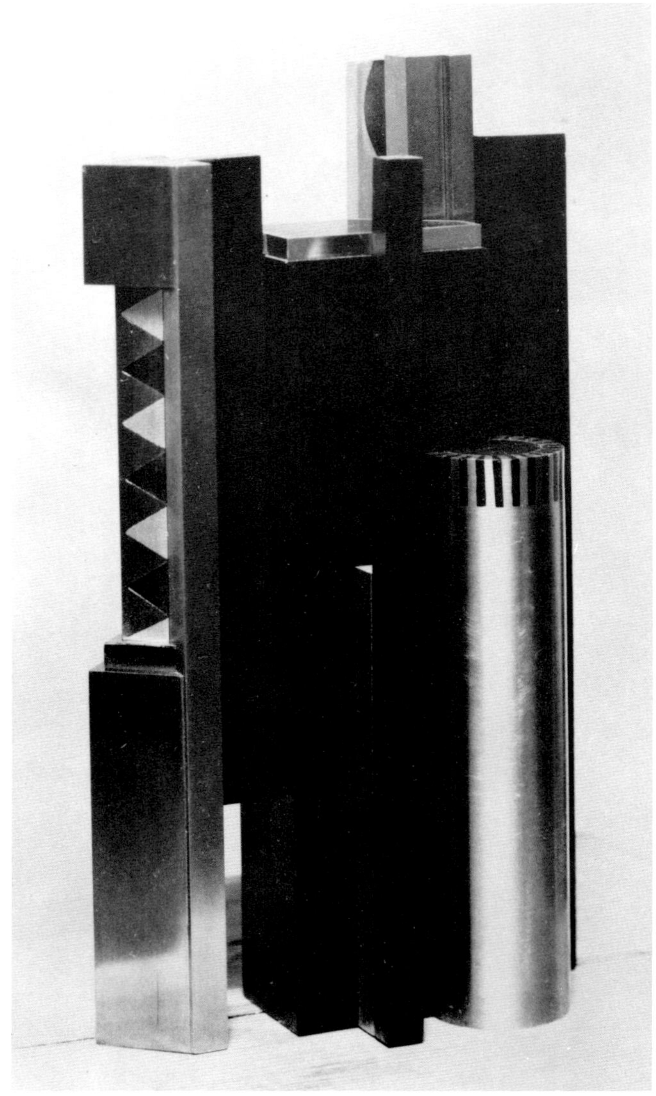

forms against the skyline. The central brass form is like a slim sky-scraper with setbacks, the flanking triangular units resemble the con-tour of the Flatiron Building, and the cylindrical forms recall silos or smokestacks.[19] In his metal buildings or skyscraper cities, Storrs made each sculpture a study in the juxtaposition of pure geometric forms as well as an idealized cityscape.

Study in Form (Fig. 73), also of steel, copper, and brass, has sim-ilar cylindrical and set-back verticals, but its zigzag patterns and wavy, curved lines make the surfaces of the individual units especially lively. By contrast, the tall, elegant *Forms in Space* (Fig. 74) has no curved elements but only slim vertical forms angled out from one another. Yet the contrast of aluminum, brass, copper, and wood creates patterns of light and dark, and the zigzag patterning adds an electric quality to a poised and stable concept. The brass, copper, and steel *Forms in Space* (Fig. 76) is ruled by a carefully calculated system of proportions

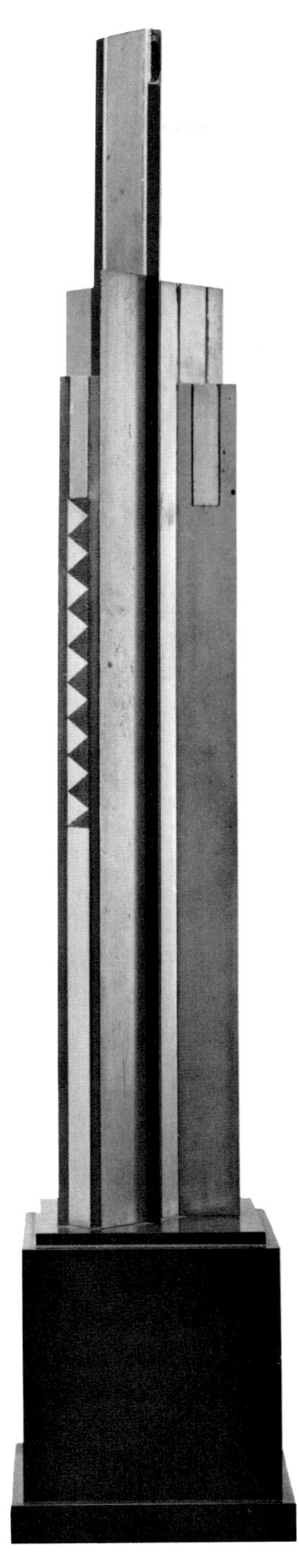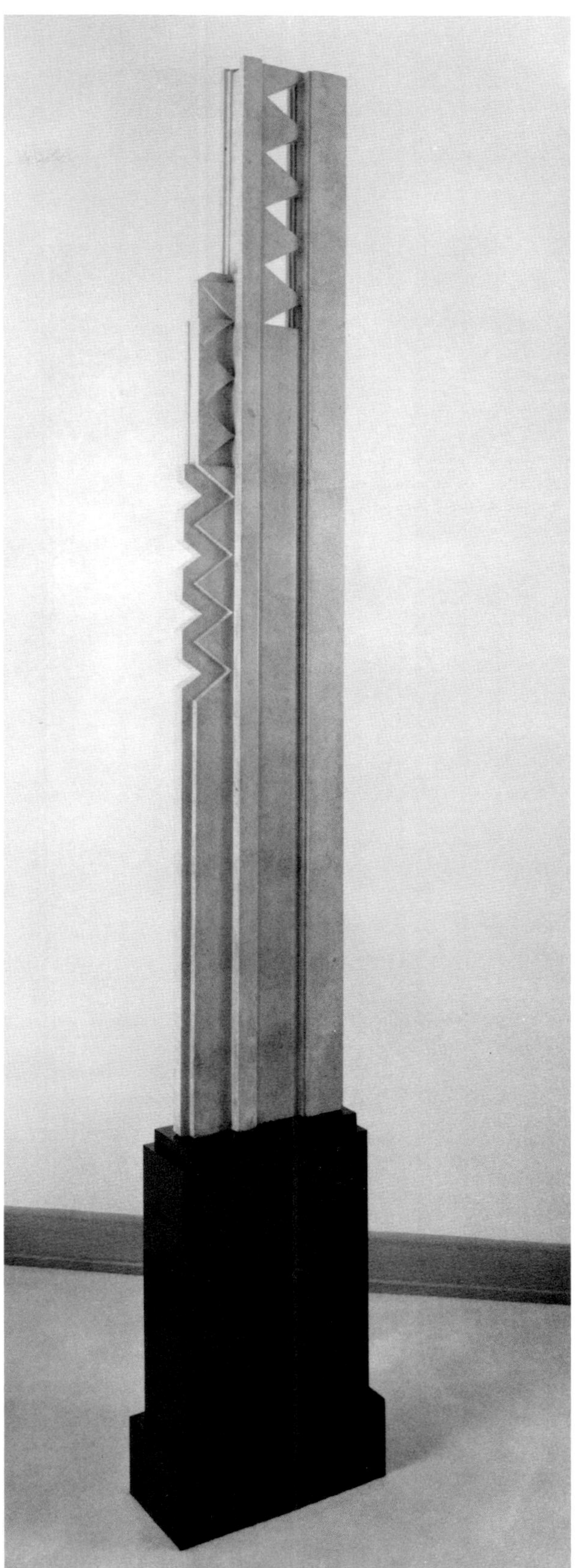

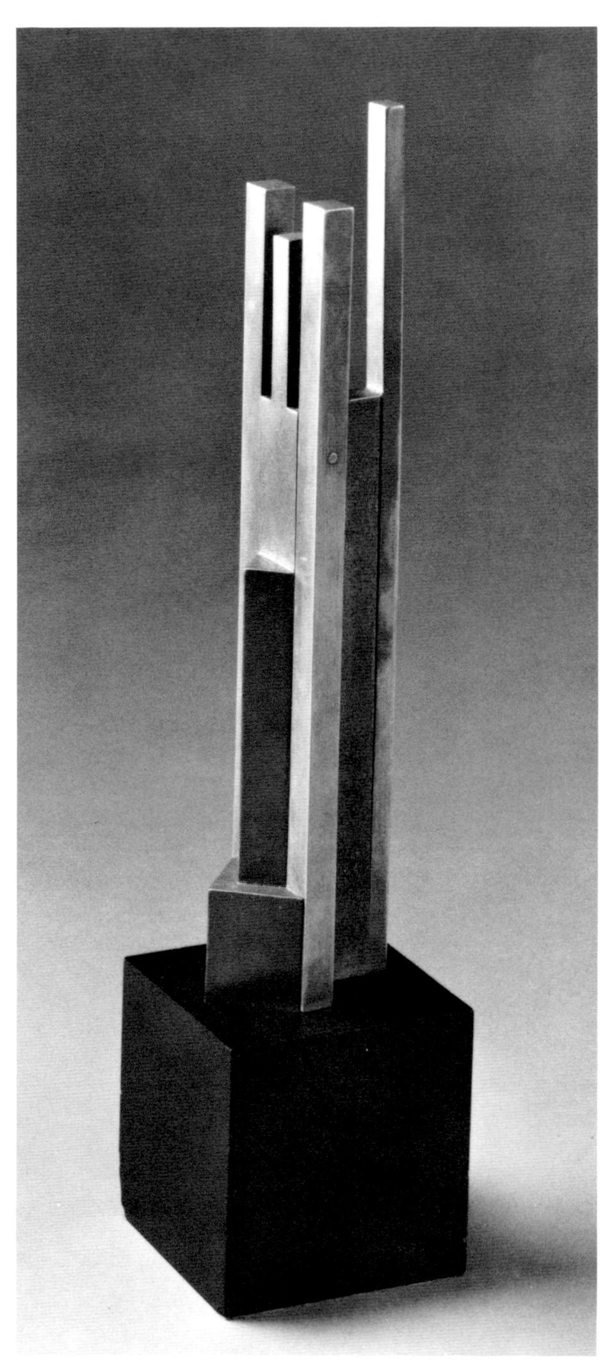

76. *Forms in Space*, c. 1924
Brass, copper, and steel
9⅛ x 1¾ x 2 (23.2 x 4.4 x 5.1)
The Museum of Modern Art,
New York; The Riklis
Collection of the McCrory
Corporation (fractional gift)

that varies the height and depth of the vertical elements to establish a sense of restraint and self-containment.

Storrs produced many ink drawings as studies for these metal sculptures, although at present no exact match can be made to an extant sculpture. Among these drawings, two reveal an intended joining of separate geometric units into a single sculpture (Figs. 78, 79); they may be working drawings for a fabricator. A third sheet of c. 1928 (Fig. 77) reveals that Storrs continued to envision such idealized sculptural-architectural forms as actual buildings, although he undoubtably knew they would never be built.

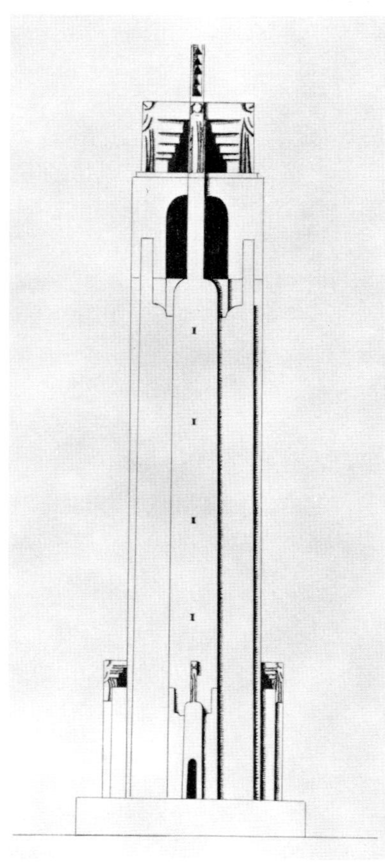

77. *Study for a*
Monumental Tower with
Sculptural Decorations, c. 1928
Ink on paper
16 x 6⁹⁄₁₆ (40.6 x 16.7)
The St. Louis Art Museum,
Missouri; Purchase, Friends Fund

78. *Design for Fabrication of*
Abstract Metal Sculpture
c. 1924–25
Ink on paper
15³⁄₈ x 10¾ (39.1 x 27.3)
Collection of Raymond J. Learsy

79. *Study for a Sculpture*
(*Forms in Space*), 1923
Ink on paper
10¾ x 8¾ (27.3 x 22.2)
The Museum of Modern Art,
New York; The Riklis
Collection of the McCrory
Corporation (fractional gift)

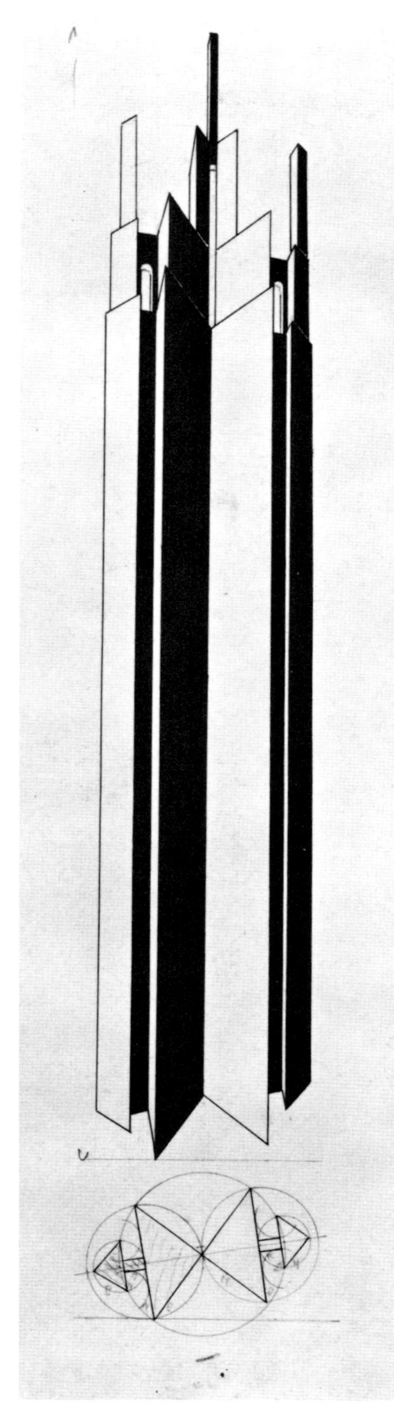

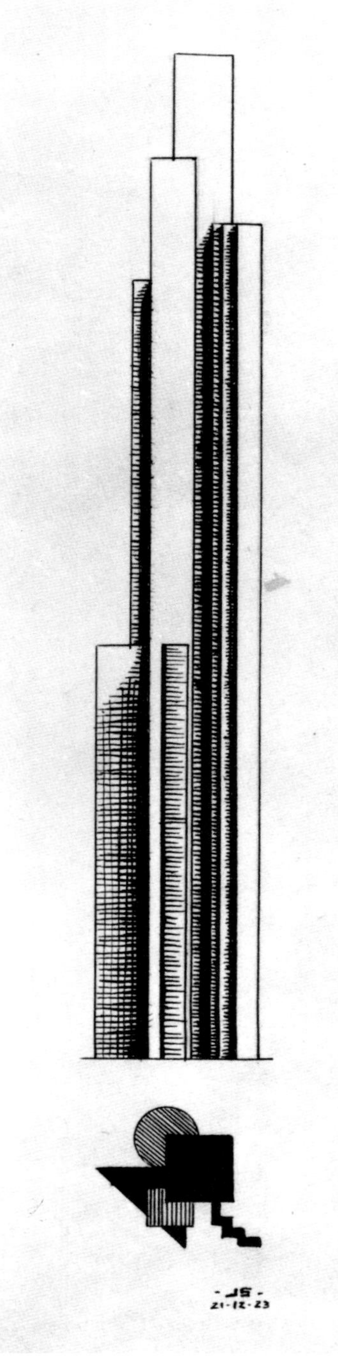

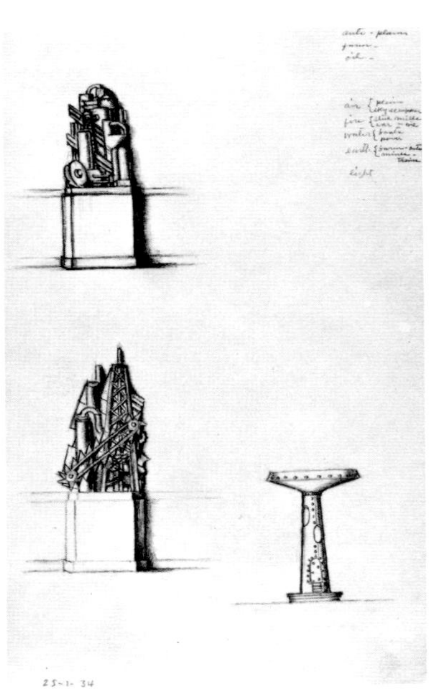

80. *Untitled*, 1934
Pencil on paper
9 x 5½ (22.9 x 14)
John Storrs Papers,
Archives of American Art,
Smithsonian Institution,
Washington, D.C.;
Gift of Monique Storrs Booz

The Skyscaper as Icon

At the same time Storrs was having mixed metal architectural sculptures fabricated, he was also creating "skyscraper icons" in marble and metal. His building clusters or skyscraper cities were groupings of urban structures. By contrast, any one of Storrs' skyscraper icons, whether made of marble or of combined metals, whether sculpted as a whole unit or created from joined parts, conveys the immediate impact of a single, individual building.

Storrs tried to create through his skyscraper sculptures symbolic images for the twentieth century. A 1934 drawing that combines machine and skyscraper forms (Fig. 80) shows that he identifies these forms with the four elements. As inscribed in the upper right hand corner, "air" is represented by the skyscraper and airplane; "fire" by steel mills, oil, and war; "water" by boats and power; and "earth" by barns, automobiles, mines, and trains. To these four elements, Storrs added a fifth element—"light."

Intellectually aware that skyscrapers could be a menace, Storrs on one level saw them as a "parade of mercantile packing casses. . . . And second handed packing cases at that."[20] For this reason, his own skyscraper sculptures did not imitate existing buildings. He seems to have been more impressed with the interpretation of skyscrapers in photography and art than with the structures themselves. He certainly knew the skyscraper images of Joseph Stella, John Marin, Georgia O'Keeffe, and Charles Sheeler—including Sheeler's photographs, which had been published in a 1927 issue of *Cahiers d'Art* that Storrs kept in his library.[21] In sculpture, however, skyscraper imagery was an unexplored field.

Storrs turned such a skyscraper sculpture as *New York* (Fig. 81) into a symbolic icon, like the totem poles and houseposts of the Pacific Northwest that he knew so well. Made of bronze inlaid with steel, *New York* deifies a single building, making it express an entire urban metropolis. Only the most positive aspects of the city are concentrated within this single image—sophistication, the sense of optimism implicit in tall buildings that reach for the sky, and the interaction of the old and the new, like the interaction of bronze and shining steel. For Storrs, the very concept of verticality represented the spiritual, the line projected into infinity, the growth toward the sun and the sky, while he felt that "all that is heavy & brutal is well expressed by the horizontal."[22] *New York* was reproduced on the cover of the Société Anonyme checklist for the international group exhibition held at The Brooklyn Museum in 1926.[23] The reproduction of Storrs' work on this cover indicates its power as a totemic emblem, a distillation not only of the spirit of New York but of the very essence of modernism. Yet in 1966, *New York* was brought to Edith Halpert, whose Downtown Gallery was then handling the Storrs estate, by a woman who had found it in a Goodwill Industries thrift shop.[24]

A most striking use of the skyscraper image as totem or icon is the white marble skyscraper, over six feet high, *Forms in Space No. 1*

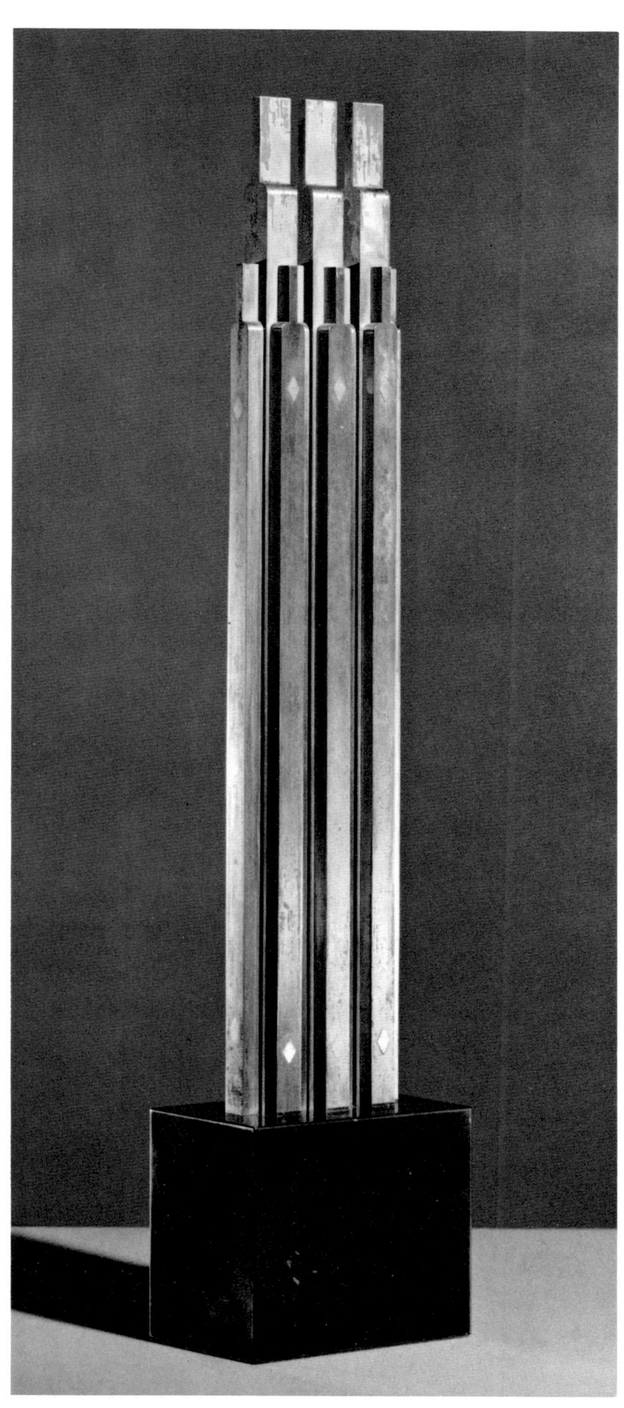

(Fig. 54) of c. 1924. The sculpture is simple and unadorned except for the zigzag motifs incised on the front and back surfaces. The very simplicity of this sculpture and its total adherence to symmetry cause us to view this work as a single image rather than as joined forms. Due to the purity of the white marble, the large scale, absolute symmetry, clarity of form, and carefully calculated proportions, this skyscraper sculpture is the most classicizing of Storrs' architectural sculptures of this period. He here implies that the skyscraper, in utopian form, could be a new temple for modern living.

71   Architectural Forms in Sculpture

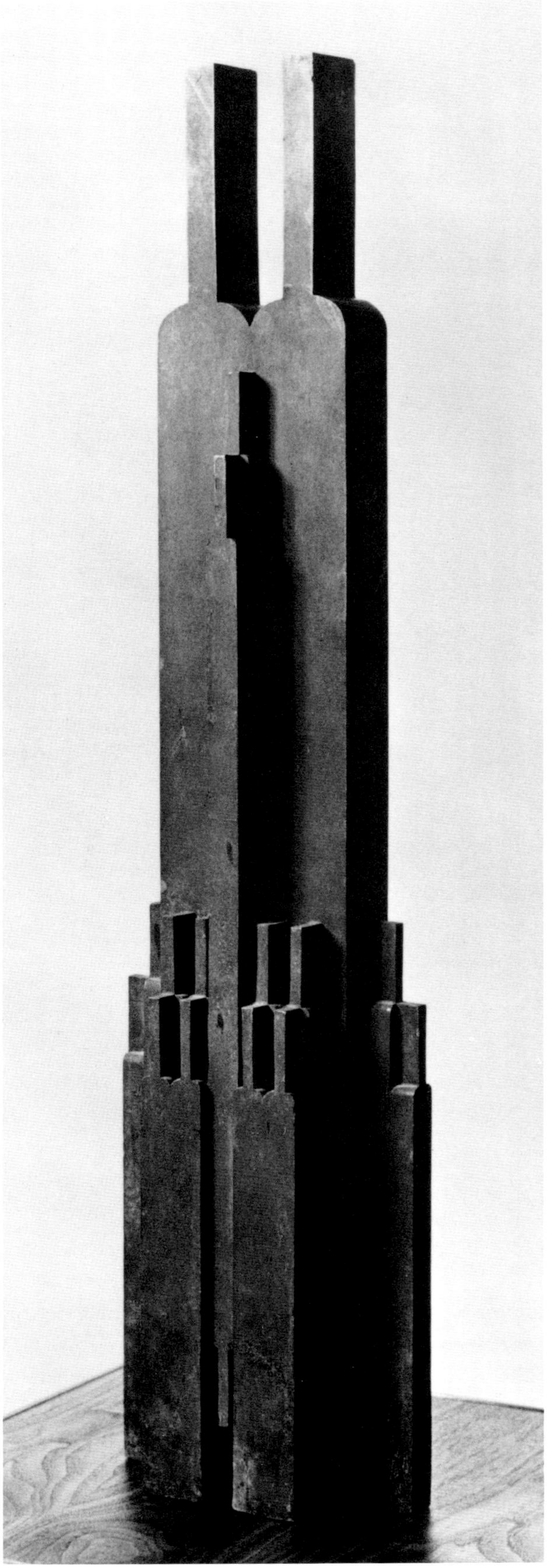

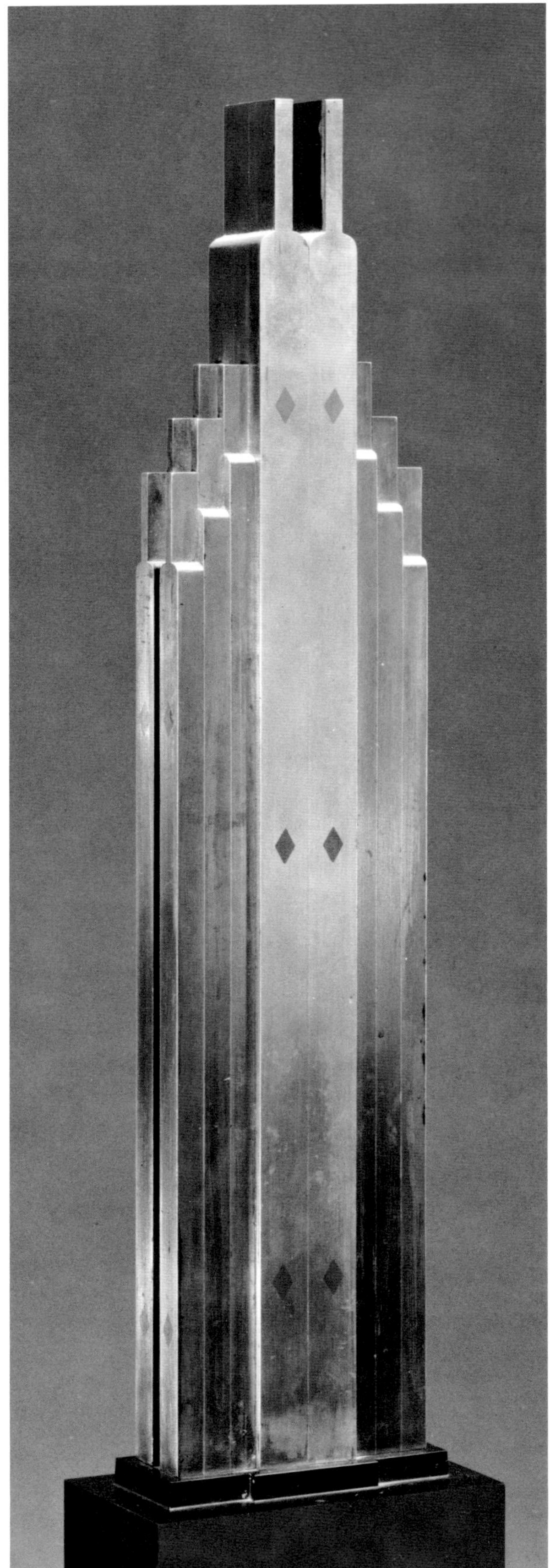

82. *Study in Architectural Forms*, 1927
Steel
31 x 6 x 5 (78.7 x 15.2 x 12.7)
Collection of Mr. and
Mrs. Raymond D. Nasher

83. *Forms in Space*, c. 1927
Steel and copper
20½ x 4 x 1⅝ (52.1 x 10.2 x 4.1)
The Metropolitan Museum of
Art, New York; Purchase, 1967,
Bequest Fund

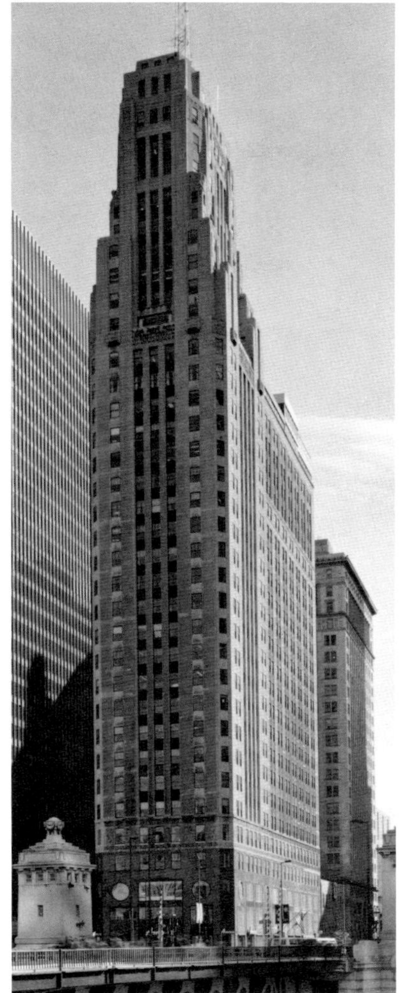

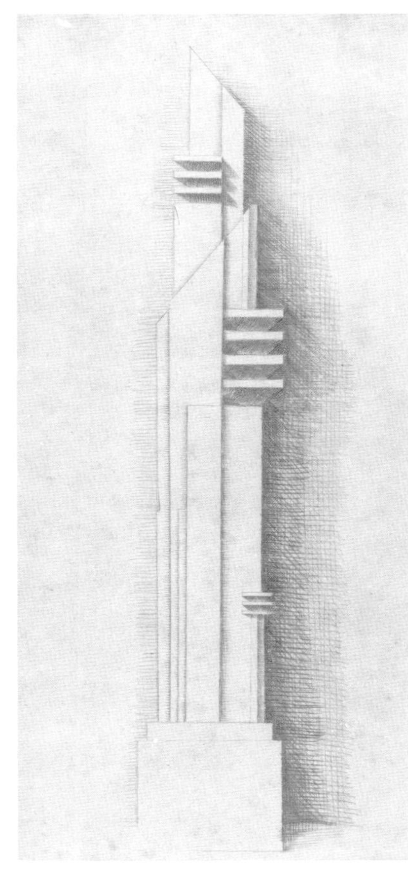

84. John A. Holabird and
John Wellborn Root, Jr.,
architects
333 North Michigan Avenue,
Chicago, 1928

85. *Study for Architectural Sculpture*, 1929
Silverpoint on paper
13¼ x 10¼ (33.7 x 26)
Estate of Monique Storrs Booz;
courtesy of Robert Schoelkopf
Gallery, Ltd., New York

With the economic depression of the late 1920s, Storrs was forced by financial necessity to begin spending the requisite eight months a year in America in order to receive the full measure of his inheritance from the trust fund his father had set up for him. Although he regularly spent summers in France and visited whenever possible, by December 1927 he had moved to Chicago.[25]

Storrs' return to the United States coincided with another exhibition of his sculpture at the Arts Club of Chicago. Although he also showed figurative sculpture and drawings in pencil and silverpoint, he exhibited as numbers 1 through 12 works entitled *Studies in Form*, in stone and metal; it was doubtless these *Studies in Form* that the French critic Maurice Reynal, in his catalogue essay for the show, found to accord with the "magnificent static power of the American skyscraper."[26]

One of the twelve original *Studies in Form* is the imaginative steel skyscraper, whose title changed during the years to *Study in Architectural Forms* (Fig. 82). Its paddlelike repeated motif, not found on any particular building, is used by Storrs again and again in his sculpture and drawings. Similarly, he invented almost all of his

73   Architectural Forms in Sculpture

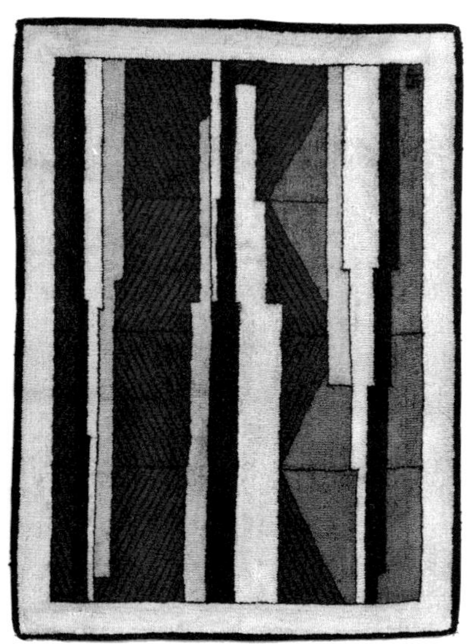

86. *Diagonals*, 1928
Hand-hooked wool rug,
designed by Storrs
64 x 46 (162.6 x 116.8)
Estate of Monique Storrs Booz;
courtesy of Robert Schoelkopf
Gallery, Ltd., New York

skyscraper distillations. Rather than simulate any one building, he captured the essence of the skyscraper concept in the Art Deco style that constituted the American contribution to the skyscraper phenomenon.

Only once did Storrs model a skyscraper sculpture on a known building. The shape and proportions of *Forms in Space* (Fig. 83) bear a striking similarity to the skyscraper built by Holabird and Root at 333 North Michigan Avenue in Chicago (Fig. 84). Constructed in 1927–28, the building was the first Art Deco skyscraper in Chicago,[27] and Storrs' sculpture can probably be given the same date. Yet *Forms in Space* is hardly a copy of the actual skyscraper; rather, Storrs has simplified, refined, and heightened the various elements contained within the generalized form of the building.

Storrs also explored skyscraper images in silverpoint, responding to the challenges and special demands of that medium (Fig. 85). He liked the evanescent, flexible line afforded by silverpoint and, since he sought to capture luminosity in his skyscraper sculptures, he was also attracted to silverpoint's light-reflecting qualities.[28]

Storrs even rendered the skyscraper image in a rug he designed in 1928 (Fig. 86). *Diagonals* incorporates skyscrapers into a zigzag landscape that resembles that of the American Southwest. The zigzag pattern immediately conjures up associations with the Navaho rugs that Storrs enjoyed collecting. Through the use of pure geometry he made this combination of the wonders of nature and the sophisticated urban wonders of man work in tandem. Once again, as in *Auto Tower* (Fig. 48), he used a punning double image, for the landscape is most evident when *Diagonals* is seen horizontally, while the skyscrapers appear when the rug is turned ninety degrees. Color also helps differentiate the forms; the skyscrapers are rendered in grays and beiges, all tonal, urban shades, while the landscape is in blues and greens.

Notes

1. John Storrs to Marguerite Storrs, February 23, 1923, AAA, JSP, 5, John & Marguerite Storrs correspondence 1923: "I have arranged with the Arts Club to have an exhibition of Stella's & my work which will open April 14th to April 26th. . . . " That Storrs specifically wanted Stella's *New York Interpreted* is indicated by Katherine Dreier's letter to him, April 6, 1923, AAA, JSP, 4, Correspondence 1923: "I sent you a telegram stating that I would try to see whether we could handle the situation so that the Arts Club of Chicago could have the five big Stella panels of 'New York Interpreted.' I hope I can handle it so that you all may not be disappointed, and at the same time, that he will not lose the chance of selling these very valuable pictures."

2. John Storrs, "Museums or Artists," *The Little Review*, 9 (Winter 1922), p. 63.

3. Storrs' architectural drawings of this type date chiefly from 1914, 1915, and 1916; many of them are in the estate of Monique Storrs Booz.

4. Draft letter, undated, AAA, JSP, 4, Fragments of letters. Some corrections in this draft letter were made by Marguerite Storrs, but it is clear that the section Storrs wished to omit from his final letter he crossed out himself.

5. Frank Lloyd Wright, *An Autobiography* (New York: Horizon Press, 1977), pp. 204–05. Wright considered the straight line itself as an abstraction.

6. Wright's role as a progenitor of the Art Deco movement has been well noted; see especially Jeffrey Wechsler, "Machine Aesthetics and Art Deco," in *Vanguard American Sculpture: 1913–1939*, exhibition catalogue (New Brunswick, New Jersey: Rutgers University Art Gallery, 1979), pp. 85–104. Wechsler discusses the connections of Wright and Storrs with Art Deco and uses the examples of

Wright's *Nakoma* and *Nakomis* (the terra-cottas date from 1924) to show the Art Deco characteristics in Wright's sculptures.

7. AAA, Downtown Gallery Papers, "A Catalogue of the Works of John Storrs, 1915." Storrs' listing is "7/2/14 Femme Dansant sur une Colonne—26½ cm. Platre et Bronze"; this date appears on the existing bronze.

8. Ibid. Storrs' own listing is "2/9/13 Tête sur le Pilastre, variation de 6/28/13" with dimensions given for the bronze as 23 cm. Storrs' entry for 6/28/13 describes the piece as "Homme Chantant, A Head." The date of 6/28/13 appears on the existing bronze.

9. AAA, JSP, 9, Financial records & ledgers, "Etchings and Poems *sent out.*" Storrs' entry reads, "Head of Vicomte Inoye in polished silver bronze. Made 1918—sold to him Oct 26 1922. . . . "

10. John Storrs to Marguerite Storrs, 1/5/23, AAA, JSP, 5, John & Marguerite Storrs correspondence, 1923.

11. Ibid. Storrs does not mention Iannelli by name but writes that Byrne, "took me in auto out north to visit the studio of his partner a sculptor—who does all small stuff for him—they are both very interested in what I am doing & promed give me work to do on their next big job. They will both be over this summer. . . . "

12. Alfonso Iannelli to John Storrs, July 9, 1924, AAA, JSP, 4, Correspondence 1924: "Inclosed [*sic*] please find the 600 fr. for the piece of sculpture. I feel that I shall enjoy the influence of this so much and shall be anxious for it to arrive." R.A. Lennon, "Two Works of Art in Odd Adventure," *The Art World Magazine*, March 3, 1925, John Storrs Scrapbook, Robert Schoelkopf Gallery, Ltd., New York, p. 8, reports that "Mr. Byrne, an architect met Storrs during the course of the sculptor's last Chicago exhibition some two years ago. Last summer, while in Paris, he purchased from the artist two of his newer conceptions, works of a purely mechanistic character, to the evolution of which Storrs had but recently turned his attention. Mr. Byrne arranged for the shipment of the two pieces to Chicago before he himself returned." The article reproduces the sculpture now known as *Study in Pure Form (Forms in Space No. 4)* (Fig. 84). Possibly the second piece that Byrne had shipped did not belong to him but to Iannelli, and

Byrne simply facilitated the shipping by sending both under one name.

13. One of the pier elements in the dining room of Wright's Imperial Hotel in Tokyo bears a chevron pattern that grows into a Wrightian "tree of life" motif. This same motif, which can also be read as a series of inverted Indian arrowheads, had appeared in Wright's window for the Darwin Martin House of 1904. Robert Schoelkopf kindly pointed out the visual connection between the Darwin Martin window motif and Storrs' *Architectural Form* (Fig. 62).

14. The comparison between the Larkin columns and Storrs' *Study in Form (Architectural Form)* becomes more telling if the round globes and sculpture on the top of the columns, the work of Richard Bock, are omitted. Henry-Russell Hitchcock, *In the Nature of Materials: The Buildings of Frank Lloyd Wright, 1887–1941* (reprint, New York: Da Capo Press, 1982), p. 51, writes that critics of the twenties generally disapproved of these sculptured groups. Storrs may have heard such rumblings and perhaps his *Study in Form (Architectural Form)* is an attempt to simplify and thus purify the Larkin columns.

15. This diary-sketchbook is in AAA, JSP, 1, Diary 1909, 1910, 1919.

16. Many of John Storrs' sculptures, among them *Architectural Forms No. 3*, had been in storage at the Lefèvre-Foinet warehouse in Paris. In 1981, over two hundred of them were shipped back to the United States and are now either among the works in the Monique Storrs Booz estate or estate works that are presently in the Robert Schoelkopf Gallery in New York.

17. F.G. in "Round the Studios," *New York Herald Tribune*, European edition, January 25, 1925, p. 4, in describing a visit to Storrs' Paris studio. He added that Storrs had advanced to making "studies in pure form, with no representation whatsoever involved . . . . It is the architectural element which is now the controlling factor in his work."

18. Of the ten identical sculptures, fabricated by the industrial firm of G. Sueur, Paris, the one presently in the Munson-Williams-Proctor Institute (Fig. 69) came from the collection of Barry Byrne. Others are in The Hirshhorn Museum and Sculpture Garden, and private collections in Paris, Rhode Island, and New York. During the 1980s, recent fakes of *Study in Pure Form (Forms in Space*

No. 4) have appeared on the market. Among other factors that characterize them as fakes, they differ in measurement and assembly from the pieces in the original edition.

19. See Paul D. Schweizer, "Skyscraper Sculpture: John Storrs Acquired by the Museum," *Munson-Williams-Proctor Institute Bulletin* (November 1983), unpaginated, describing the effects of the metals in *Study in Pure Form (Forms in Space No. 4)*: "These metals have been crafted together with machine-like precision, creating a tapered shaft that is sleek and beautifully proportioned. Its polished forms have been arranged with an eye to the mutually contrasting effects created by the natural colors of the various metals."

20. Entry, 9/8/15, AAA, JSP, 1, Diary 1914–1916.

21. *Cahiers d'Art*, 4–5 (1927).

22. Entry, 9/8/15, AAA, JSP, 1, Diary 1914–1916.

23. Katherine S. Dreier, *An International Exhibition of Modern Art*, exhibition catalogue (New York: The Brooklyn Museum, 1926); see also Ruth L. Bohan, *The Société Anonyme's Brooklyn Exhibition* (Ann Arbor, Michigan: UMI Research Press, 1982).

24. Edith Halpert to James Harithas, April 15, 1969, exhibition files, The Corcoran Gallery of Art, Washington, D.C.

25. A letter from R. G. Toffany, Cadillac Motor Company, Chicago, to John Storrs, 20 E. Delaware Place, Chicago, December 23, 1923, AAA, JSP, 4, Correspondence 1927, congratulates Storrs on the purchase of a Cadillac Sedan from the used-car department.

26. "About the Works of John Storrs," in *Sculpture by John Storrs*, exhibition catalogue (Chicago: Arts Club of Chicago, 1927). See also Reynal's corrected text in French, "Sur l'oeuvre de John Storrs," AAA, JSP, 1, Critical & Historical Comments on Storrs.

27. See Ira J. Bach, ed., *Chicago's Famous Buildings* (Chicago and London: The University of Chicago Press, 1980), pp. 61–62.

28. For Storrs' attraction to silverpoint, see Bruce Weber, *The Fine Line: Drawing with Silver*, exhibition catalogue (West Palm Beach, Florida: Norton Gallery & School of Art, 1985), esp. pp. 20–21, with accompanying notes.

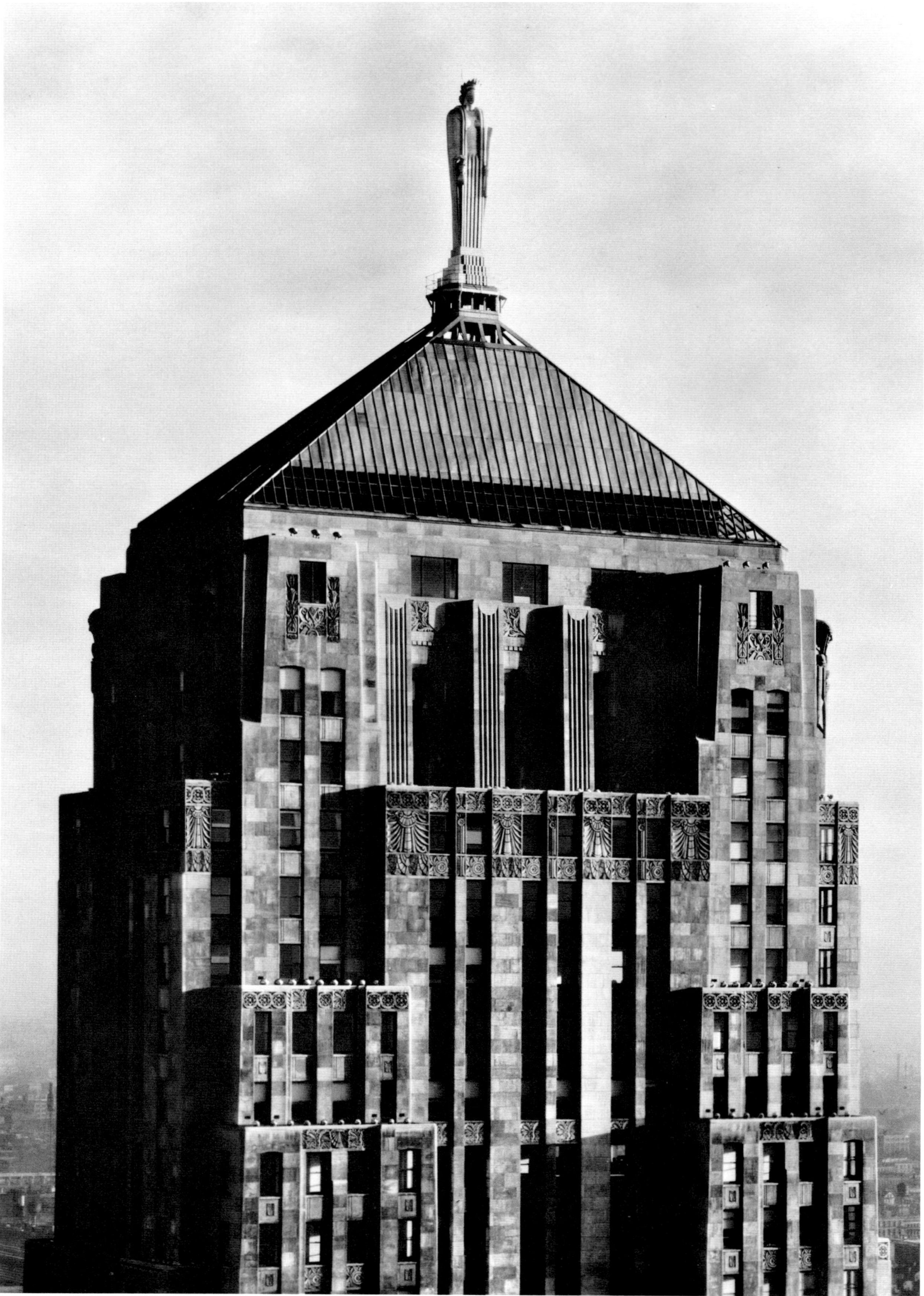

V. Commissions from Architects 1928–1930

John Storrs had three major commissions in the works by 1929: he had completed a model for a statue of *Ceres*, the Roman goddess of grain, for the Chicago Board of Trade Building; he was working on a statue of *Christ* for the Church of Christ the King in Cork, Ireland; and he had submitted sculpture designs for a monument to honor American naval heroes in Brest, France. In the first two works, which were of necessity figurative, Storrs embraced the opportunity to create architectonic sculptures on a monumental scale.

Ceres for the Chicago Board of Trade Building

Storrs' thirty-one foot high *Ceres* (Fig. 89) was the ultimate Art Deco goddess. She encapsulated the Neoclassical tendencies of the movement, while her coolly seductive, machine-tooled body—made of polished cast aluminum—prefigured the streamlining of the 1930s. She is as sleek and smooth as the newest, bullet-shaped trains that sped down the tracks. In one of his scrapbooks, Storrs saved a photograph of *Ceres* and the new Commodore Vanderbilt streamliner as they were seen at Chicago's La Salle Street station (Fig. 88). The handwritten caption, "modern train to modern statue," declares his intention.

Storrs felt strongly that his first task was to make his statue "in architectural harmony with the building on which it was to stand.[1] A view of the uppermost portion of the Art Deco Board of Trade Building (Fig. 87) shows that the fluting in *Ceres'* gown, which also acts as the fluting in a classical column, exactly echoes the stripings of the roof and columns below. As Storrs said, "the vertical lines of the building itself are retained in the lines of the statue."[2] Storrs had been given total liberty by the architects John A. Holabird and John Wellborn Root, Jr., who merely set their blueprints before him. Because the top of the building was a simple pyramid, Storrs did not want a visually dynamic piece. He decided that the statue would have to function like a finial, with the entire figure conceived as a column and its surface articulation.[3]

Storrs also took into consideration the curving forms of the interior of the Chicago Board of Trade Building (Fig. 90). The curves of *Ceres'* shoulders and draperies echo the multiple, swelling forms of the interior design. Thus, by linking his statue with the exterior and interior of the building, Storrs was applying one of the basic principles of Art Deco design—the unification of all form into a continuous, flowing totality.

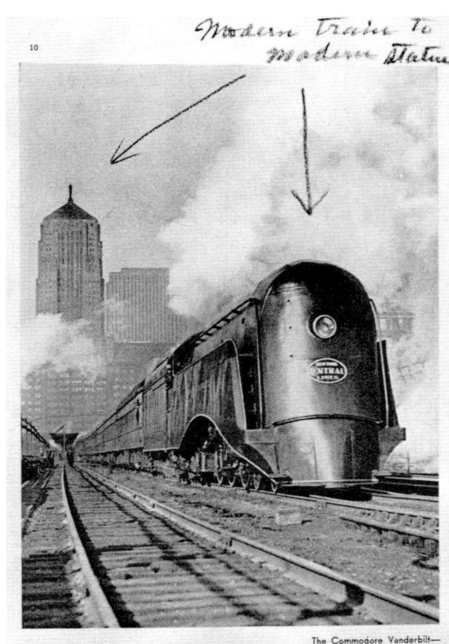

88. Magazine reproduction with
Storrs' handwritten notation,
The Commodore Vanderbilt in
La Salle Street station, Chicago,
with the Board of Trade
Building in left background
John Storrs Scrapbook,
Robert Schoelkopf Gallery, Ltd.,
New York

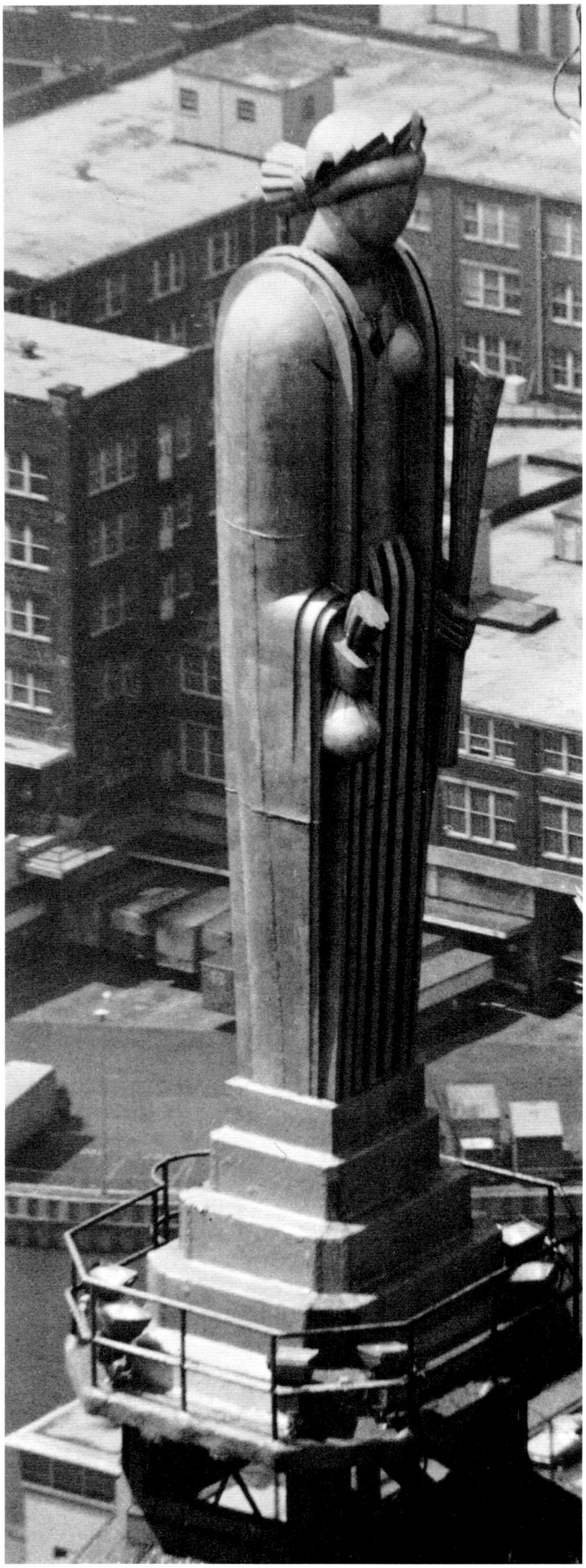

89. *Ceres*, c. 1929
Aluminum
372 (944.9) high
Board of Trade Building, Chicago

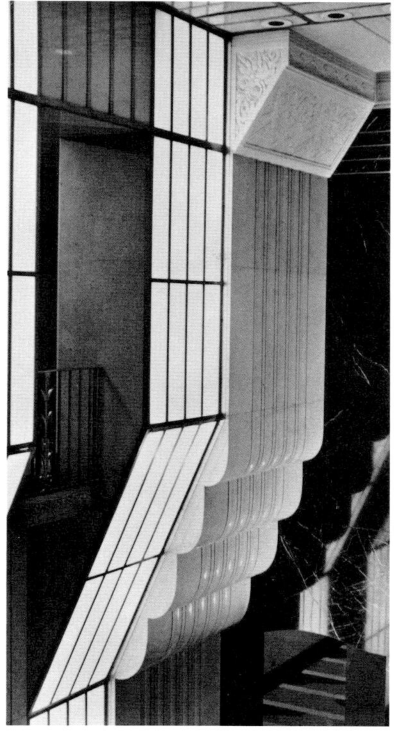

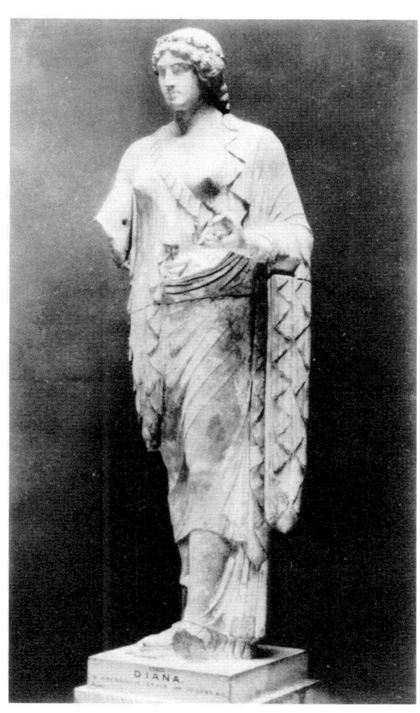

90. John A. Holabird and
John Wellborn Root, Jr.,
architects
Interior of the Board of
Trade Building, Chicago, 1928

91. Postcard kept by Storrs of the
Greek Archaistic statue of *Diana*
in the British Museum, London
John Storrs Papers,
Archives of American Art,
Smithsonian Institution,
Washington, D.C.;
Gift of Monique Storrs Booz

Storrs' next consideration was for the work's symbolic value; he felt that *Ceres* should symbolize the organization that the building was to house.[4] The Chicago Board of Trade was then (and still remains) the world's number one grain market. Decorative panels on the interior are detailed with sheaves of wheat and the exterior relief sculptures show figures holding, respectively, a sheaf of wheat and an ear of corn. Storrs' *Ceres* also holds a sheaf of wheat—with Art Deco zigzag detailing—in her right hand and in her left a grain trader's sample bag, originally used to show samples of the grain being traded so that buyer and seller could agree on quality.[5]

In his efforts to create a simple, columnar sculpture, a streamlined goddess for an Art Deco skyscraper, Storrs turned both to ancient and contemporaneous sources. A postcard that he kept among his papers shows that one ancestor of *Ceres* was the Greek Archaistic statue of *Diana* in the British Museum (Fig. 91).[6] The conical geometry of *Diana*'s breasts would not have escaped Storrs' notice, and the zigzag patterning of the draperies is captured in the zigzag motif on the sheaf of wheat that *Ceres* holds. The contemporary sculpture of Constantin Brancusi seems to have asserted itself as well in *Ceres*' physiognomy, or rather, lack of physiognomy. Storrs' *Ceres* shares with Brancusi's *Mlle. Pogany, II* of 1920 (Albright-Knox Art Gallery, Buffalo) a minimal face and a severe hairstyle, although *Ceres* lacks features altogether. Storrs had visited Brancusi's studio in the early 1920s and thus would probably have been familiar with the polished bronze *Mlle. Pogany, II* and with Brancusi's featureless marble *Head of a Woman*; Storrs was still dining with Brancusi in 1927.[7]

92. *Ceres*, c. 1929
Steel
26 x 6½ x 5 (66 x 16.5 x 12.7)
The Art Institute of Chicago;
Gift of John N. Stern

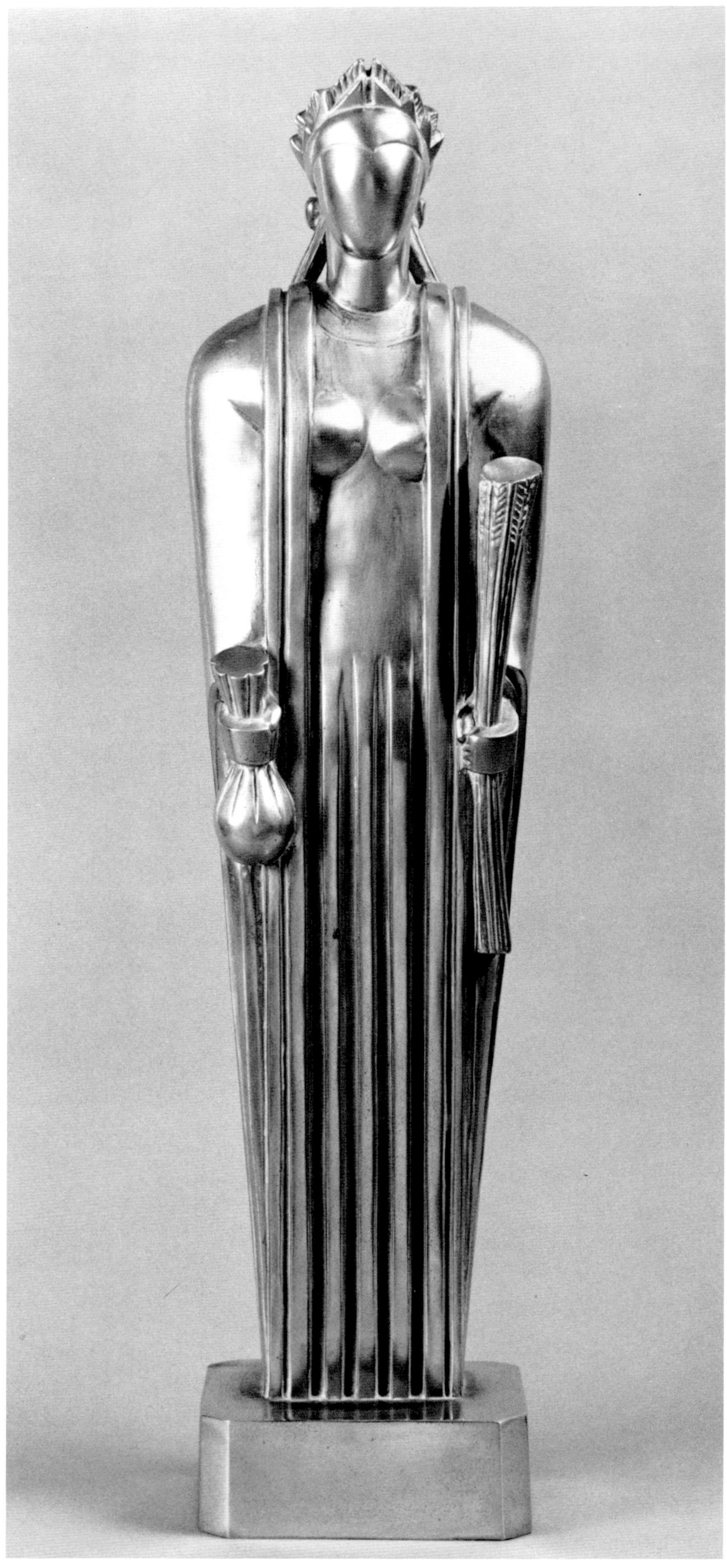

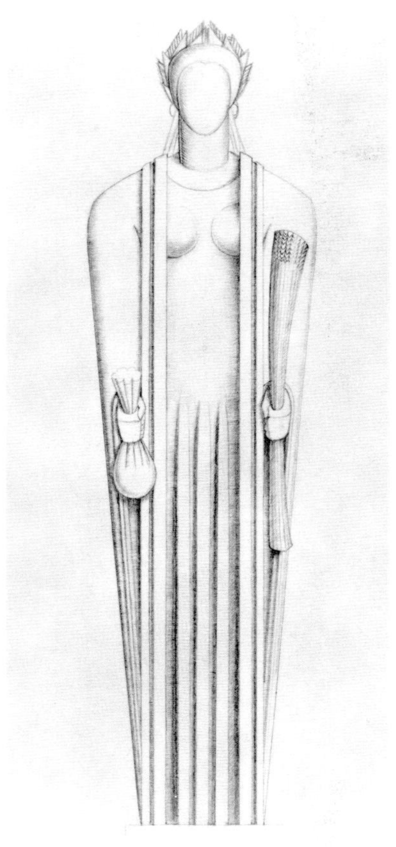

93. *Ceres*, c. 1929
Pencil on paper
14¾ x 6⅝ (37.5 x 16.8)
Collection of Stephens Inc.,
Little Rock, Arkansas

94. *Bust of Ceres*, c. 1929
Bronze
7¼ x 6⅜ x 3⅝
(18.4 x 16.2 x 9.2)
Estate of Monique Storrs Booz;
courtesy of Robert Schoelkopf
Gallery, Ltd., New York

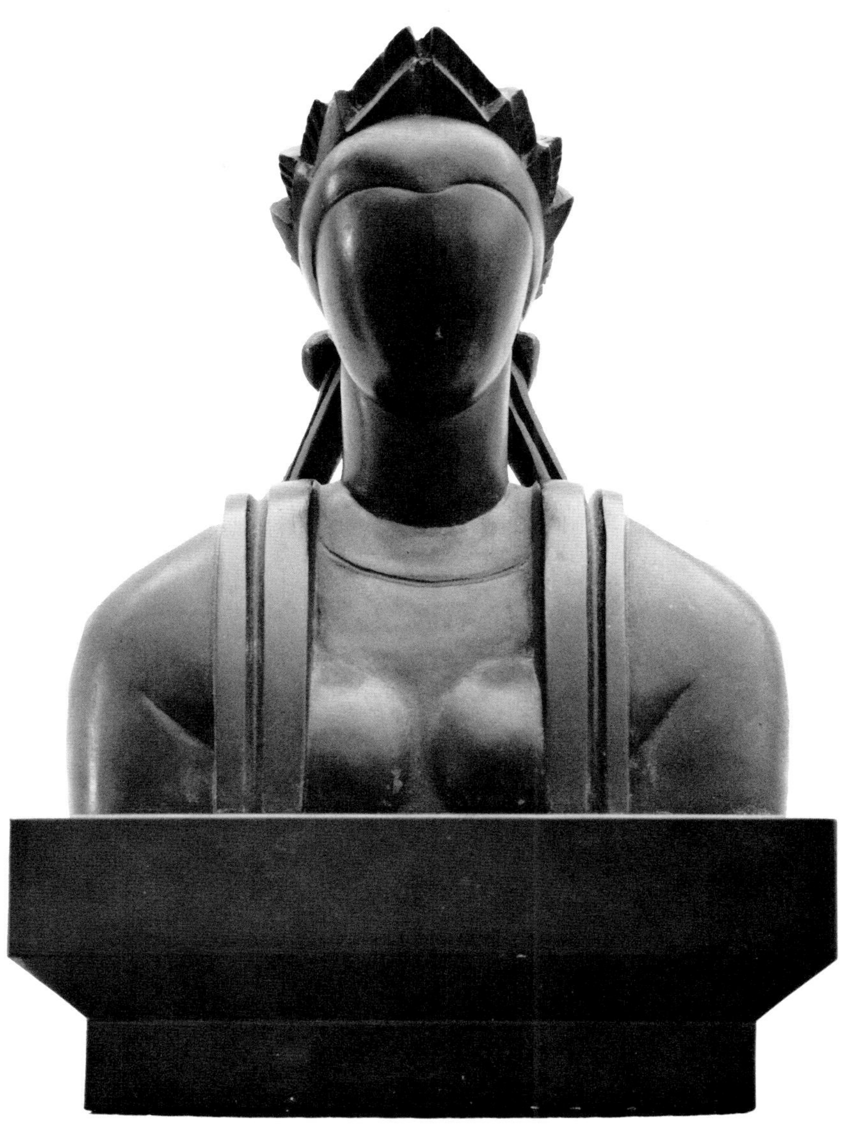

Ceres had lasting ramifications for Storrs' development as an artist. He evolved a figural type—an idealized, classicizing woman—that was to resurface in his sculpture, drawings, and graphics for the rest of his career. First he had the *Ceres* image cast in smaller sizes in various materials. One of these smaller versions, in cast chrome steel (Fig. 92), has a neat chignon tied with a bow instead of the cut-sheaf-of-wheat ponytail of the monumental statue. A highly finished drawing (Fig. 93) and a small bust (Fig. 94) both show this same hairstyle. From this point on, Storrs never entirely abandoned his use of the Ceres type and his penchant for the streamlined goddess led to silverpoint drawings of women, many of them portraits or nudes, of incredible skill and delicacy.

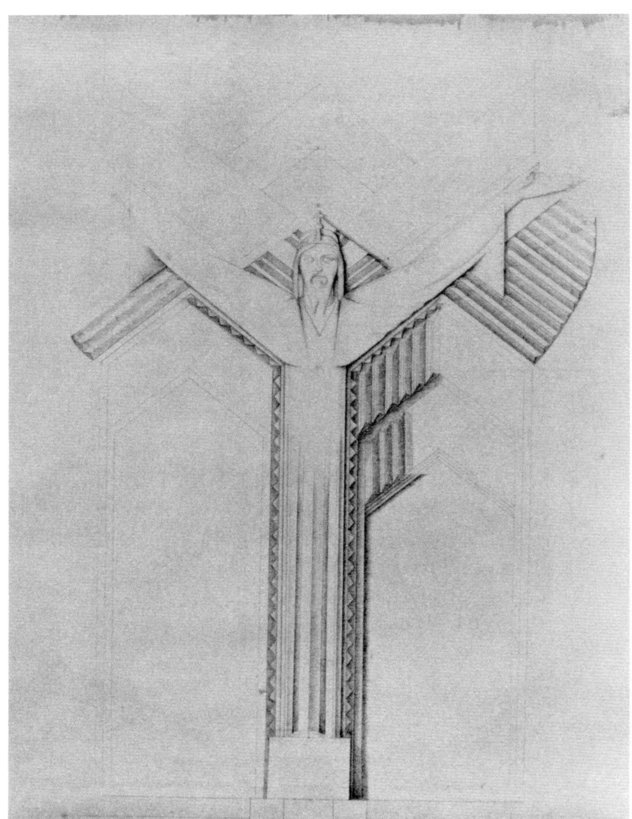

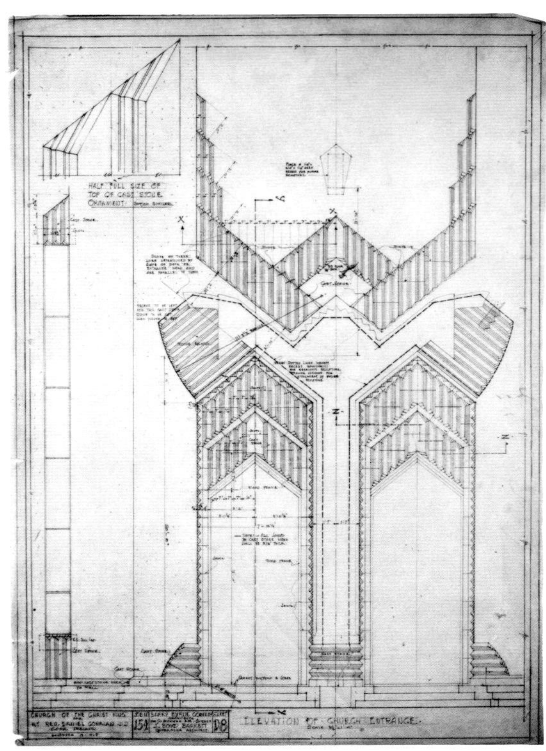

95. *Study for Christ, for the
façade of the Church of Christ
the King, Cork, Ireland*, c. 1929
Pencil on paper
29 x 23 (73.7 x 58.4)
Estate of Monique Storrs Booz;
courtesy of Robert Schoelkopf
Gallery, Ltd., New York

96. Barry Byrne, architect
Elevation of main entrance of
the Church of Christ the King,
Cork, Ireland, c. 1930

Christ for the Church of Christ the King, Cork, Ireland

Storrs probably received the commission for a monumental Christ
figure for the Church of Christ the King in Cork in 1928—for in May
of that year, Barry Byrne, the architect for the church, was in touch
with him.[8] Byrne owned a sculpture by Storrs and had once promised
him work on a major project (see p. 60). Like Storrs, Byrne was a firm
believer that structure and ornament should be integrated.[9]

Work on the church began in March 1929. By early July, Storrs
had visited Cork to see the initial work and in December he started to
make sketches for the *Christ* figure (Fig. 95).[10]

The Church of Christ the King is a rare example of an Art Deco
church. It was considered innovative in its adaptation of the liturgical
service to modern structural forms.[11] The floor plan shows the characteristic Art Deco octagon shape and the exterior (Fig. 97) and interior are punctuated by repeated serrated parallelisms and stepped
motifs, while a chevron motif accentuates the main entrance (Fig. 96).

It seems likely that the general configuration of Storrs' statue was
predetermined since it was to be slotted in between the cast stone
decorative embellishment on the entrance; the upraised arms of the
figure thus result from Byrne's design. This position, combined with
the draped, striated "sleeves" Byrne designed, resembled wings. The

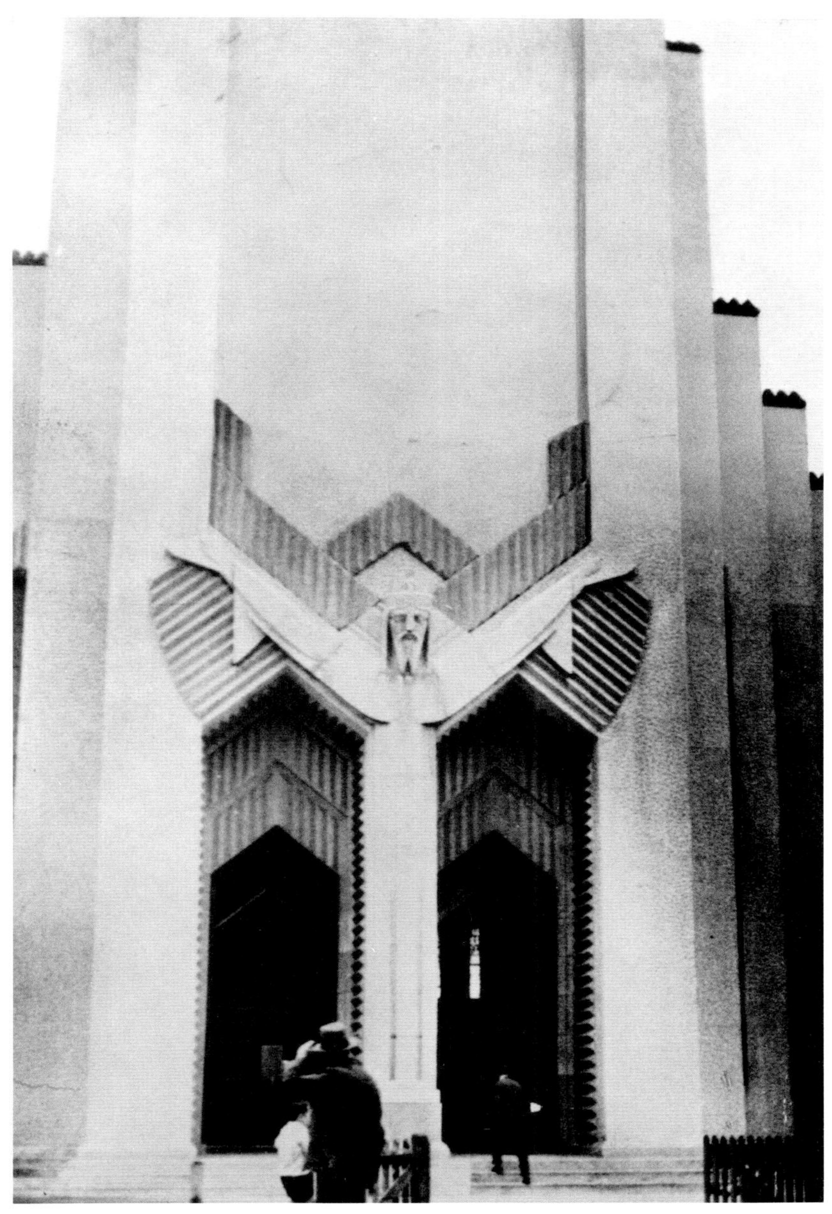

configuration thus offered Storrs a fresh opportunity to work with one
of his favored themes, that of the winged figure (see pp. 29–35)—and
also strive to surpass the winged figures created by other contemporary
sculptors who worked with architects, such as Richard Bock in his sculpture for the Larkin Building (Fig. 57).[12] In fact, if we seek a secular
ancestor for Storrs' *Christ*, Bock's pier capital (Fig. 58) done for
Wright's Midway Gardens is surely part of the family tree.

In July 1929, Storrs' drawing for *Christ* was approved by Boyd
Barrett, the supervising architect, and Storrs signed a contract for the
project.[13] He then made a small plaster relief, just over two feet
high (Fig. 98), showing how the sculpture would look at the church
entrance. Then, in Paris, where he spent most of the summer and
winter of 1929–30, he made a nine-foot-high model (Fig. 100), cast in

83   Commissions from Architects

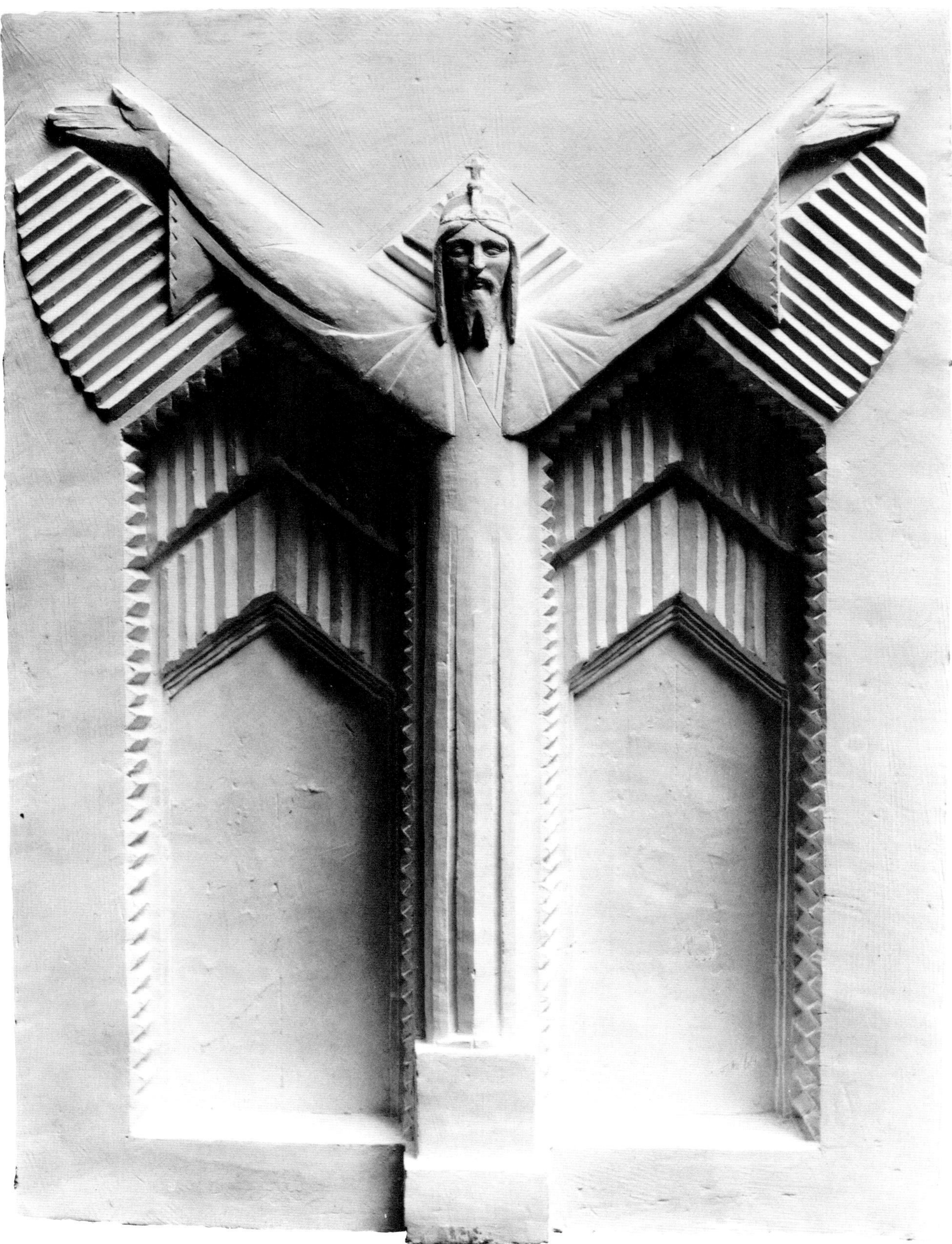

98. *Christ*, 1929
Plaster
26¼ x 19¼ x 4
(66.7 x 48.9 x 10.2)
Musée, Mer, France

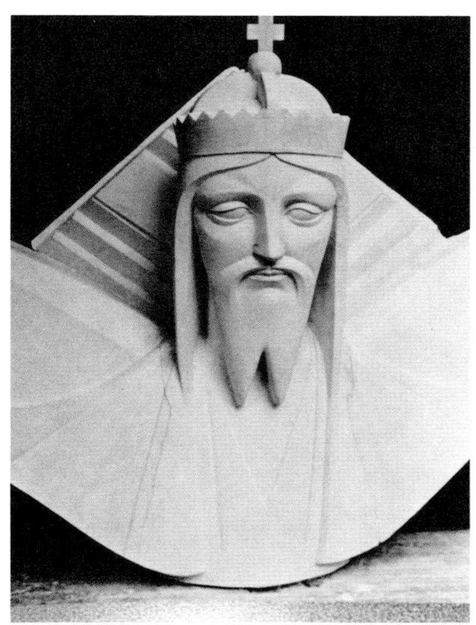

99. *Christ*, c. 1930
Plaster
Whereabouts unknown

100. *Christ*, 1929–30
Plaster
108 (274.3) high
Whereabouts unknown

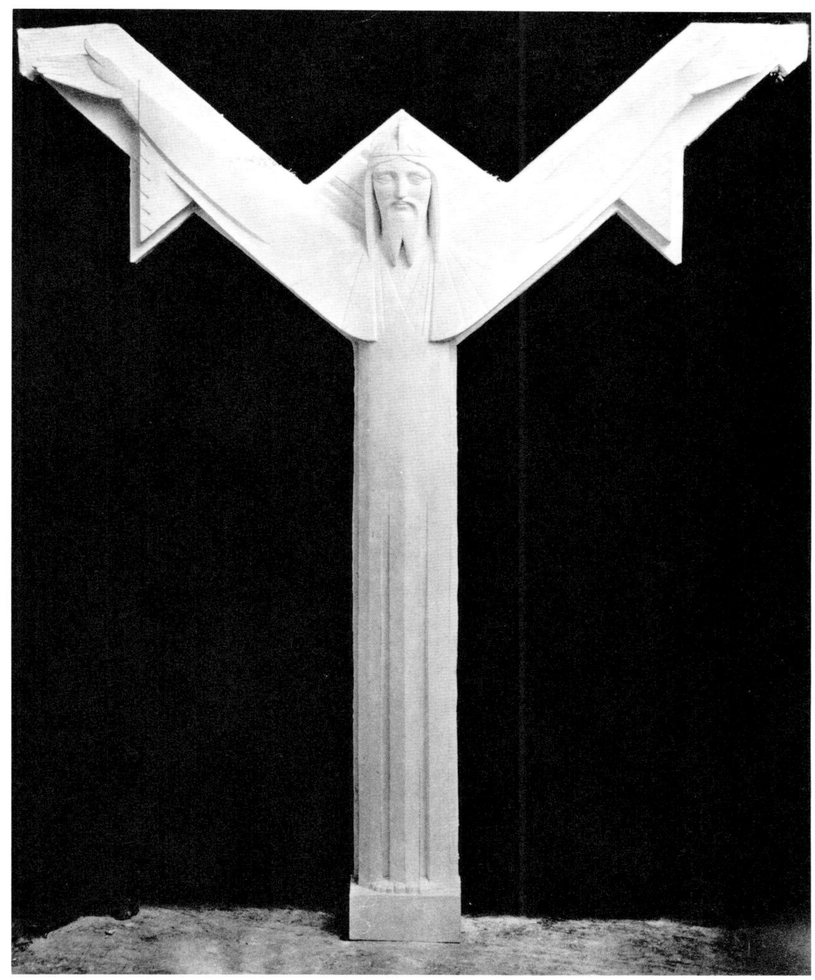

plaster in separate parts, which was completed by February 1930.

In the development from the small plaster relief to the nine-foot model, the face became more impassive and generalized, with the sharply divided beard, calm expression, and narrowing eyelids giving it an exotic, Eastern flavor. Clearly, Storrs continued to be of a universal, mystical religious persuasion, and fascinated by Eastern religions.

Storrs sent photographs of both works to Barry Byrne in Chicago in February 1930. Byrne was upset; he liked the small plaster relief better than the nine-foot model.[14] Although he wrote that "The conception has nobility—more than that can scarcely be said of any art work," he remained critical.[15] The design, he objected, had an unfortunate "cut" look, as if for fine stone, the "V" of the clothes at the neck was too literal, and he questioned whether the scale of the figure's detail would hold its place against the "ornament" of the architecture. Boyd Barrett complained that the crown was small and undignified and the figure "unduly plain and severe."[16]

In a later model for the head of the statue (Fig. 99), Storrs did change *Christ*'s crown, making the brim more prominent and adding a serrated edge. Also, under the barrage of criticism, he was persuaded to accept less money than originally agreed upon for his sculpture.[17]

85   Commissions from Architects

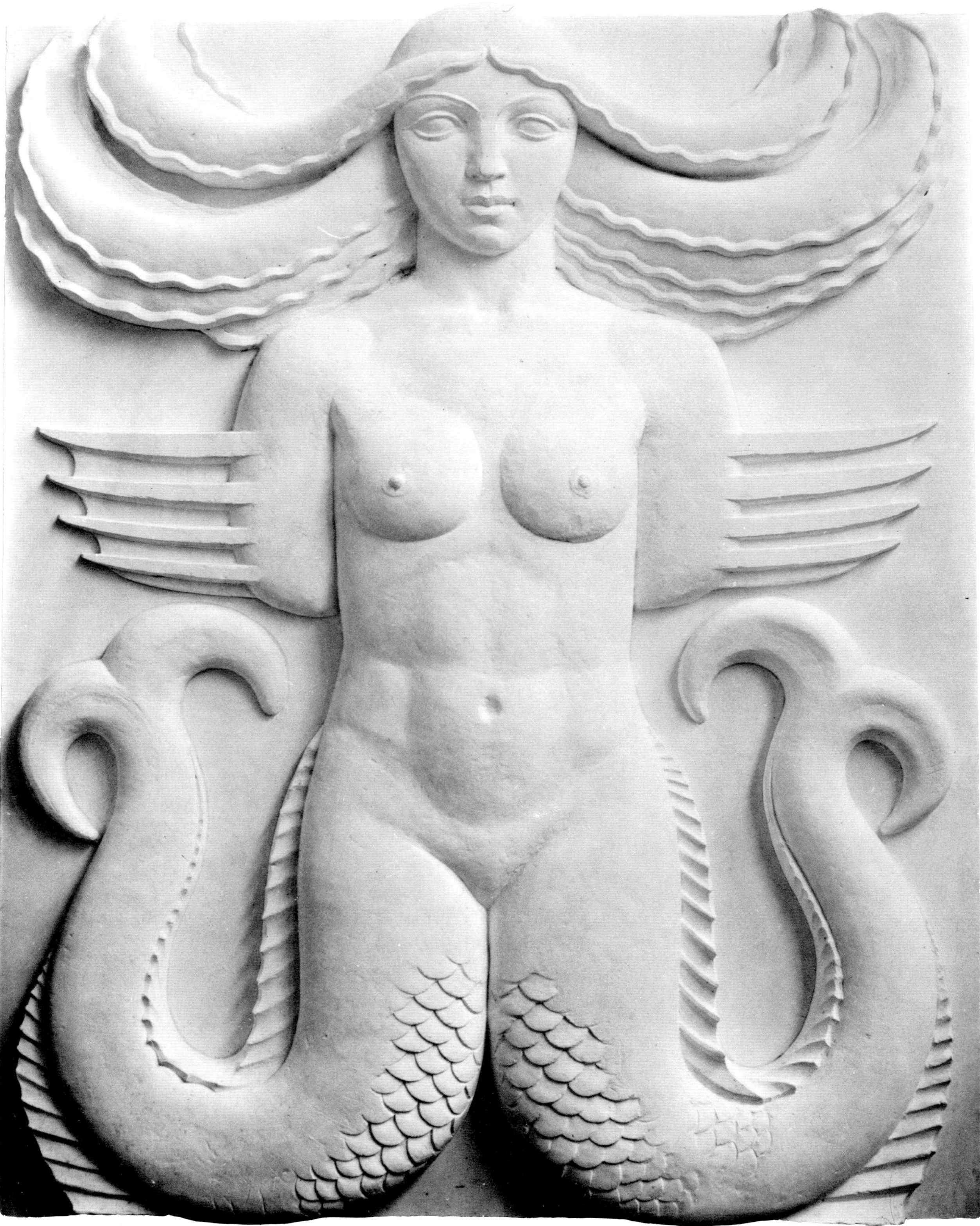

Sculpture for the United States Naval Monument, Brest, France

The United States Naval Monument at Brest, France, which com-
memorated the services of the American Navy in European waters
during World War I, was the third large project that Storrs worked on
during the late 1920s. He received the commission to create sculpture
for this monument through the architect Ralph Milman, at that time
senior partner in the Chicago firm of Howard Shaw Associates.[18]
Storrs' name had been suggested to Milman by Arthur Aldis, a trustee
of the Art Institute of Chicago. Aldis, Milman wrote to Storrs, said
that, "you might be interested in working with us on a monument we
are doing at Brest for the American Battle Monuments Commission....
I know Mr. Shaw was interested in your work and he, as you no
doubt remember, wished to use one of your figures on the Roosevelt
Monument here in Chicago. The sculptural opportunities on our
design are not so great but we feel they are very important and we
would like the work to be done by someone who could give it character
and distinction."[19]

Storrs submitted his models and preliminary drawings for the
sculpture to the American Battle Monuments Commission and they
were approved in June 1929. As originally erected (Fig. 103), the
granite monument was striking during the day and dramatically lit at
night. Its general form—a four-square columnar shaft rising upward
at three stepped levels—bears a family resemblance to that of the Art
Deco skyscrapers of the period.

Storrs was responsible for all the relief sculpture, relief panels,
and decorative sculpture on the monument. He supplied the actual
sketches and models, while the carving was done by the stone carver of
his choice, Edmondo Quattrocchi, whose studio was in Montrouge,
France, and who was also working for Frederick MacMonnies.[20] Storrs'
designs for the Brest monument incorporated such standard nautical
and American naval images as American eagles, the coat of arms and
shield of the United States, the Navy shield, Neptune's trident, crossed
anchors, fish, seashells, and stars. Nevertheless, in certain panels,
Storrs was able to exercise his imagination more freely. His panels of
mermaids (Fig. 101) and seahorses (Fig. 102) show his taste for fixed
symmetry, extreme simplification, strong silhouettes, and bold contrasts of patterning. His mermaid panel especially reveals his characteristic sense of humor. To solve the asymmetrical problem of the
typical mermaid's single tail, Storrs has given her twin tails and she is
awash in her wavelike hair. And, still fascinated by the theme of the
winged figure, he made the mermaid's fins into rudimentary wings;
she thus becomes a creature both of sea and air, with all the boldness
of a figurehead on an old sailing vessel.

The original monument, dedicated in 1937, was destroyed by
German bombs on July 4, 1941. In 1955, the American Battle Monuments Commission proposed to rebuild it and contacted the original
architect, Ralph Milman, as well as Storrs.[21] Storrs' original drawings
for the reliefs and photographs of the reliefs were used to create the

*101. Model for Mermaid
for the United States Naval
Monument, Brest, France, c. 1929*
Plaster
Destroyed in World War II

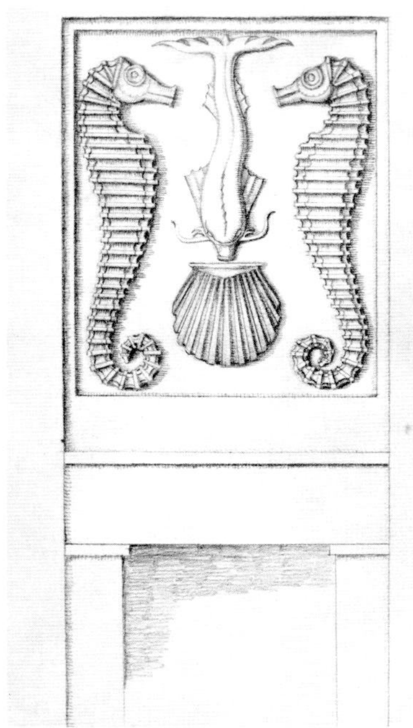

102. *Untitled (Sketch for Relief Panel of Seahorses for the United States Naval Monument, Brest, France)*, c. 1929
Pencil on paper
10½ x 7¼ (26.7 x 18.4)
John Storrs Papers,
Archives of American Art,
Smithsonian Institution,
Washington, D.C.;
Gift of Monique Storrs Booz

103. Ralph Milman, architect
The United States Naval
Monument, Brest, France,
as seen in the 1930s
Destroyed in World War II

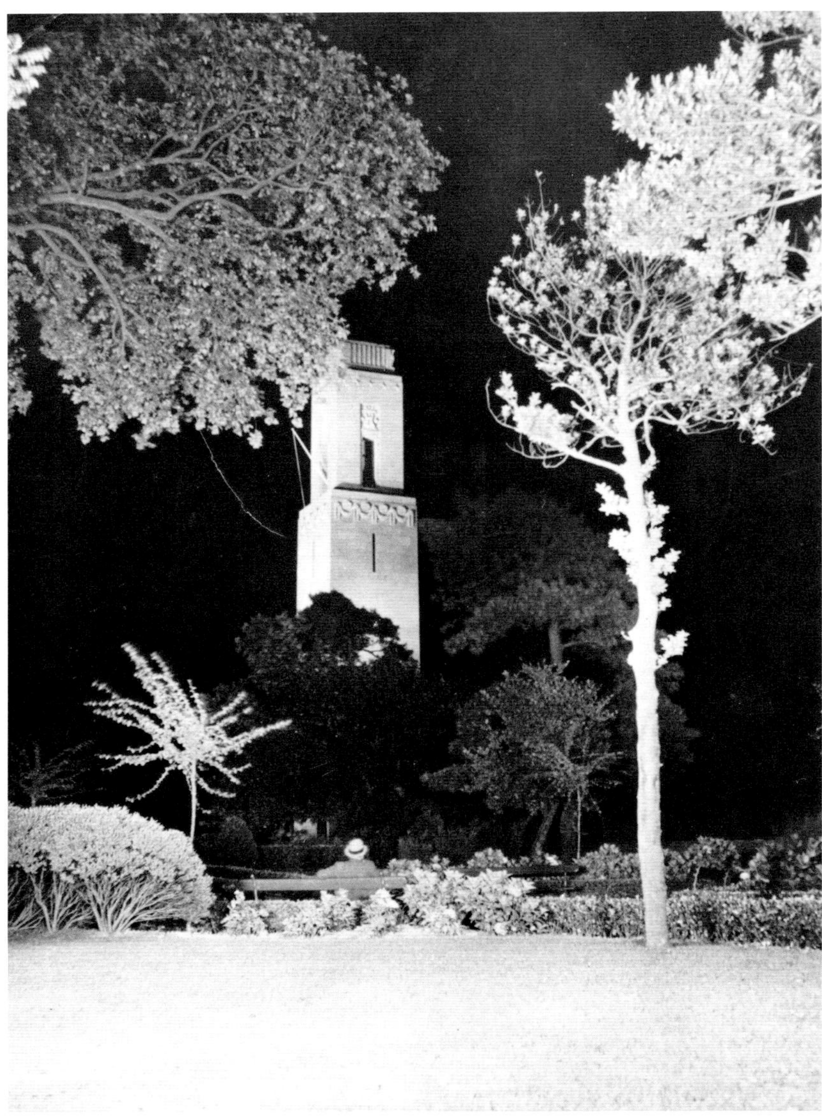

new sculpture, intended to replicate the originals. However, Storrs was not asked to make the new plaster models but only to suggest, criticize, and approve them; apparently, the price he asked to make the new models was considered too high.[22] Aside from these limited activities, Storrs had little to do with the sculpture for the rebuilt monument, dedicated in 1960, although the designs derive from his original inspiration. One can still appreciate, however, the fertility of Storrs' concepts, even when his choices were limited by the necessity of using certain customary motifs. In one case, he filled a small sheet of paper with rough sketches of over thirty different ideas for panels and individual motifs.[23] Such a creative outpouring shows Storrs' energy and enthusiasm for the few commissions he did receive in his lifetime.

Notes

1. As quoted in Philip Hampson, "Ancient Goddess in Modern Form to Command City," *Chicago Sunday Tribune*, May 4, 1930, section 2, p. 14.

2. Ibid.

3. Interview, radio broadcast, November 10, 1934, Station KYW, Chicago; text in AAA, JSP, 1, Critical & Historical Comments on Storrs.

4. Hampson, "Ancient Goddess in Modern Form to Command City."

5. Ibid. See also Chesly Manley, "Board of Trade is World's No. 1 Grain Market," *Chicago Sunday Tribune*, December 12, 1954, section 1, pp. 6–8, where it is explained that, more recently, paper bags containing grain samples are used for trading and these samples are carefully tested and graded according to quality by state inspectors.

6. The postcard is located in AAA, JSP, 4, Postcards (1st folder thus marked).

7. Storrs' entry, July 14, 1924, AAA, JSP, 1, Diary 1924, reads: "Dinner with Miss Dreiur & others at Brancuy's after Dome with Ford Jane Heap etc. till 4 a.m." Entry, March 28, 1927, AAA, JSP, 1, Diary 1927, "dinner at Brancui with Carpenters & Duchamp." Ibid., on a slip of paper, Storrs wrote the address, "Broncusi, 8 Impasse Bousin, 152 rue du Vaugirard."

8. A cryptic letter from Byrne to Storrs, May 5, 1928, AAA, JSP, 4, Correspondence 1928, says in part: "The statue of St. Michael is favorably considered and they want a drawing. When can I get it and how quickly? Inform me as soon as possible as I must give them an answer." No sculpture exists by Storrs that can be identified as a St. Michael nor any drawing that seems to pertain to what may have been an unrealized project.

9. See Sally Kitt Chappell, "Barry Byrne," in *Barry Byrne, John Lloyd Wright: Architecture & Design* (Chicago: Chicago Historical Society, 1982), esp. p. 26.

10. Storrs' entry, July 5, 1929, AAA, JSP, 1, Diary 1929, reads, "leave Cork for Dublin"; ibid., the entry for December 23, 1929, reads, "Began sketch for Cork."

11. See Sally Anderson Chappell, "Barry Byrne: Architecture and Writings," Ph. D. dissertation, Northwestern University, Evanston, Illinois, 1968, pp. 102–03, and James Johnson Sweeney, "Barry Byrne and New Forms in Church Construction," *Creative Art*, 2 (September 1932), pp. 61–65.

12. As early as 1906, Storrs had been impressed by the Christ figure being created by his teacher, Arthur Bock (see p. 11). Decades later, his recollection was still vivid: "I was terribly impressed by an all-most finished statue of a Christ with arms extended in an atitude of beniddection that was all of fifteen feet in height, little immagening that some day I would be called on to make one of twice that heighth"; AAA, JSP, 2, Writings 1947, brown book, describing Bock's studio.

13. A letter from J.R. Boyd Barrett, Cork, to John Storrs, Paris, July 23, 1929, AAA, JSP, 4, Correspondence 1929, says he is enclosing the contract form to be signed and returned, and he has returned Storrs' drawing on the 9th. He asks Storrs to send him a tracing of the original drawing.

14. Byrne's many objections to Storrs' sculpture were based on photographs Storrs sent to him, as per Byrne's letter, February 27, 1930, AAA, JSP, 4, Correspondence 1930.

15. Ibid.

16. Boyd Barrett to John Storrs, September 11, 1930, from letters still remaining in the Monique Storrs Booz estate; access through the courtesy of Michelle Storrs Booz.

17. Ibid. Storrs' note on this letter reads, "Saw Barrett in Paris—26–9 I agreed to accept 100 Lbs off balance to be paid at once."

18. Hampson, "Ancient Goddess in Modern Form to Command City."

19. Ralph Milman to John Storrs, August 22, 1928, AAA, JSP, 6, Commission File, Brest Memorial, Paris (2nd folder thus marked).

20. For Storrs' choice of Quattrocchi, see Major X.H. Price, American Battle Monuments Commission, to John Storrs, March 5, 1931, AAA, JSP, 6, Commission File, Brest Memorial, Paris (2nd folder thus marked).

21. Storrs' original plaster models had been placed as decorations inside the shaft of the monument and thus were also destroyed in 1941; see his draft letter, undated, to "Dear Gen. North," AAA, JSP, 6, Commission File, Brest Memorial, Paris (2nd folder thus marked). Only a single half-sized model of one of the reliefs still remains. Measuring 29 x 22⅝ x 1½ inches, it is in the Musée Régional, Arts et Traditions de l'Orléanais, Château Dunois, Beaugency, France. It depicts an eagle surmounting a shield with crossed anchors behind it.

22. See the correspondence between Storrs and Colonel Jack D. Mage, March–July, 1955, AAA, JSP, 6, Commission File, Brest Memorial, Paris (2nd folder thus marked).

23. Measuring 10½ x 7½ inches, this sheet of pencil sketches is in AAA, JSP, 6, Commission File, Brest Memorial, Paris (1st folder thus marked).

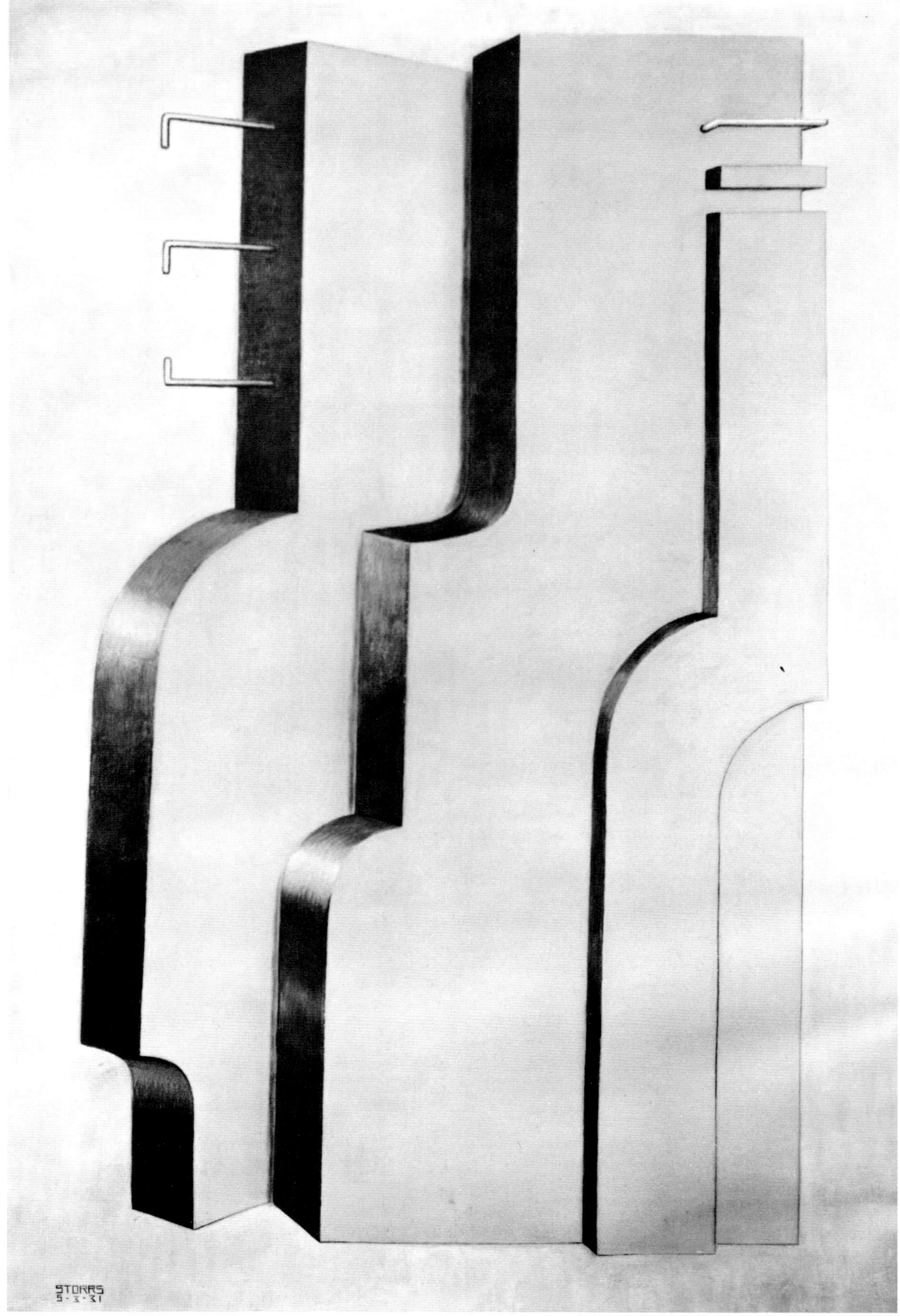
STORRS
5-3-31

104. *Double Entry*, 1931
Oil on canvas
45½ x 30¼ (115.6 x 76.8)
Collection of Mr. and Mrs.
Barney Ebsworth

Painting

In 1930, at the age of forty-five, John Storrs began to paint seriously.
Several factors may have contributed to his decision to take up another
form of expression so late in his career. He had no new commissions in
1930 and there was little commercial market for his sculpture. Moreover, he had reached a stage in his development where, lacking architectural commissions, he would have preferred to have his smaller
sculptures cast in bronze, fabricated in metal, or preserved in marble.
But the hardships of the Depression had hit the Storrs family, and
all of these methods were expensive. Canvas and paint, on the other
hand, were relatively inexpensive.

Storrs was not without experience—or talent—in painting. As a
student at the school of the Pennsylvania Academy of the Fine Arts, he
had been placed by Thomas Anschutz, then chief instructor and head
of the faculty, in the advanced painting class. Anschutz thought his
work was poetic and possessed an unusual, refined, and beautiful
sense of color.[1]

Not unexpectedly, Storrs' earliest paintings in the 1930s look like
paintings of his own unexecuted sculpture. In the first, dating from
December 14, 1930 and titled *Man and Woman* (Fig. 105), two sculptural forms are juxtaposed to create a visual tension in the space
between them, suggesting a psychological stress between the sexes.
A primitivizing male profile is on the left, a more rounded female
profile on the right. With mouths open, and facing in opposite directions, they clearly oppose one another. Without the assistance of the
title, they might simply be two polychromed abstract forms, flattened
by the use of black paint and made volumetric through the suggestion
of light reflections.

Storrs' first exhibition of paintings took place at the Chester H.
Johnson Galleries in Chicago in 1931. Among the paintings exhibited
were some of his most accomplished and revealing works: *Double
Entry* (Fig. 104), *Portrait of an Aristocrat* (Fig. 106), and *Politics*
(Fig. 107). Again, Storrs deals with the depicted forms as if they were
sculptures—in these examples, shallow sculptural reliefs. In *Portrait
of an Aristocrat* and *Politics*, the forms cast shadows, and in *Double
Entry* they appear to reflect light. In each case, the painted forms are
presented as if they were actual objects set in a limited space.

Conceptually, these paintings constitute Dada gestes. Whereas
once, in such early terra-cotta figures as *Modern Madonna* (Fig. 8) or
Dance (Fig. 28), Storrs had painted his sculptures, now he made paint-

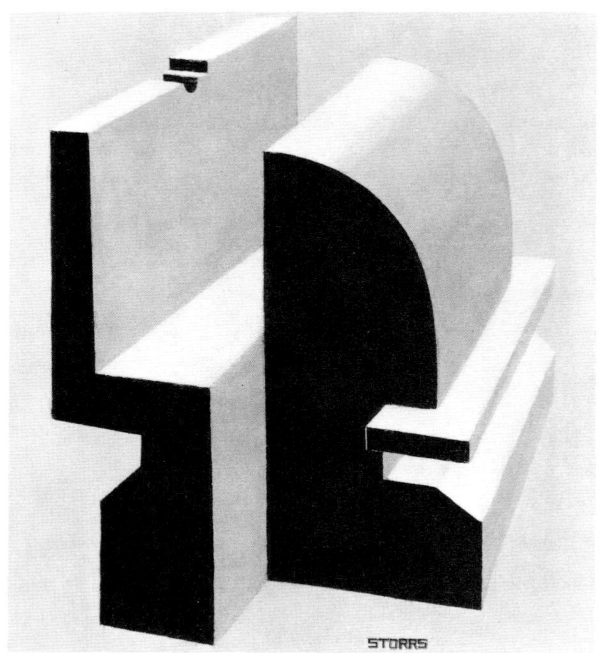

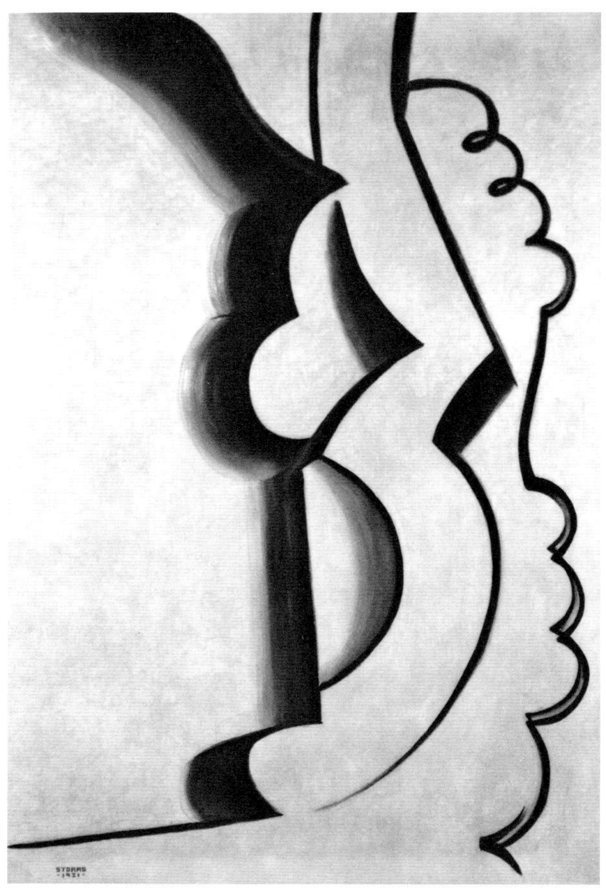

105. *Man and Woman*, 1930
Oil on canvas
14 x 12 (35.6 x 30.5)
Collection of Harvey and
Françoise Rambach

106. *Portrait of an Aristocrat*,
1931
Oil on canvas
44 x 30 (111.8 x 76.2)
Collection of
Edward R. Downe, Jr.

107. *Politics*, 1931
Oil on canvas
40 x 40 (101.6 x 101.6)
Estate of Monique Storrs Booz;
courtesy of Robert Schoelkopf
Gallery, Ltd., New York

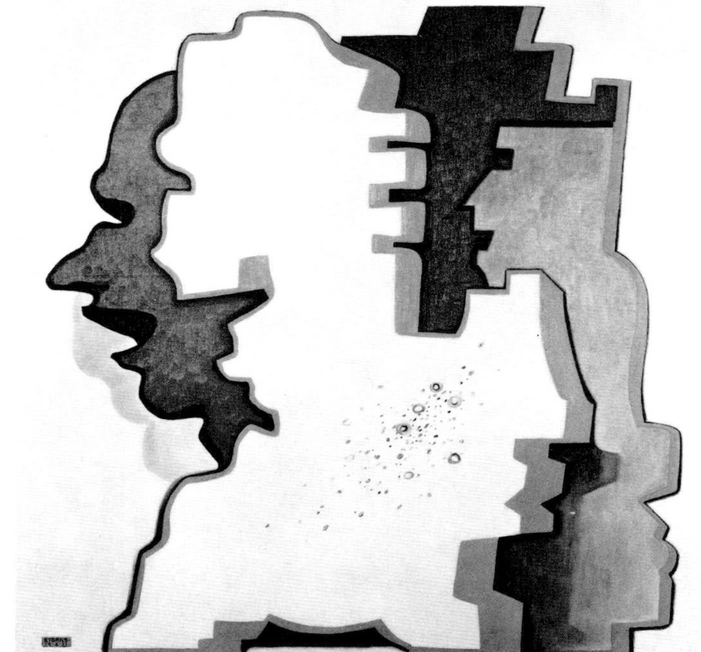

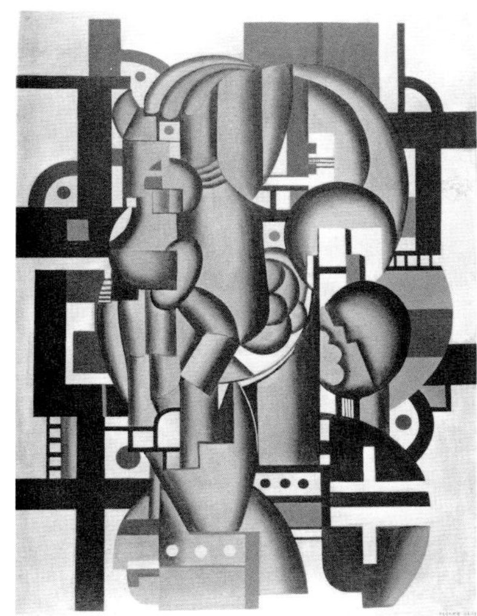

108. Fernand Léger
Composition in Blue, 1921–27
Oil on canvas
51⅛ x 38⅛ (129.9 x 96.8)
The Art Institute of Chicago;
Gift of Charles H. and
Mary F.S. Worcester

109. *Genesis*, 1932
Oil on board
31¾ x 26 (80.6 x 66)
Private collection

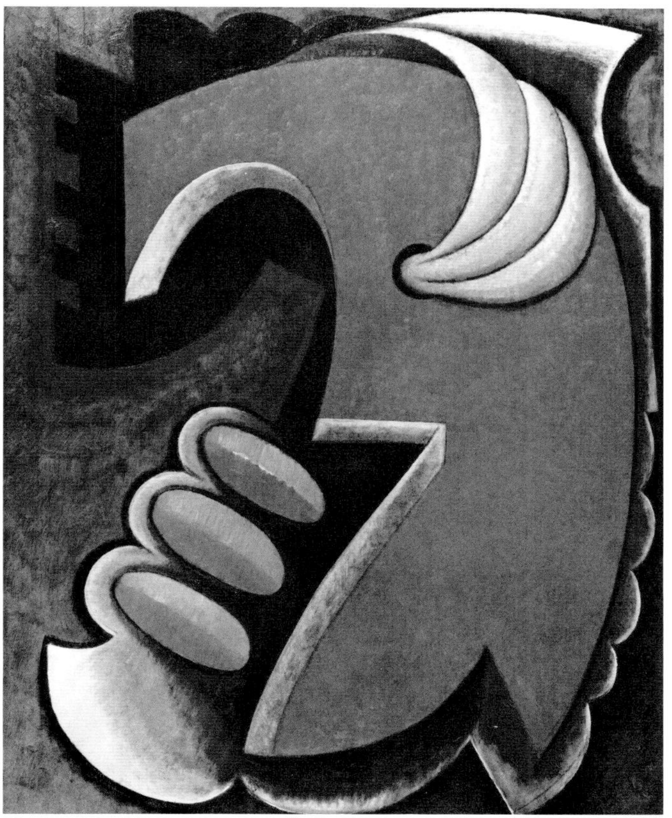

ings of sculptural forms, even approximating the materials of sculpture. In *Portrait of an Aristocrat*, the gray, mottled surface presents a simulacrum of grained marble, while the hues in *Double Entry* resemble the coloration of rose granite. In *Politics*, the surface is painted to look pitted like stone or cast stone. These paintings thus become a kind of punning on the entire subject of sculpture.

Human or humanoid profiles appear in many of Storrs' paintings, frequently in the form of male-female contrasts, sometimes totemic, often amusing, always seeking the essence of the sexes—contentious in *Man and Woman*, haughty and self-satisfied in *Portrait of an Aristocrat*. The male-female profiles in *Double Entry* are conceptually enriched by the title, which usually refers to two horses in a race that come from the same stable. Hence the man and woman can be viewed as the original contenders in the human race. Such a double-edged title reveals Storrs' continuing enjoyment of visual and verbal puns.[2]

In *Politics*, it is possible to discern at least six profile faces, ranging from human to animalistic, in various stages of confrontation. The open mouths and fierce, savage expressions represent the animosity that can be unleashed in political discourse. Such paintings provided seeds for Storrs' later sculpture of the mid-1930s, where machine and architectural forms are combined with primitivizing human profiles or figures (pp. 106–10).

It was Léger who had the greatest influence on the surrealistic character of Storrs' paintings.[3] Both had spent time in each other's

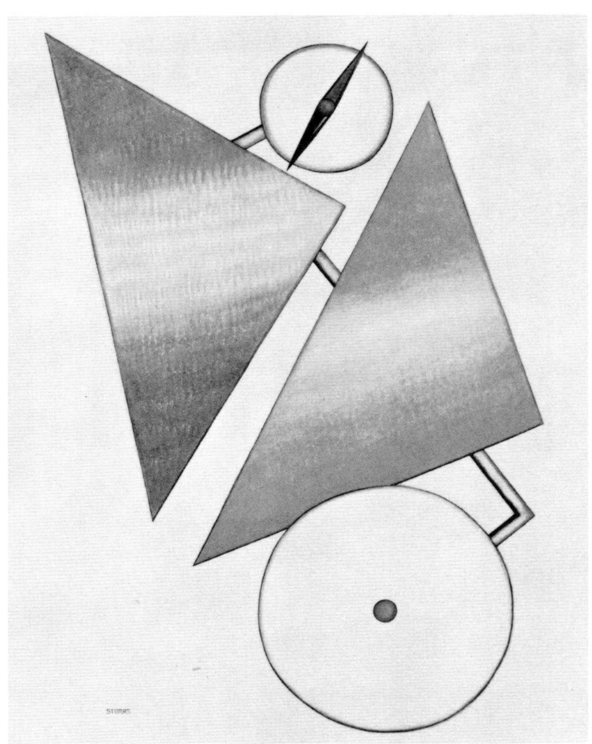

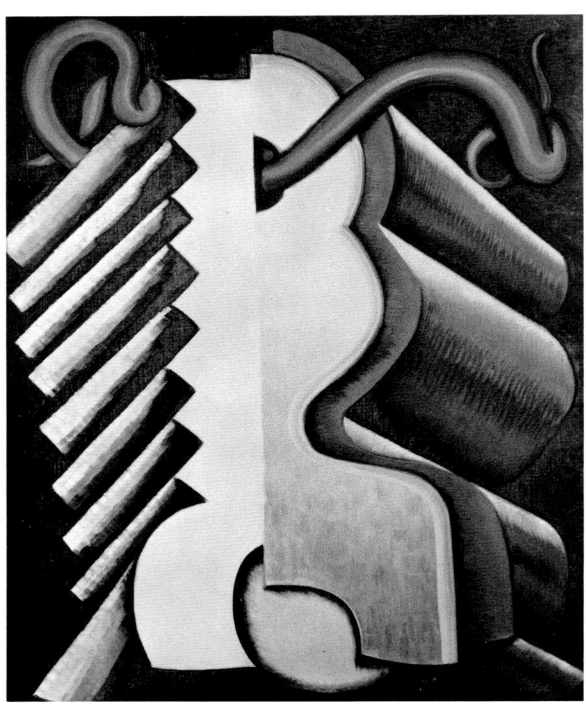

studios and, in 1930, when Léger visited Storrs' Paris studio, Storrs reported that Léger was "very much surprised to see all my abstract things."[4] In 1928, Storrs selected Léger's *Composition in Blue* (Fig. 108) for purchase by the Art Institute of Chicago.[5] The work therefore represents exactly the sort of Léger canvas that Storrs most admired. A comparison of Léger's *Composition in Blue* and Storrs' *Genesis* (Fig. 109) is telling. While the Léger painting is more mechanistic and complex, a close relationship exists between the individual biomorphic forms—the curved ones, like bananas or snakes, the ovoid lozenges, as well as the arcs; and Storrs transforms one of Léger's dots into an "eye" for his primitivizing profile head.

Male and female symbols of reproductive processes are evident in the seed and phallus forms of *Genesis*, Storrs own title for the work.[6] As with *Double Entry* or *Politics*, word and image are again closely related in Storrs' creative process. In *Genesis*, however (like Storrs' early poem, Fig. 3), the two become absolute visual coordinates.

Storrs seems to have appropriated several modes of Surrealist expression. *Abstract No. 1* (Fig. 110) comes close to the wit of Picabia's early mechanistic drawings and paintings. Like Picabia, Storrs humorously combines human, mechanical, and sexual references. It is possible to see this assembling of machine forms as a profile face, tilted downward with the points of the triangles forming an open mouth, sharp nose, and chin. The circular form serves simultaneously as an eye and a vaginal slit. Seen in this context, the large circle below could represent a "body" with a navel.

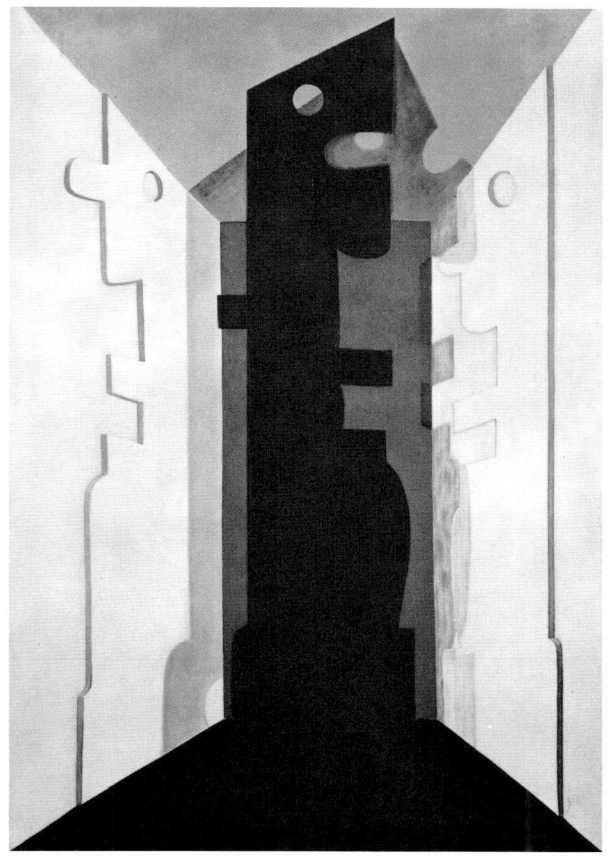

112. *Monologue*, 1931
Oil on canvas
57¼ x 38¼ (145.4 x 97.2)
Collection of Raymond J. Learsy

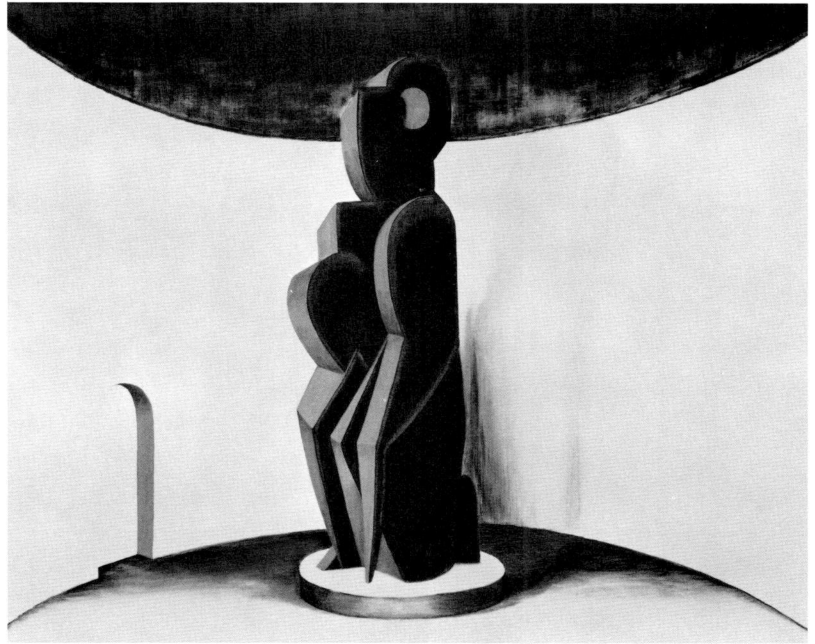

113. *The Idol (Figure in a Circular Room)*, 1936
Oil on canvas
25½ x 31½ (64.8 x 80)
Collection of
Edward R. Downe, Jr.

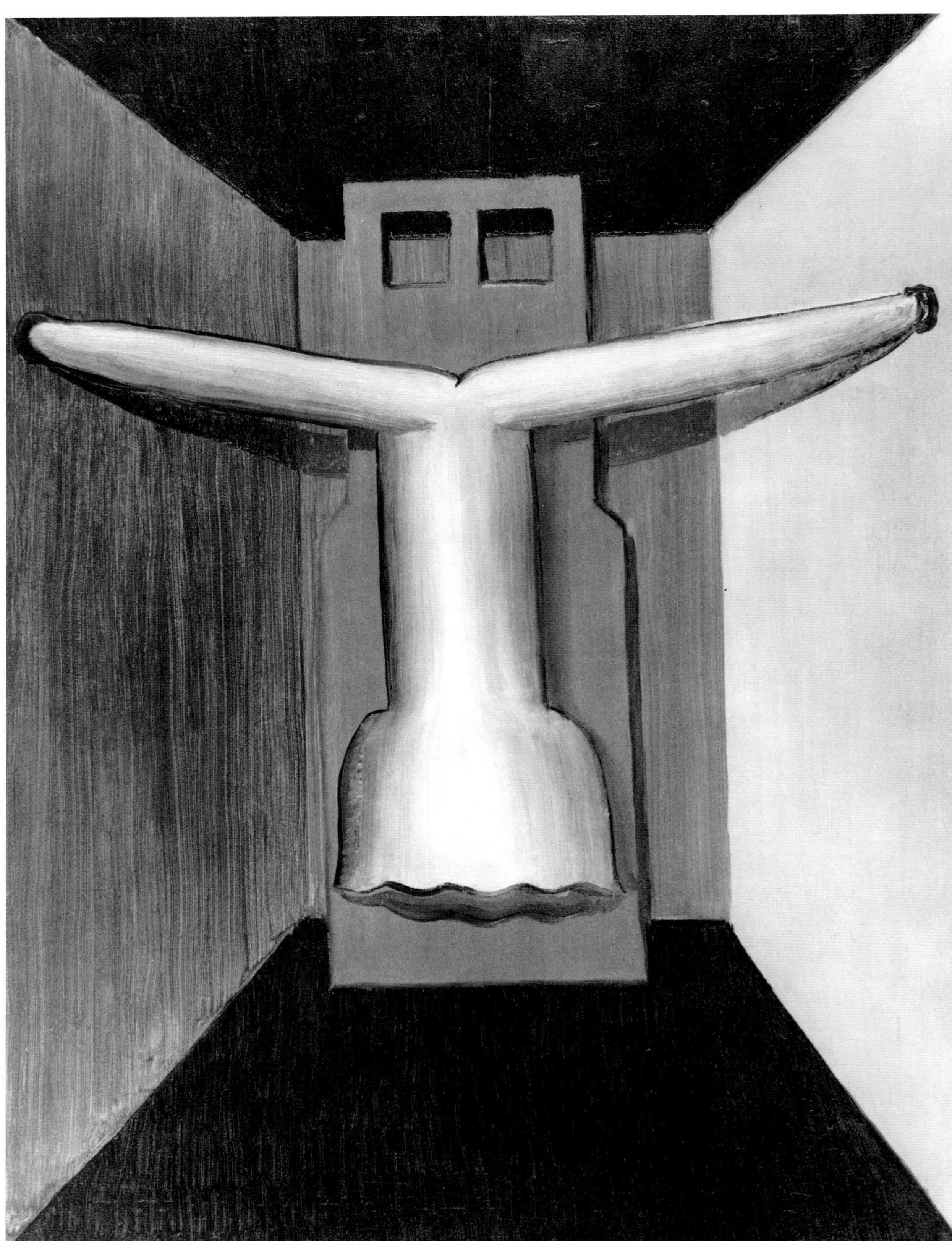

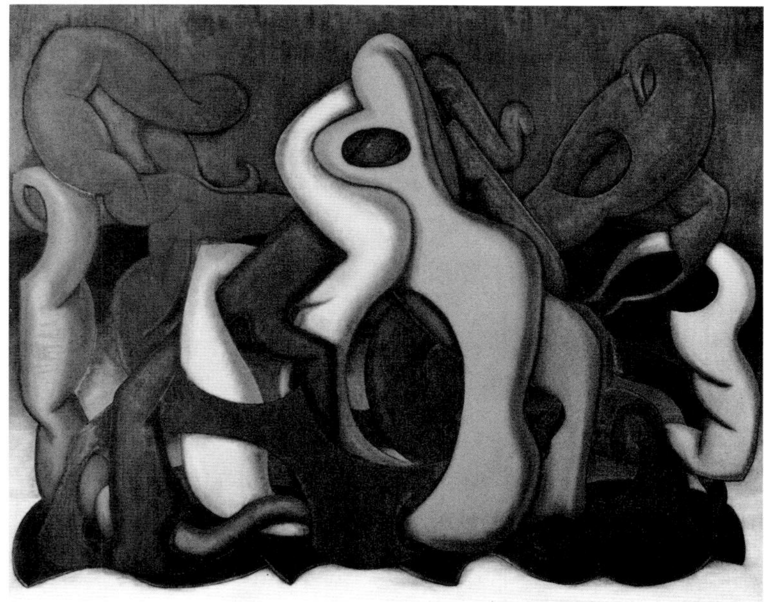

114. *Room 13*, c. 1931
Oil on wood
16 x 13½ (40.6 x 34.3)
Private collection

115. *The Battle*, 1936
Oil on canvas
34 x 49 (86.4 x 124.5)
Private collection

116. *Untitled*, 1936
Oil on masonite
43 x 42½ (109.2 x 108)
Private collection

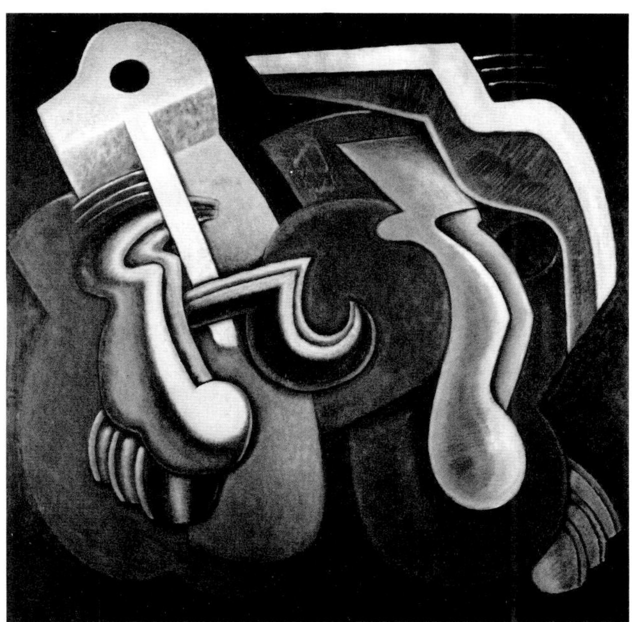

In the same year as *Genesis* and *Abstract No. 1*, Storrs painted *Green and White Sculpture* (Fig. 111). Here again, he seems to be probing an unrealized sculpture. There are angular and rounded profiles, and the eye of the rounded one is pierced by a snakelike intestinal form. The painting has an emotional force and brutality associated with the most basic, primitive emotions.

There are several other paintings that reveal a darker side of Storrs' nature—an attraction to the horrific, like a child who finds excitement in being frightened. In *Monologue, The Idol (Figure in a Circular Room)*, and *Room 13* (Figs. 112–114), Storrs places a huge,

97 Streamlining and Surrealism

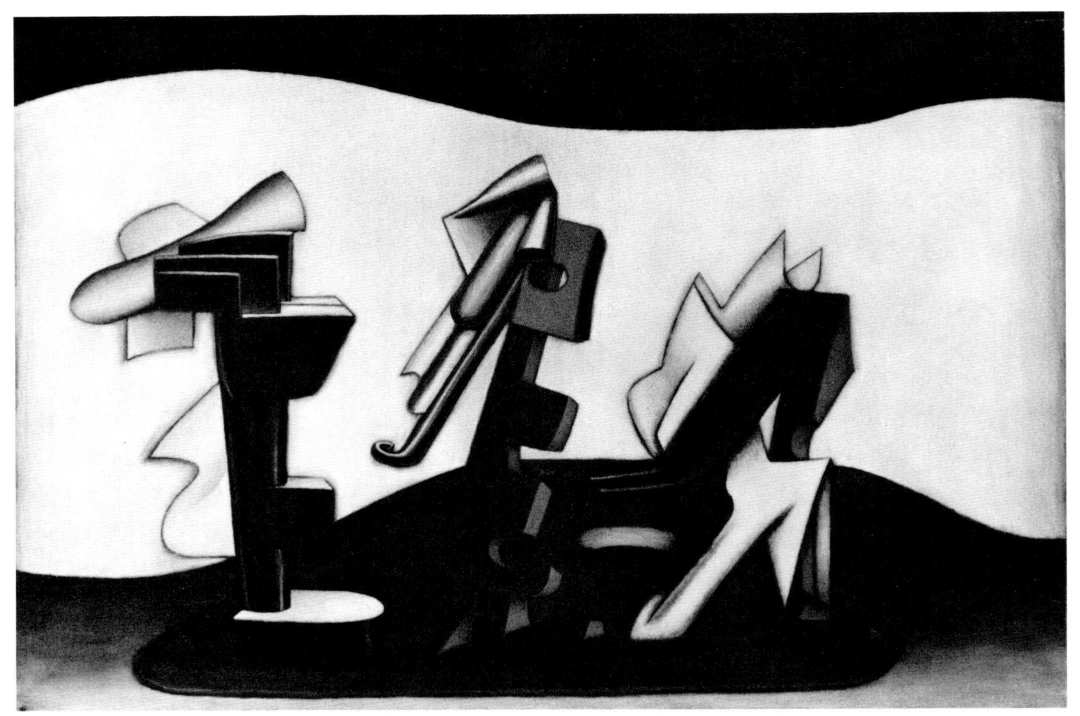

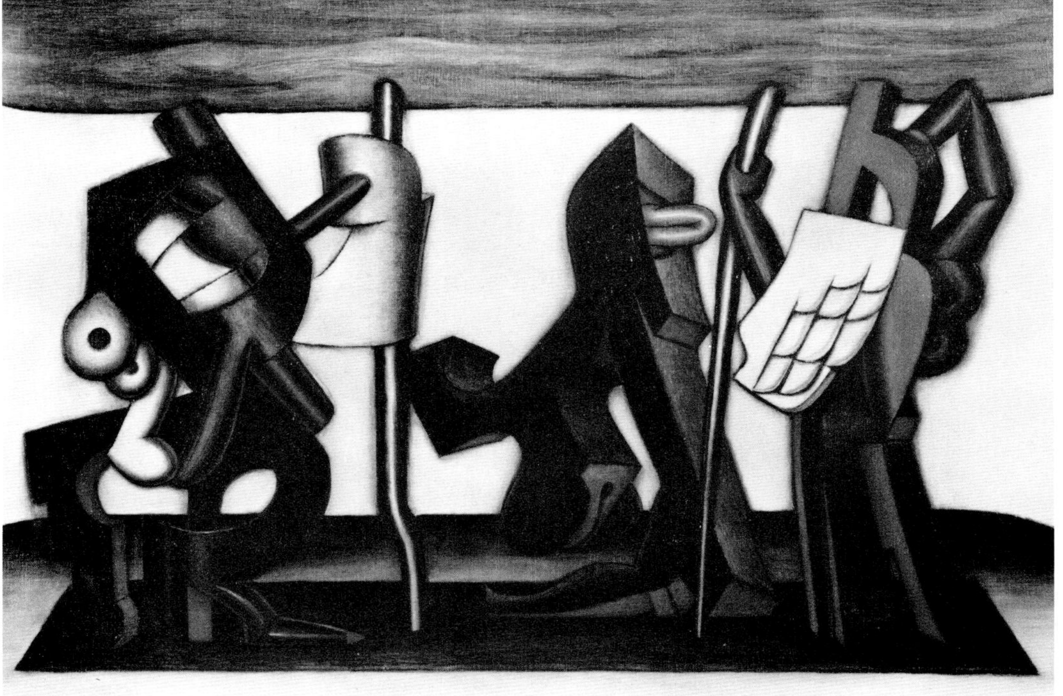

bizarre, totemic figure in a mysterious, yet plausible architectural space.[7] Each of the sculptural objects depicted—the mysterious flat shape that casts inexplicable shadows, the enormous idol with its huge round eye and swollen stomach, and the curious suspended form that resembles a cow's skull—could serve as icons for some instinctual, primeval worship.

As the 1930s progressed, Storrs' paintings became increasingly surreal, a characteristic also found in his abstract sculpture of this period (Figs. 130–137). Storrs developed his own brand of quirky, hybrid Surrealism and, in formal terms, he began to set his images into motion. Thus *The Battle* (Fig. 115) is a scene of monster figures in combat, made all the more frightening because the figures are partial —torsos without limbs, agonized, screaming heads, and sometimes only intestinal shapes. An untitled painting (Fig. 116), dating from 1936, depicts a kind of mechanical wind-up toy; its head is a key that generates the forward motion of the body. The robot figures of *Walking on the Grass* (Fig. 117) advance like mechanized toys or tin soldiers. In *Composition, Abstract Forms* (Fig. 118), these robot toys take on the equipage of medieval knights on a battlefield that is also a stage set. In such paintings, Storrs may have been responding to the worsening political situation in Europe.

A Century of Progress: The 1933 Chicago World's Fair

Monique Storrs Booz, the artist's daughter, often said that her father began painting while waiting for the committee of A Century of Progress to make up its mind. She probably meant that the committee was debating about the sculptures Storrs had offered to execute for the Administration Building.[8]

Finally, in January 1932, Storrs received a formal contract to prepare sketches, studies, and models for a single freestanding group of sculptures for the head of the north ramp of the Hall of Science, four bas-relief panels for the north wall between the pylons, and two other bas-reliefs, one for either side of the speaker's rostrum.[9]

The themes of all of Storrs' sculptures for the Hall of Science were clearly set by the committee for the Fair.[10] The four bas-relief panels were to represent Natural Science, Mathematics and Mechanics, Chemistry, and Physics, that is, the four divisions of science. A 1932 photograph (Fig. 119) shows Storrs and an assistant at work on *Natural Science* and *Mechanics*. As appears to have been his method in all his monuments, Storrs began with several alternative ideas. Two pencil sketches depict a man moving a rock (Fig. 120) and a seated man with a cogwheel (Fig. 121).

For the freestanding statue placed in a niche at the top of the ramp of the Hall of Science, Storrs created *Knowledge Combatting Ignorance*, symbolized by a man struggling with a snake (Fig. 122). Because his statue stood at the end of the Avenue of Flags, the main entrance to A Century of Progress, it was the dominating sculpture of the Fair

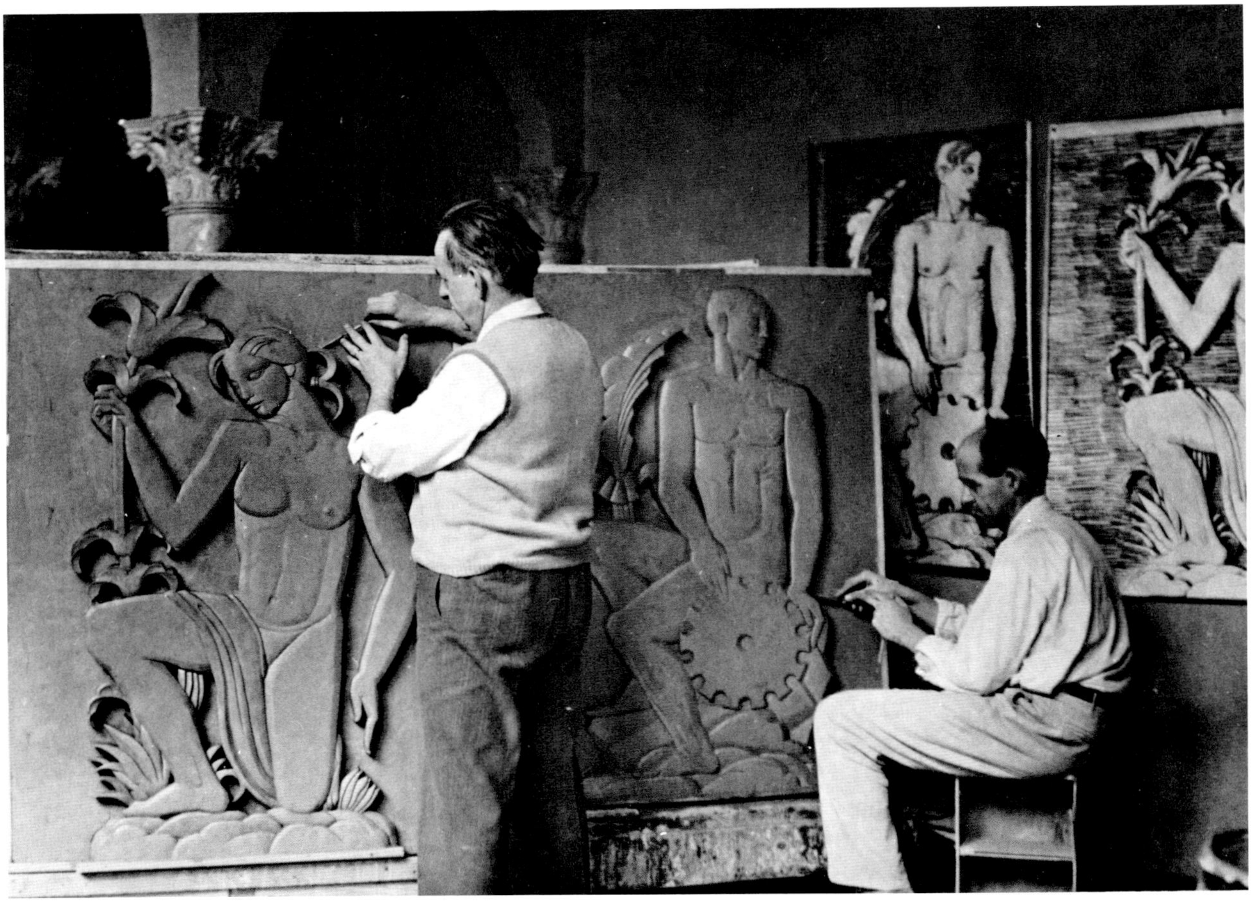

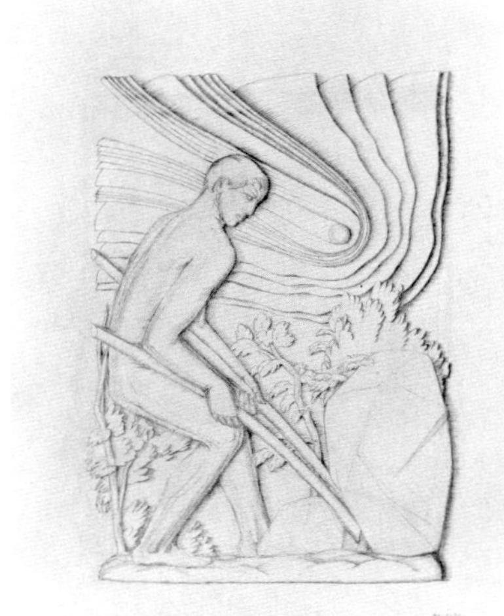

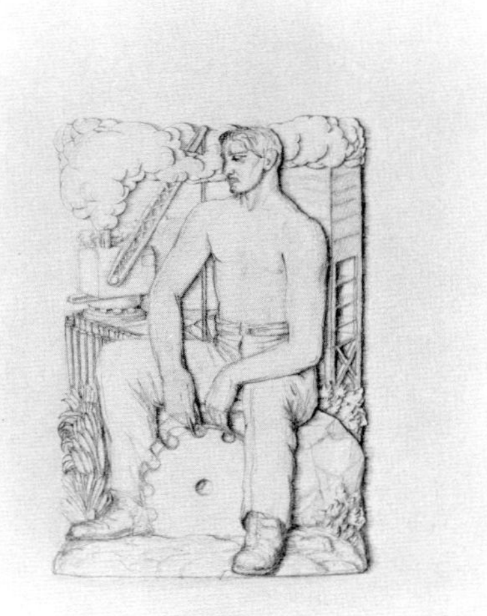

119. Photograph of Storrs
and his assistant working on the
reliefs for the Hall of Science
at the 1933 Chicago
World's Fair, 1932
John Storrs Papers,
Archives of American Art,
Smithsonian Institution,
Washington, D.C.;
Gift of Monique Storrs Booz

120. *Study for Hall of Science
Reliefs, 1933 Chicago World's
Fair: Man Moving Rock*, 1932
Pencil on paper
12¾ x 9¾ (32.4 x 24.8)
Estate of Monique Storrs Booz;
courtesy of Robert Schoelkopf
Gallery, Ltd., New York

121. *Study for Hall of Science
Reliefs, 1933 Chicago World's
Fair: Man and Industry*, 1932
Pencil on paper
13 x 9¾ (22.9 x 24.8)
Estate of Monique Storrs Booz;
courtesy of Robert Schoelkopf
Gallery, Ltd., New York

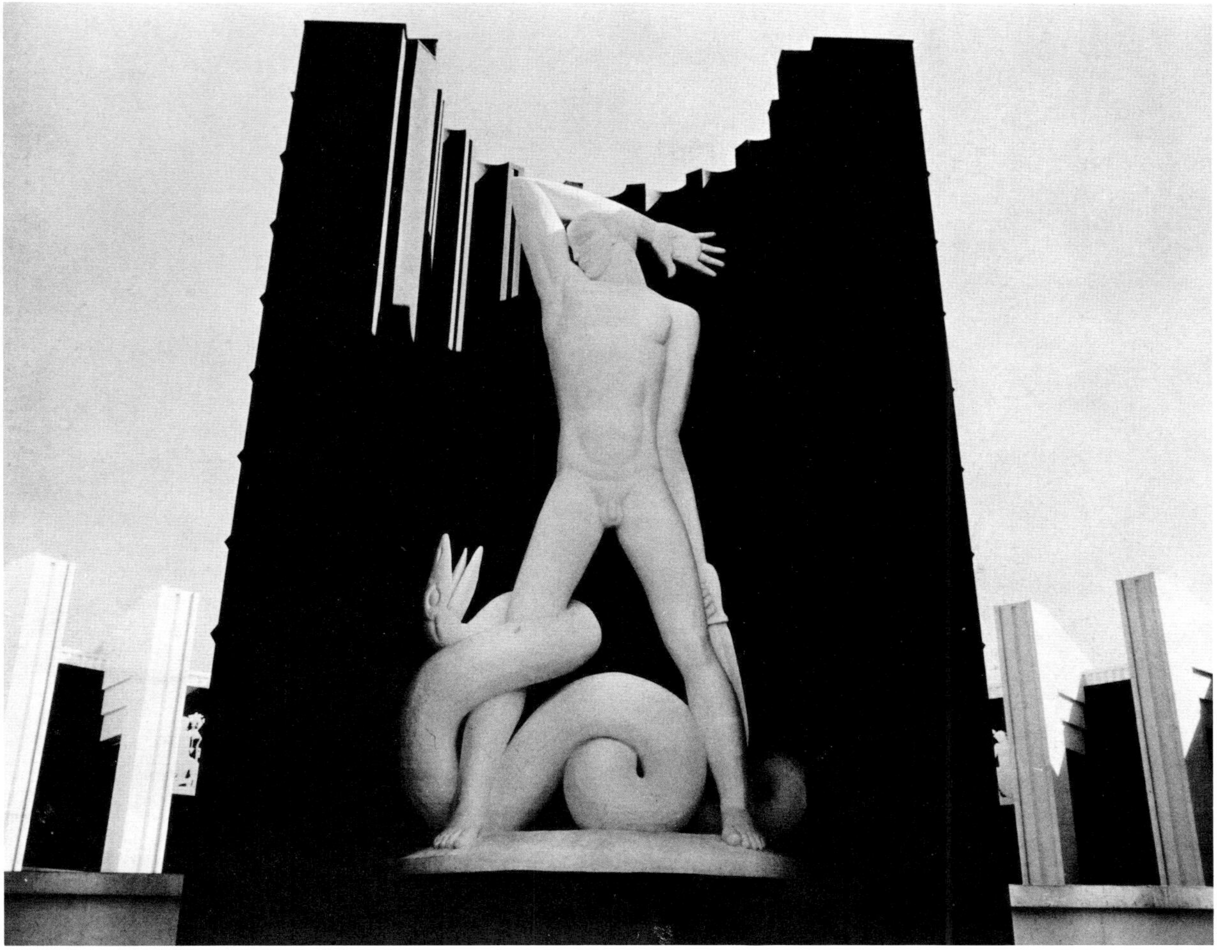

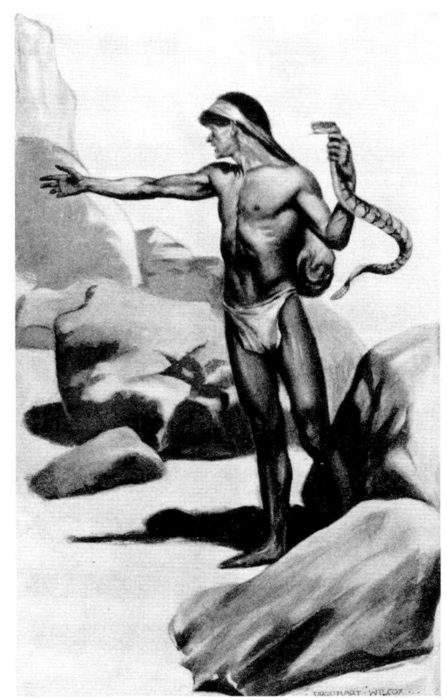

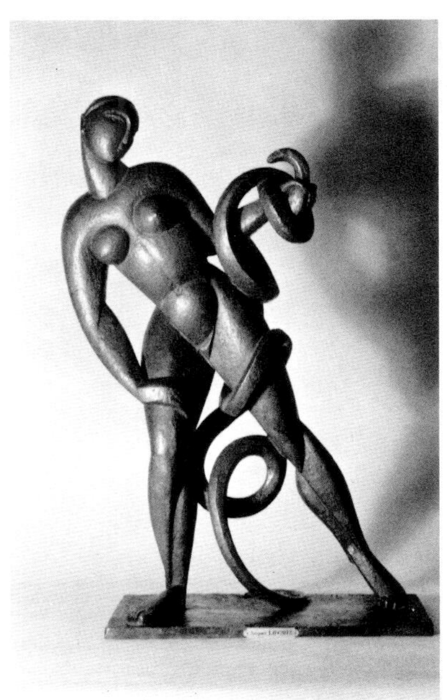

122. *Knowledge Combatting
Ignorance*, in niche designed by
Paul Cret, 1933
Plaster
252 (640.1) high
1933 Chicago World's Fair,
north entrance
Whereabouts unknown

123. Urquehart Wilcox
Illustration, c. 1903–04,
in a Storrs scrapbook (upper left)
Archives of American Art,
Smithsonian Institution,
Washington, D.C.;
Gift of Monique Storrs Booz

124. Jacques Lipchitz
Woman with Serpent, 1913
Bronze
25 (63.5) high
The Barnes Foundation,
Merion, Pennsylvania

125. *Study for Left-hand Panels
of Speaker's Rostrum,
Hall of Science, 1933 Chicago
World's Fair*, c. 1932
Pencil on paper
10 x 13 (25.4 x 33)
Collection of
Edward R. Downe, Jr.

126. *Model of Speaker's
Rostrum, Hall of Science, 1933
Chicago World's Fair*,
view with placement of
right-hand panels
Plaster
Whereabouts unknown

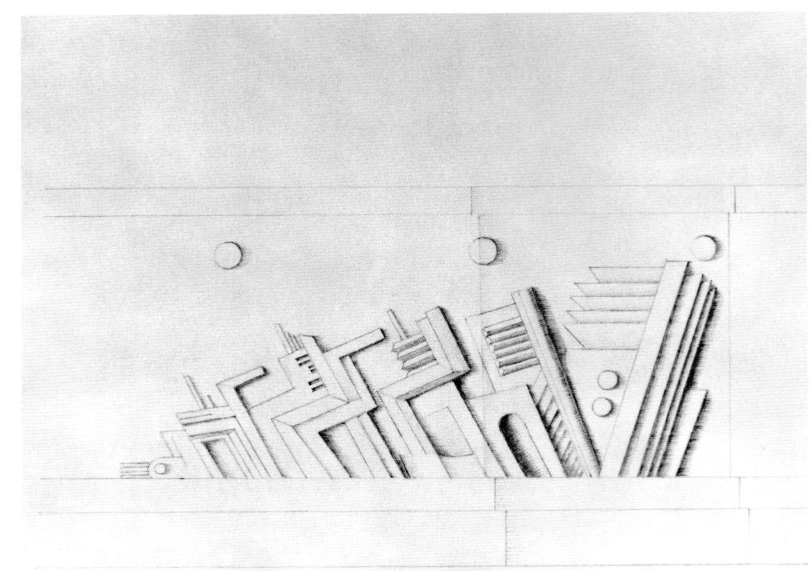

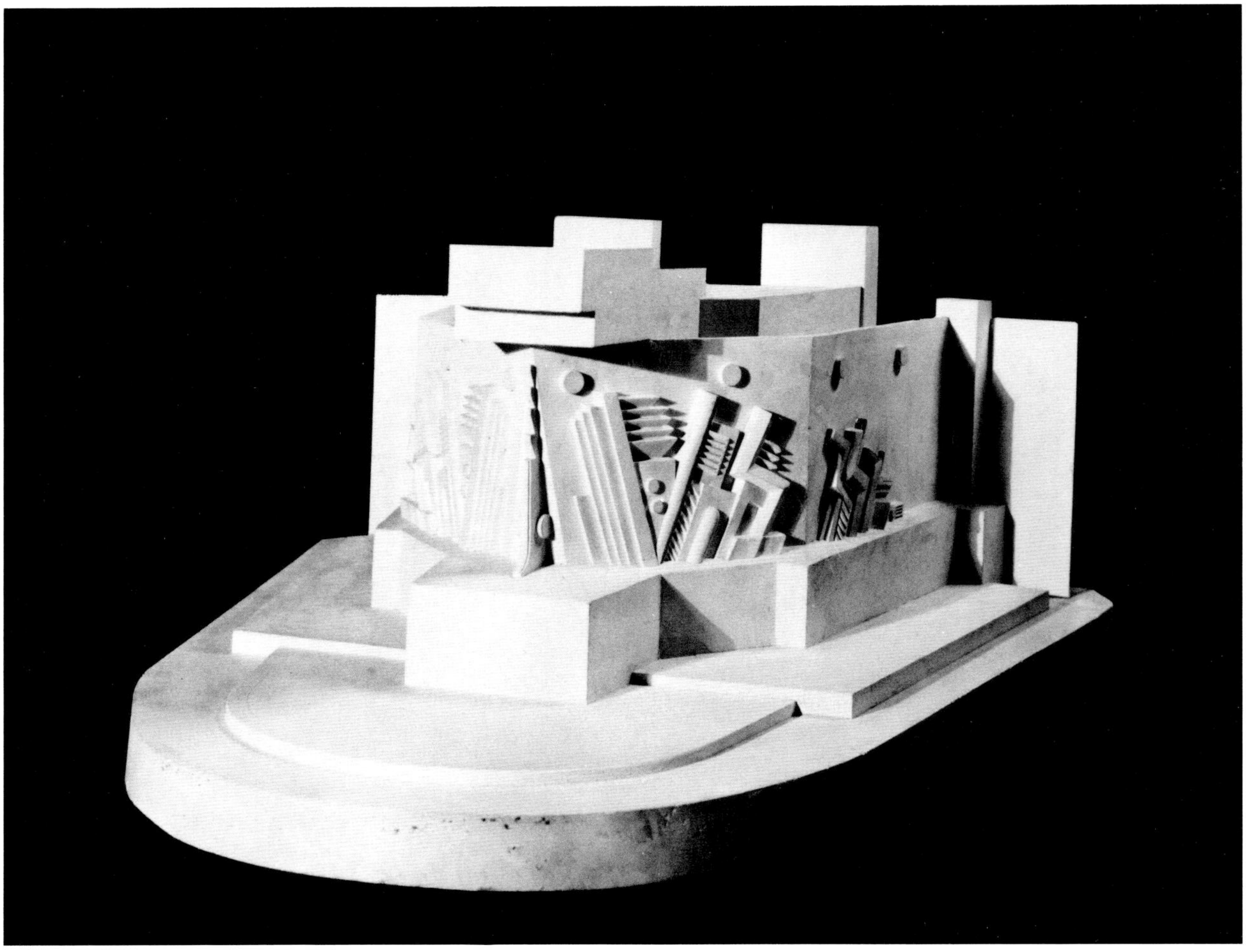

and its spirit and theme were felt to encapsulate the very essence of that exposition.[11]

"The Man and the Serpent," as Storrs sometimes called *Knowledge Combatting Ignorance*, used a gesture—an arm flung back behind the head—which was characteristic of several of his earlier works, including his *Joan of Arc* relief (Fig. 19).[12] Storrs seems to have viewed the snake image as something frightening, evil, and yet seductive, as he had in *Green and White Sculpture* (Fig. 111). In his boyhood scrapbook, he saved an exotic popular illustration by Urquehart Wilcox of a muscular man in a loincloth grasping a snake (Fig. 123). He probably also saw Jacques Lipchitz's 1913 bronze *Woman with Serpent* (Fig. 124) in Lipchitz's studio; it had also been reproduced in a 1930 issue of *Cahiers d'Art*, where it was entitled *Snake Charmer*.[13]

Storrs third commissioned sculptural project for the Hall of Science, the bas-reliefs for the speaker's rostrum, was stopped short of completion when the Fair organizers decided not to build the rostrum.[14] He had conceived the panels as abstract, geometric, and architectonic, and they would have been his most provocative, advanced sculptures for the Fair.

Originally, the theme of the two bas-reliefs was to have been "Services of Science to Humanity." One relief would show "Protective Service by Control of Disease," and the other, "Constructive Service by Harnessing Natural Forces." Either Storrs or the Fair committee jettisoned the former concept while retaining the latter. An early sketch for the rostrum panels with notations in Storrs' handwriting shows that he intended his geometrized images to represent aspects of communication—specifically, the telephone, automobile, boat, train, and airplane. A highly finished drawing (Fig. 125) clearly shows how Storrs planned his two panels to work together as a single unit. A photograph of his model for the rostrum (Fig. 126) reveals that he expected to use these panels, joined, on both sides of the rostrum. One panel (Fig. 128), repeated in mirror image, would have been on the narrower, forward part, with the other (Fig. 127) appearing at the sides.

As first conceived, the speaker's rostrum had roughly the shape of the prow of a boat, and Storrs conceptualized the entire structure as a kind of steamship. How else to explain the repeated circular disks that band the upper segments of the panels? They simulate the portholes on a steamship, a not unexpected association for a traveler like Storrs who claimed to have crossed the Atlantic forty-three times between 1907 and 1939.[15] To the customary Art Deco motifs in these panels— zigzags, stepped patterns, parallelisms—Storrs added his personalized vocabulary of architectural forms, such as buildings tilted sideways, arches, and doorways.

As late as February 1933, Storrs was still under the impression that his rostrum panels were to be erected in the Hall of Science. A month earlier, he had received a commission for a standing figure representing *The Legislative Branch* for the front of the Fair's government building.[16] When the rostrum project was cancelled, it became

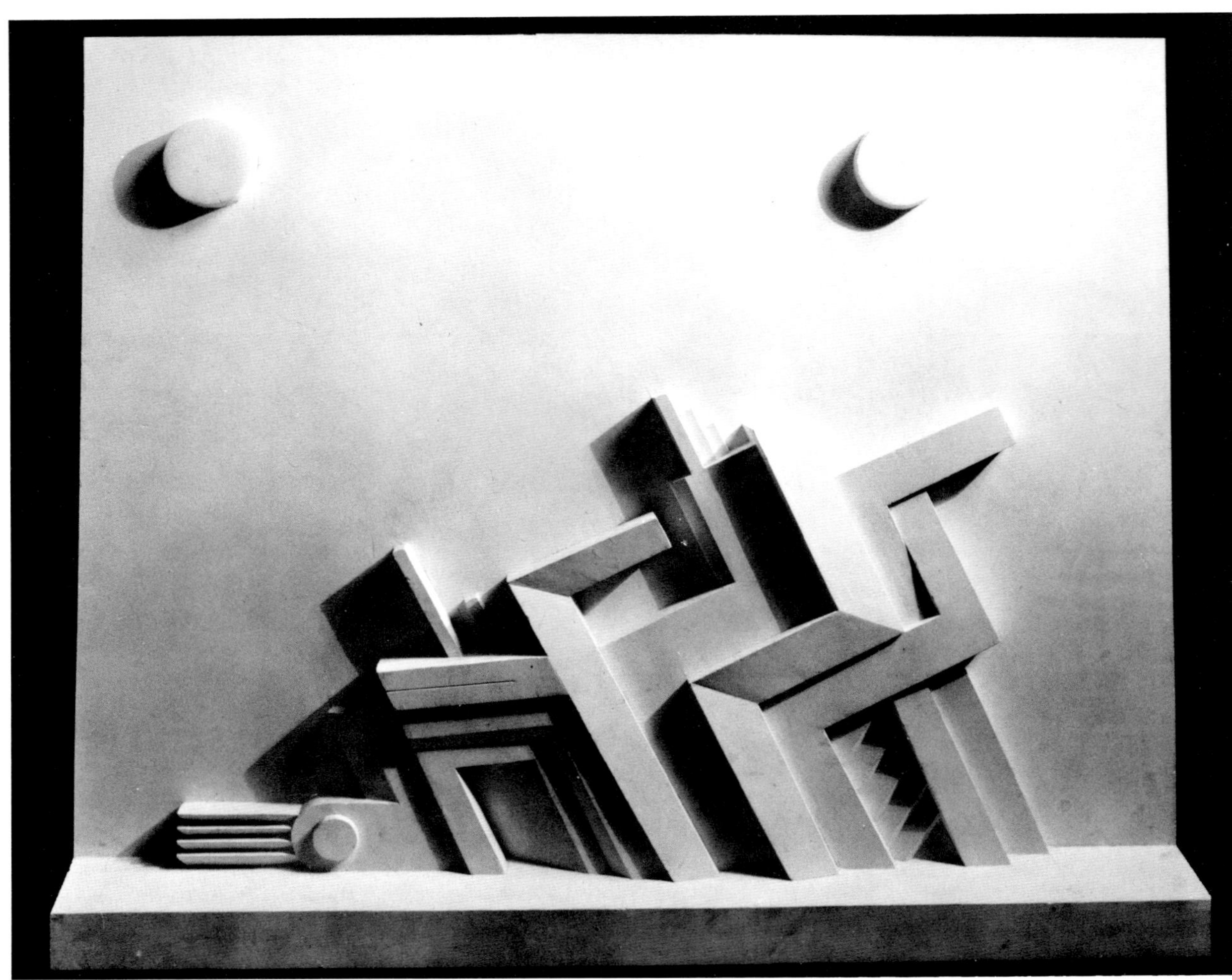

127. *Model for Left-hand Panel
of Speaker's Rostrum,
Hall of Science,
1933 Chicago World's Fair*
Plaster
Whereabouts unknown

opposite:

128. *Model for Left-hand Panel
of Speaker's Rostrum,
Hall of Science,
1933 Chicago World's Fair*
Plaster
Whereabouts unknown

129. *The Legislative Branch,*
installed in front of the
Government Building at the
1933 Chicago World's Fair
Whereabouts unknown

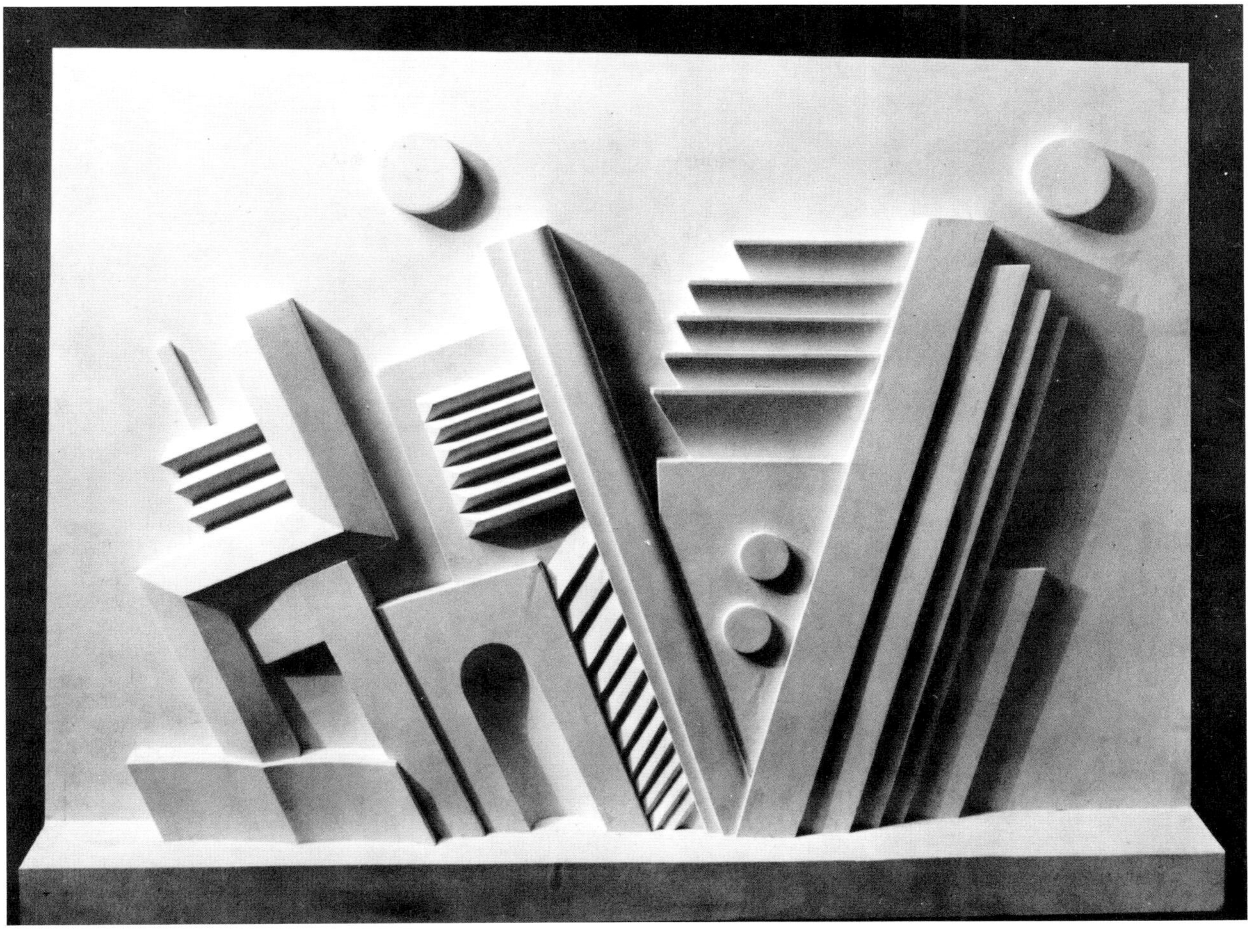

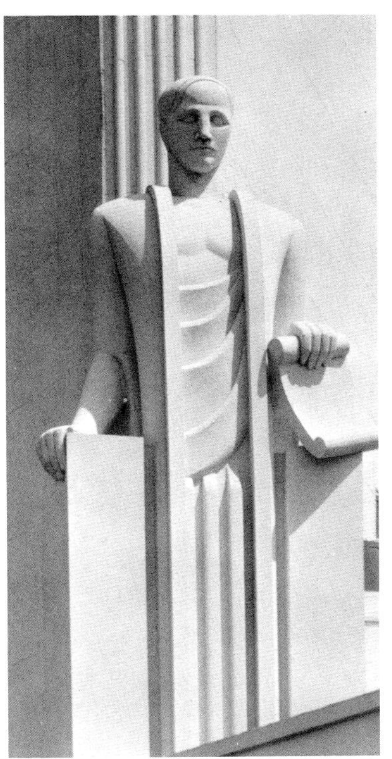

apparent that *The Legislative Branch* had been given to him as a sop. No wonder it was lifeless (Fig. 129). Moreover, it was intended to form part of a triumvirate of standing figures, with the *Executive* and *Judicial* statues executed by Raoul Josset and Loredo Taft, respectively. Storrs' statue would merely be slotted in between those of Josset and Taft, and had to conform to the prior sketches and silhouettes provided by Josset.[17] Thus, before Storrs ever made his own first sketch, the form of the statue was locked into place.

Funds received from his work at A Century of Progress kept Storrs temporarily afloat, but by March 1934 he had to join the P.W.A.P. (Public Works of Art Project), receiving a weekly check of $38.25.[18] There is no indication that Storrs produced any sculpture under the P.W.A.P., but he did execute paintings.[19]

Storrs also entered a variety of competitions for public commissions during the 1930s. Among these were the competition for sculpture for the Worcester Art Memorial, the Texas Centennial Exposition, the Post Office Building in Washington, D.C., the courtroom of the New Jersey Court House and Post Office, and the Federal Triangle in Washington, D.C. In all cases, he either lost the competition or withdrew before a final decision had been made.[20]

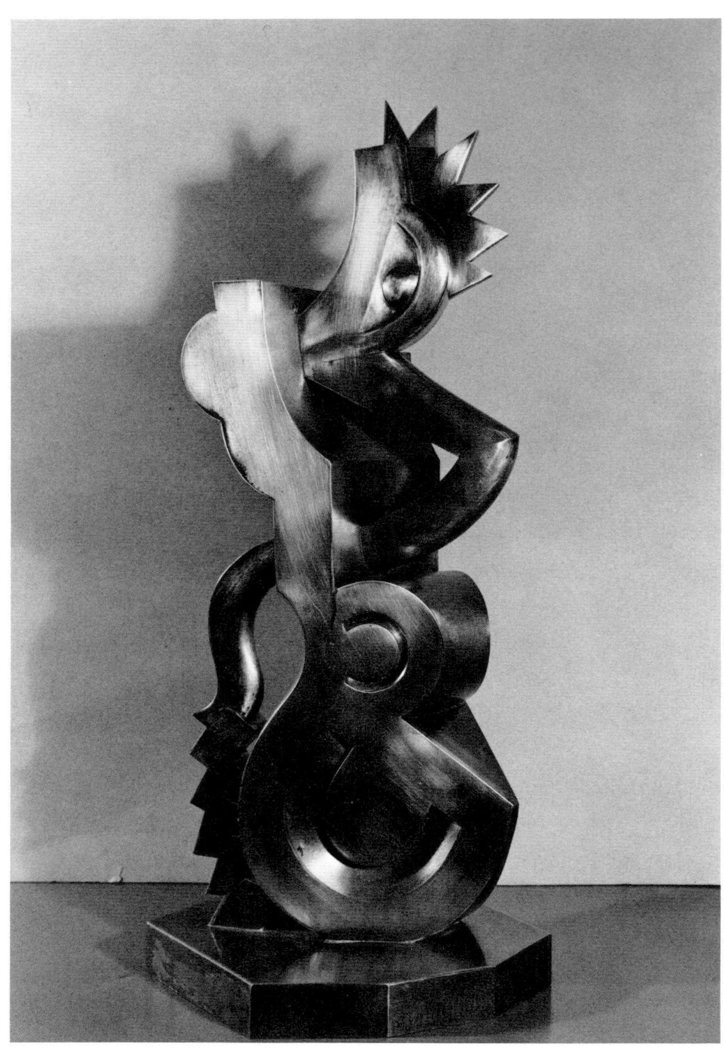

130. *Cock of the Morning*
(*The Spirit of Morning*), c. 1934
Aluminum, brass, and copper
35½ x 12¾ x 10¼
(90.2 x 32.4 x 26)
Private collection

Abstract Sculpture 1934–1938

After completing his work for the 1933 Chicago World's Fair, Storrs executed independent abstract sculptures—works unencumbered by architects' demands or the exigencies of commissions. In formal terms, these sculptures were of two types: figurative works of essentially Cubist structure updated to emulate the smooth, hard lines and surfaces of current industrial design; and abstractions that remained primitivizing, also related to Cubism and with Art Deco motifs, but now sleeker and more curvaceous. In content, these works reveal a shift in emotional temperature and a deepening of expressive power, as well as more profound psychological implications. Several of the sculptures, for example, project a spiky aggressiveness and assertiveness that stop just short of brutality. Only Storrs' natural elegance of line and form reins in these forces.

In the spring of 1935, Storrs had his first significant show of sculpture in seven years at the Albert Roullier Galleries in Chicago. About the sculptures, the Chicago art critic C.J. Bulliet wrote, "He

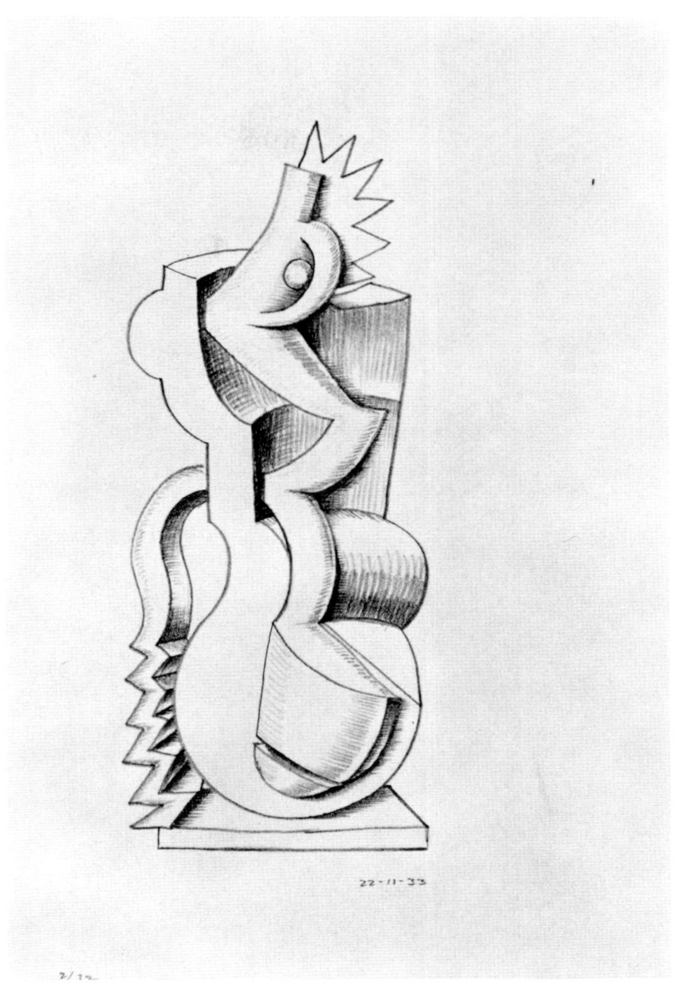

131. *Study for Cock of the Morning*, 1933
Pencil on paper
9¼ x 6 (23.5 x 15.2)
Estate of Monique Storrs Booz,
courtesy of Robert Schoelkopf
Gallery, Ltd., New York

produces abstract forms, stern and relentless, but at the same time architecturally and emotionally impressive."[21]

One of the sculptures exhibited in the Roullier Galleries was *Cock of the Morning* (Fig. 130), which Storrs called *The Spirit of Morning*.[22] The sculpture forms a striking contrast to his first attempt to symbolize the times of day, his 1915 bronze *Morning* (Fig. 5). *Cock of the Morning*, with its swelling curves and jagged forms, fairly bursts with the energy of the new day. The serrated explosion at the top of the sculpture is simultaneously a cock's comb and the stylized rays of a sunrise. A snakelike organic form twists through the piece. The many implied connections with the human body, the suggestion of body parts and profile heads, serve to make this sculpture an expression of an awakening life-force. As with so many of Storrs' sculptures of the 1930s, these multileveled images are still more apparent in his sketches (Fig. 131), perhaps because the silhouettes of the individual forms are more clearly seen.

A second sculpture in the 1935 exhibition was *Composition Around Two Voids* (Fig. 132). Made of stainless steel, this gleaming

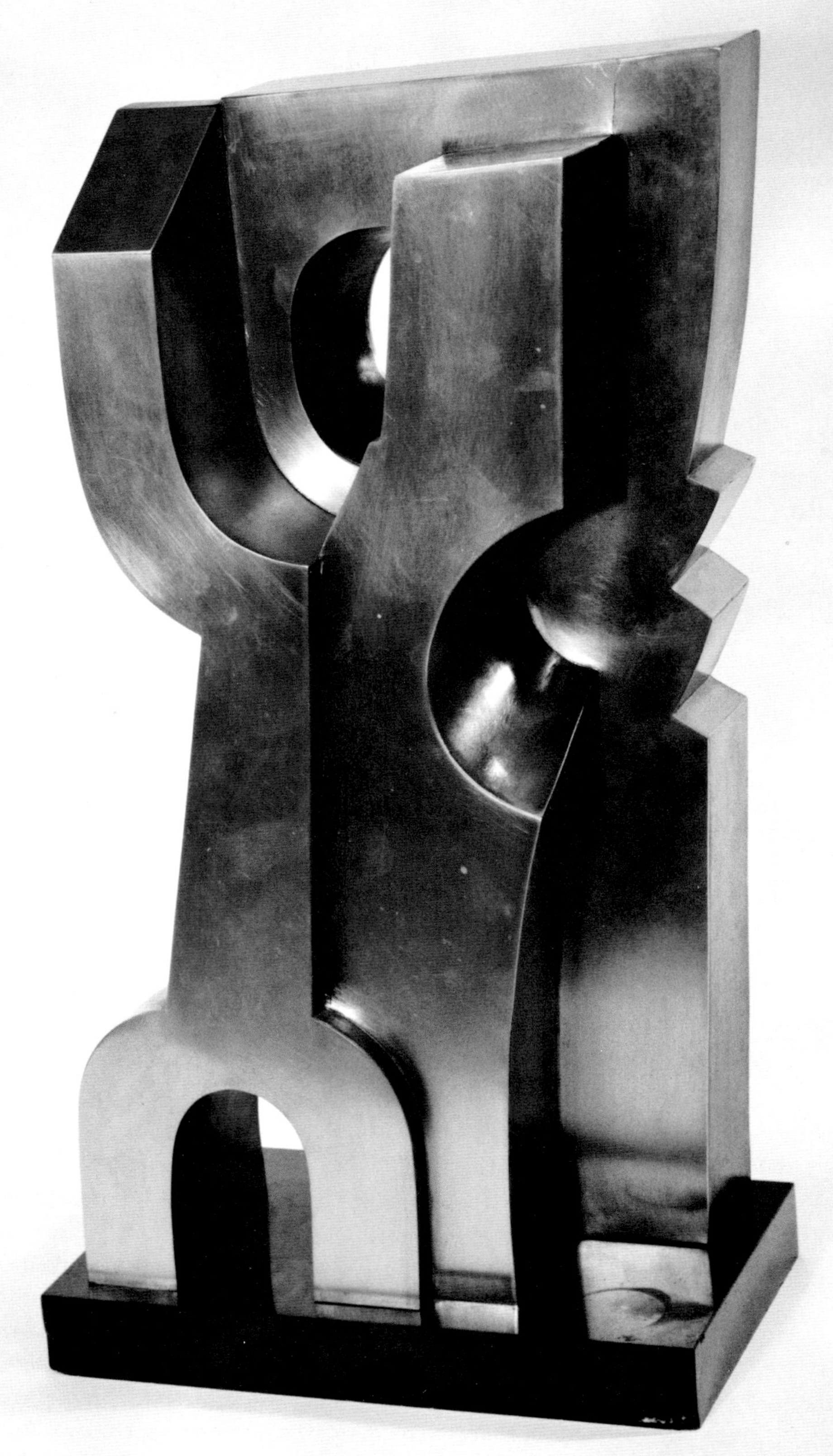

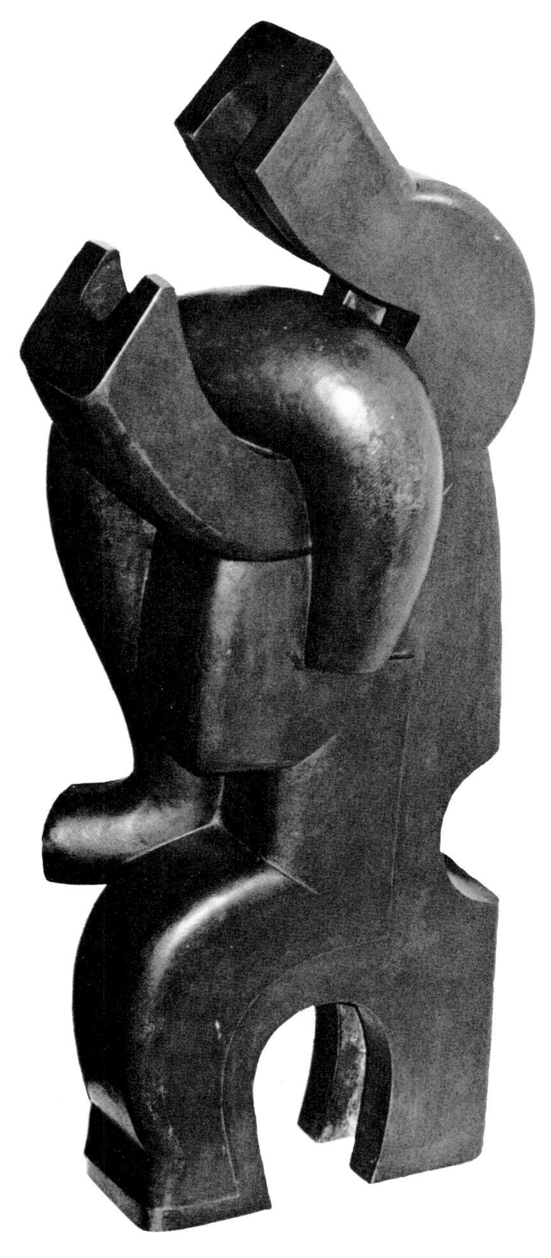

architectonic work has all the earmarks of a Precisionist sculpture concerned with machine imagery and industrial building forms. The units give the impression of tools, perhaps wrenches or pliers. Yet when we compare *Composition Around Two Voids* with Storrs' 1931 painting *Politics* (Fig. 107) it is evident that primitivizing profile faces also appear in the sculpture. The profile toward the front has a curved, open mouth and huge eye, while the profile just behind it has a snub nose and sharp profile mouth; the former profile appears masculine, the latter, feminine. If we look at the negative space surrounding the female profile, still a third silhouette profile emerges, facing in the opposite direction. It now becomes possible to read the upright wrench form as a standing totemic figure with widespread legs and upraised arms; the "eye" of the masculine profile becomes the "head" of this

109   Streamlining and Surrealism

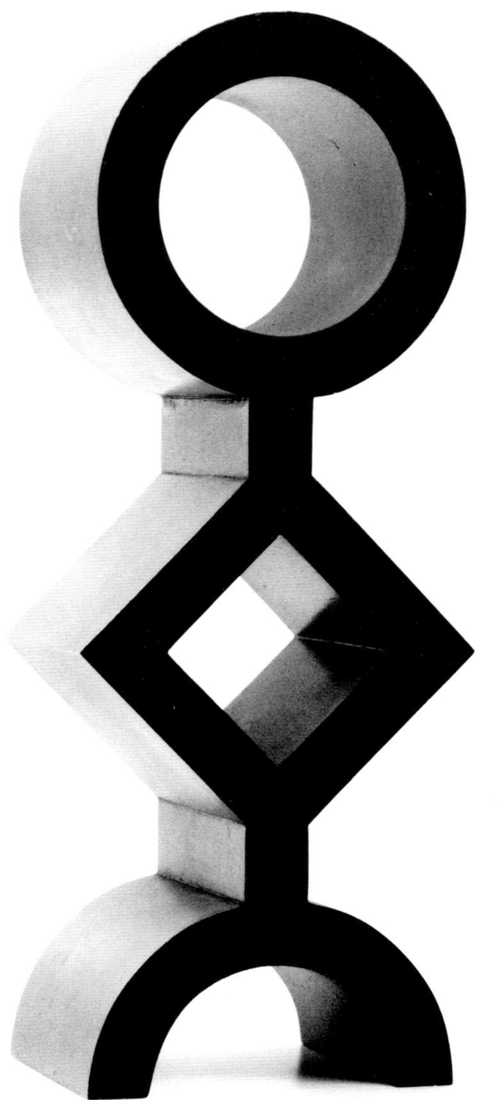

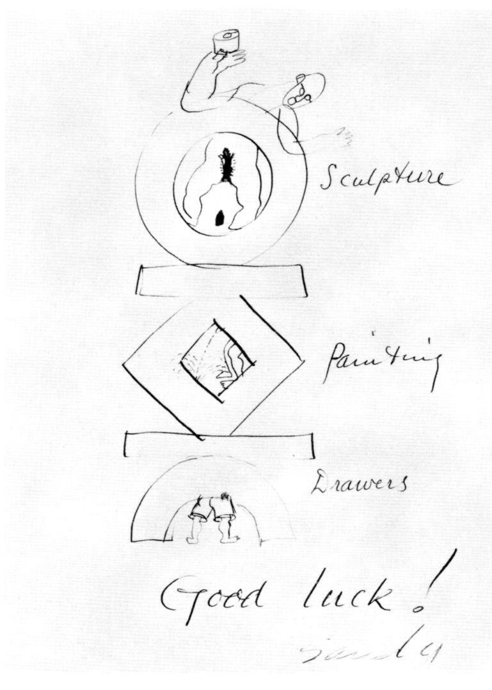

figure. Such a use of signs functioning in two separate systems simultaneously is not unusual, either in modern or tribal art or in Storrs' own work.[23] Once one looks beyond the play of machine forms here to see the strange fierce visages and the standing totemic figure, the sculpture becomes more frightening and operates at a deeper emotional level. It is exactly this intensified experience that Storrs sought to convey in his abstract sculptures of the 1930s.

A related sculpture of c. 1934, the bronze *Abstract Figure* (Fig. 133) can be seen simply as a snakelike intestinal form attached to mechanical parts. However, viewed from a frontal position, it is clearly a warlike, aggressive figure. Like *Composition Around Two Voids*, it employs the same primitivizing form—a standing idol or totem figure with upraised arms and legs spread wide apart. The space between the legs in both sculptures forms an arch or tunnel—even in these psychologically intense works Storrs never left architecture far behind. But his responses to architecture here are internal: a tunnel is

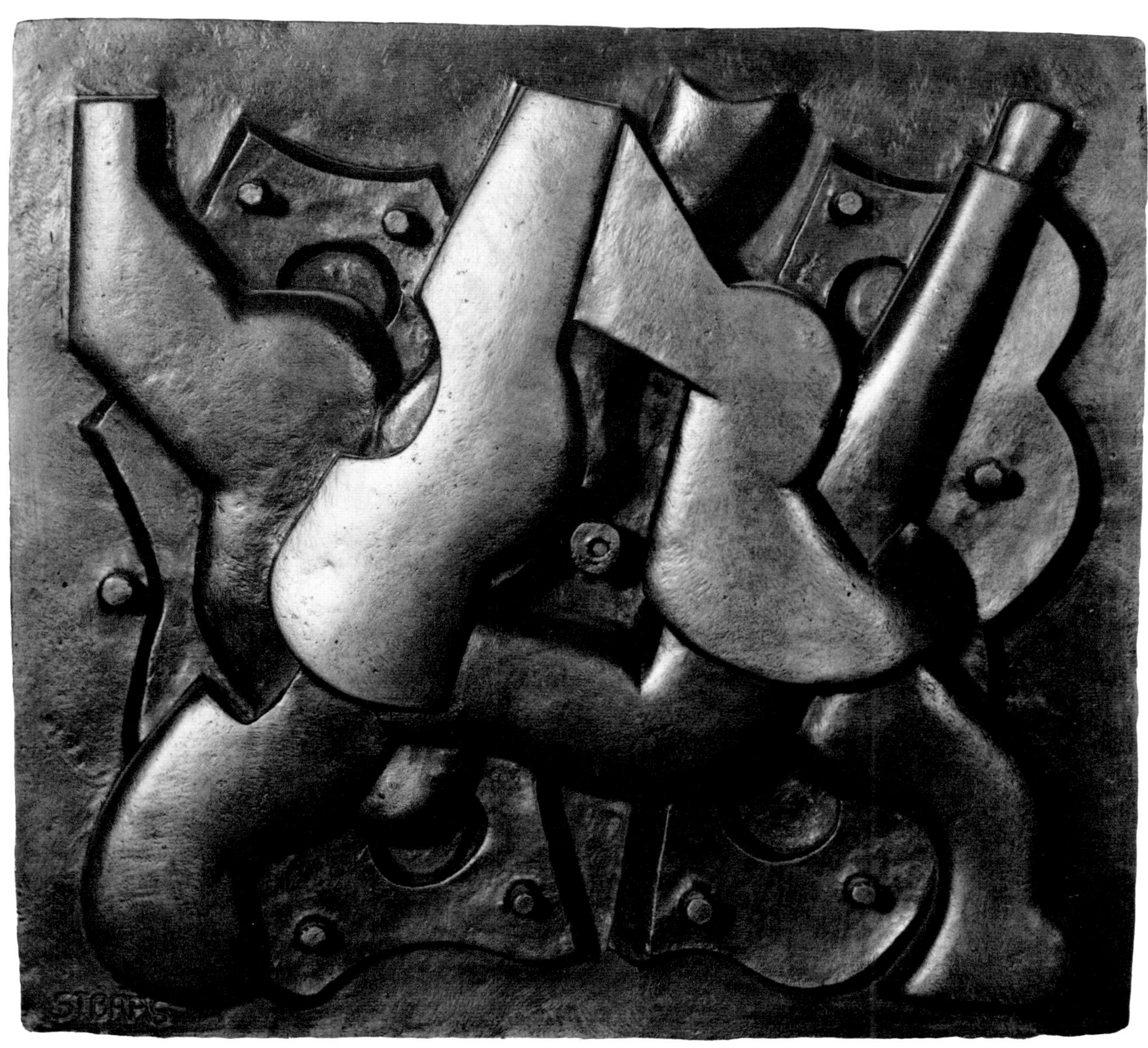

136. *Opposing Forms*, c. 1936
Bronze
9¾ x 10⅛ x 1½
(24.8 x 25.7 x 3.8)
Collection of
Harry L. Koenigsberg

not just a passageway for trains but a dark, secret, private place. Again, the snakelike form may not be a reptile or intestine but, depending on whether it is seen as part of the front or back of the sculpture, a braid on an Indian brave or an elephantine snout.[24] Seen in this light, *Abstract Figure* combines the qualities of human, animal, and idol.

The close relationship between Storrs' paintings and sculptures during this period can be seen by comparing the bronze *Abstract Figure* with his 1932 painting *Green and White Sculpture* (Fig. 111).[25] The same reptilian form is evident in both works and the totemic figure is similar as well.

Another sculpture at the Albert Roullier Galleries was a small geometric steel piece, enhanced with red and black enamel, that had been created in 1920 but not cast from the original wood model until c. 1935 (Fig. 134).[26] Storrs used a sketch of this sculpture for the gallery announcement and this gave rise to a Rabelaisian response from

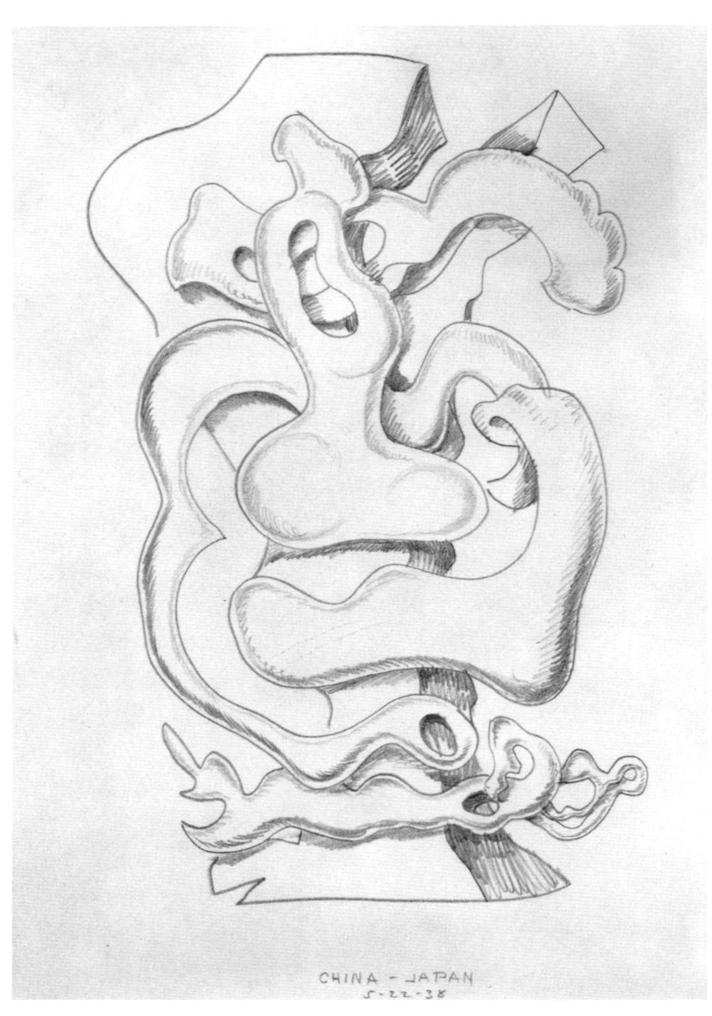

137. *China—Japan*, 1938
Pencil on paper
10⅞ x 8⅚₆ (27.6 x 21.1)
Estate of Monique Storrs Booz;
courtesy of Robert Schoelkopf
Gallery, Ltd., New York

Alexander Calder (Fig. 135), who made Storrs' design even more humanoid and added scatological comments.[27] Calder was one of a younger generation of artists who had heard of Storrs and had contacted him in Paris in 1932.[28]

About 1936, Storrs began a series of abstract relief sculptures, one group of which goes by the general title *Opposing Forms*. An example in bronze (Fig. 136) represents the several variants that Storrs created in stone and polychromed terra-cotta. In the center of the relief is what looks like the sound hole of a stringed instrument (Storrs was dedicated to music and had played the violin as a child).[29] In structure and iconography, the bronze recalls certain Synthetic Cubist reliefs by Lipchitz or Synthetic Cubist still-life paintings by Picasso and Braque that include musical instruments. However, Storrs' relief also suggests fragmented human or animal limbs. As in his 1936 painting *The Battle* (Fig. 115) or the many drawings of this period such as *China—Japan* (Fig. 137), the *Opposing Forms* relief seems to be part of his anxiety-ridden reaction to the world political situation. The depiction of convoluted, intertwined, blasted body parts continues

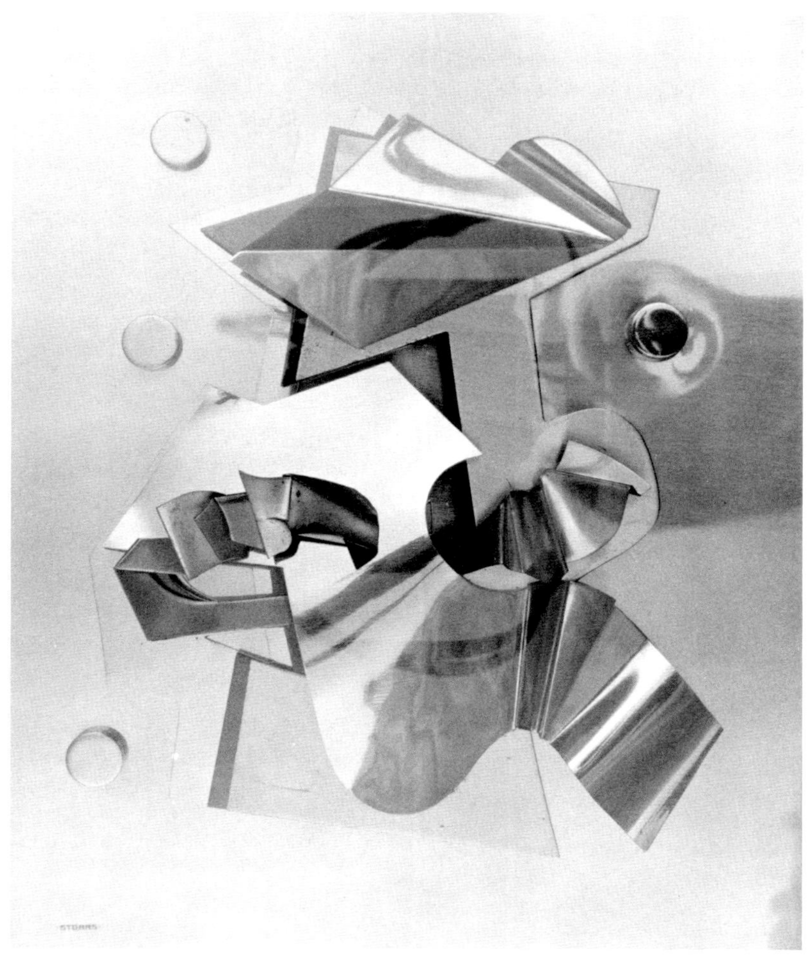

138. *Assemblage in Shadow Box*,
c. 1937
Steel, brass, and copper
13¾ x 11¾ x 2
(34.9 x 29.8 x 5.1)
Estate of Monique Storrs Booz;
courtesy of Robert Schoelkopf
Gallery, Ltd., New York

to appear in Storrs' work of the second half of the 1930s, the forms themselves becoming ever more biomorphic, fantastic, and Surrealist.

A stainless steel, copper, and brass relief that customarily goes under the title *Assemblage in Shadow Box* (Fig. 138) brings together many of Storrs' concerns of the latter 1930s.[30] The relief combines the organic and flowing with the geometric. It subverts the strict architectonic forms of Storrs' relief panels for the 1933 Chicago World's Fair (Figs. 126–128) in favor of something that approaches pure fantasy. *Assemblage in Shadow Box* is a union of shapes, some crushed and crumpled, where flickering light and shadow make the metal forms in their varied tones ever changing and evanescent.

In the decade of the 1930s, Storrs continued to execute freestanding figurative sculpture as well as portrait busts and relief portraits of important people in Chicago society. Yet it is his abstract sculptures of this period, with their complex merging of humanoid and animal, geometric and organic, tough Precisionism and fantasy, that generate the most aesthetic force.

Notes

1. Anschutz is mentioned in several of Storrs' letters to his parents but Storrs' spelling of Anschutz varies; Answtch, Auswtch, Ansutz, and Anschutz. In a letter to his mother, April 20, 1911, AAA, JSP, 6, Family correspondence, 1911, he writes: "Mr. Anschutz—while looking at one of my drawings the other day—said that it was the best portrait—in every way—that he had seen in the Academy this year—And another time—in referring to one of my skitches he said that my conception of the thing was very poetic & that my color sence was quite unusual—refined and beautiful."

2. For a slightly different description of *Portrait of an Aristocrat* and *Double Entry*, although with the same conclusions, see Noel Frackman, "John Storrs," in John R. Lane and Susan C. Larsen, eds., *Abstract Painting and Sculpture in America 1927–1944*, exhibition catalogue, Museum of Art, Carnegie Institute, Pittsburgh (New York: Harry N. Abrams, 1983), pp. 227–28.

3. Barbara Rose was the first to explore the influence of Léger on Storrs' paintings in "American Art and the Modern Theme," in *Léger and the Modern Spirit: An Avant-Garde Alternative to Non-Objective Art (1918–1931)*, exhibition catalogue (Paris: Musée d'Art Moderne de la Ville de Paris, 1982), esp. pp. 176–77.

4. Entry, January 30, 1930, AAA, JSP, 1, Diary 1930.

5. I am grateful to Courtney Donnell of the Art Institute of Chicago, whose efforts uncovered documents concerning the sale of the Léger painting in the files of the Art Institute.

6. A painting with this size, date, and title is recorded, along with a photograph of the work, in AAA, JSP, 7, brown album. C. J. Bulliet, "John Storrs Makes Debut as Painter," *Chicago Evening Post*, March 17, 1931, *Magazine of the Art World*, p. 2, reports that Storrs often titled his paintings after completion, but this does not invalidate the close connection between title and image in Storrs' creative process.

7. For an excellent discussion of *The Idol (Figure in a Circular Room)*, see Donald Kuspit, *Artists Choose Artists III*, exhibition catalogue (New York: CDS Gallery, 1984), p. 9.

8. See the following letters: Storrs to The Architectural Commission, A Century of Progress, May 15, 1930; John A. Holabird to Storrs, May 21, 1930; D.H. Burnham to Storrs, May 23, 1930; and a draft letter to "Dear John" (Holabird), 1–6–30, AAA, JSP, 6, Commission File, A Century of Progress. From these letters, it seems that Storrs submitted drawings for a sculpture or sculptures in the Administration Building. However, it was for work in the Hall of Science that he finally received a commission.

9. AAA, JSP, 6, Commission File, A Century of Progress, agreement dated January 30, 1932.

10. See Louis Skidmore, Chief of Design, A Century of Progress, to John Storrs, January 12, 1932, AAA, JSP, 6, Commission File, A Century of Progress.

11. For the iconography and importance of Storrs' sculpture at the Fair, see Jewett E. Ricker, ed., *Sculpture at A Century of Progress: Chicago 1933, 1934* (Chicago: 1934), copy in AAA, JSP, 8, Exhibition catalogs (12th folder thus marked); *Knowledge Combatting Ignorance* is discussed on p. 2.

12. In later years, Storrs became aware of his unconscious penchant for this pose. His entry for December 30, 1949, AAA, JSP, 1, Diary 1949, written when he was cleaning up his studio, notes that he had found "my relief of Jean D'Arc that I did in 1918, in full armour & that I had not seen in years & now see that I used, without thinking of it, this same pose in reverse in 1932 for my 39 ft. statue at the Chicago Fair. . . . "

13. A copy of *Cahiers d'Art*, 5 (1930) was still in Storrs' library in the home of Monique Storrs Booz as of 1983; on p. 264 is a full-page reproduction of the Lipchitz sculpture with the caption, "*Charmeuse de Serpent* (bronze) 1913. Barnes Foundation."

14. Entry, February 28, 1933, AAA, JSP, 1, Diary 1933: "See Col. Stewart he says that the Rostrum will not be done—need all the space for loudspeakers. Work afternoon."

15. A listing of biographical information in Storrs' handwriting, AAA, JSP, 1, Biography & Chronology, gives this number of Atlantic crossings.

16. The contract, dated January 9, 1933, is located in AAA, JSP, 6, Commission File, A Century of Progress.

17. Ibid. See also John Stewart, Assistant to the General Manager, Department of Works, A Century of Progress, to Storrs, January 21, 1933, AAA, JSP, 6, Commission File, A Century of Progress.

18. Entry, March 1, 1934, AAA, JSP, 1, Diary 1934: "began work for the P.W.A.P. at $38.25 per week also jury work continues as before." The "jury work" probably refers to Storrs' service on the Chicago Committee for the P.W.A.P.; his unsigned, undated draft letter, AAA, JSP, 6, Commission File, P.W.A.P., says that serving on the Chicago Committee will be an opportunity to help artists and show support for President Roosevelt.

19. Entries, March 14 and March 27, 1934, AAA, JSP, 1, Diary 1934, mention paintings done for the P.W.A.P. A photograph of a non-objective painting executed under the project is in the files of the National Archives Trust Fund, Washington, D. C., listed as 121–PWAP–18A–5.

20. For the Worcester Art Memorial, see sketches and correspondence in AAA, JSP, 6, Commission File, Worcester Memorial. For the Texas Centennial project, see letters of December 21, 1935, from the Chicago Sculptor's Association to John Storrs that tell of public monuments to be erected in Texas in 1936, AAA, JSP, 4, Correspondence 1935. For the New Jersey competition, see an undated announcement, Treasury Department, Procurement Division, inviting competition for a bronze figure of "Justice" for a courtroom in the Newark, New Jersey Post Office and Court House, and a letter from Ed Rowan, Treasury Department, Procurement Division, to John Storrs, August 1, 1935, expressing regrets that Storrs has withdrawn from the competition; both AAA, JSP, 6, Commission File, P.W.A.P. The definitive source for Storrs' attempted work for the Federal Triangle is George Gurney, *Sculpture and the Federal Triangle* (Washington, D.C.: Smithsonian Institution Press, 1985), esp. pp. 287–90 and p. 306.

21. "Around the Galleries: "John Storrs Vigorous Abstracts," *The Chicago Daily News*, February 16, 1935, p. 10.

22. In his listing of sculptures, AAA, JSP, 8, Lists of sculptures, drawings, prints and paintings, Storrs' description of the piece is "An abstract subject, 'Spirit of morning' in hammered metals." Judith Russi Kirshner, *John Storrs (1885–1956): A Retrospective Exhibition of Sculpture*, exhibition catalogue (Chicago: Museum of Contemporary Art, 1976), p. 18, refers to it by the first title.

23. William Rubin, "Modernist Primitivism: An Introduction," in *"Primitivism" in 20th Century Art*, pp. 60–62, deals with conceptualism in this imagery and the ways in which a single sign can serve more than one purpose.

24. For a good discussion of *Abstract Figure*, see Steven A. Nash in *Albright-Knox Art Gallery: Painting and Sculpture from Antiquity to 1942* (New York: Rizzoli International Publica-

tions, 1979), p. 536. Nash describes the reptilian coil in a machine-age context: "This sculpture, with its rounded brace-like forms, one opening upward and one downward to suggest a spread and solidly planted stance, and the heavy roll of metal recalling billowing smoke, presents a powerful totemistic image for the modern industrial age."

25. Ibid. A sketch for *Abstract Figure*, dated November 21, 1933, makes me hold to a date of c. 1934 for the sculpture, although Nash, ibid., suggests c. 1932 based on the date of *Green and White Sculpture*.

26. Storrs' listing, with a drawing showing this work, AAA, JSP, 8, Lists of sculptures, drawings, prints and paintings: "*Sold* to Mrs. Scheppe —$125—1935 *one* small abstract form in stainless steal with black and red enamel—made in 1920—stamped STORRS."

27. On the back of this drawing, Calder has written the word "shocking" with an arrow pointing to the

excrement in "Sculpture." The drawing has an accompanying envelope, postmarked February 28, 1935; AAA, JSP, 4, Correspondence 1935.

28. Calder's first correspondence with John Storrs is a letter dated November 7, 1932, AAA, JSP, 4, Correspondence 1932.

29. For Storrs as a violin student, between the ages of four and eleven, see AAA, JSP, 2, Writings 1942–1943, blue "The Scribble Book," pp. 98–112.

30. Although undated, the work was shown at the Albert Roullier Galleries in 1939. AAA, Downtown Gallery Papers, 132, Artists' Files: Storrs, John (Bio, Writings, Press Releases, Exh. catalogs), contains the announcement of the Roullier Galleries exhibition, "On View Five New Sculptures by John Storrs," January 28–February 11, 1939, with a listing of titles, among them an "Abstract Panel in Four Metals," surely the relief known as *Assemblage in Shadow Box*.

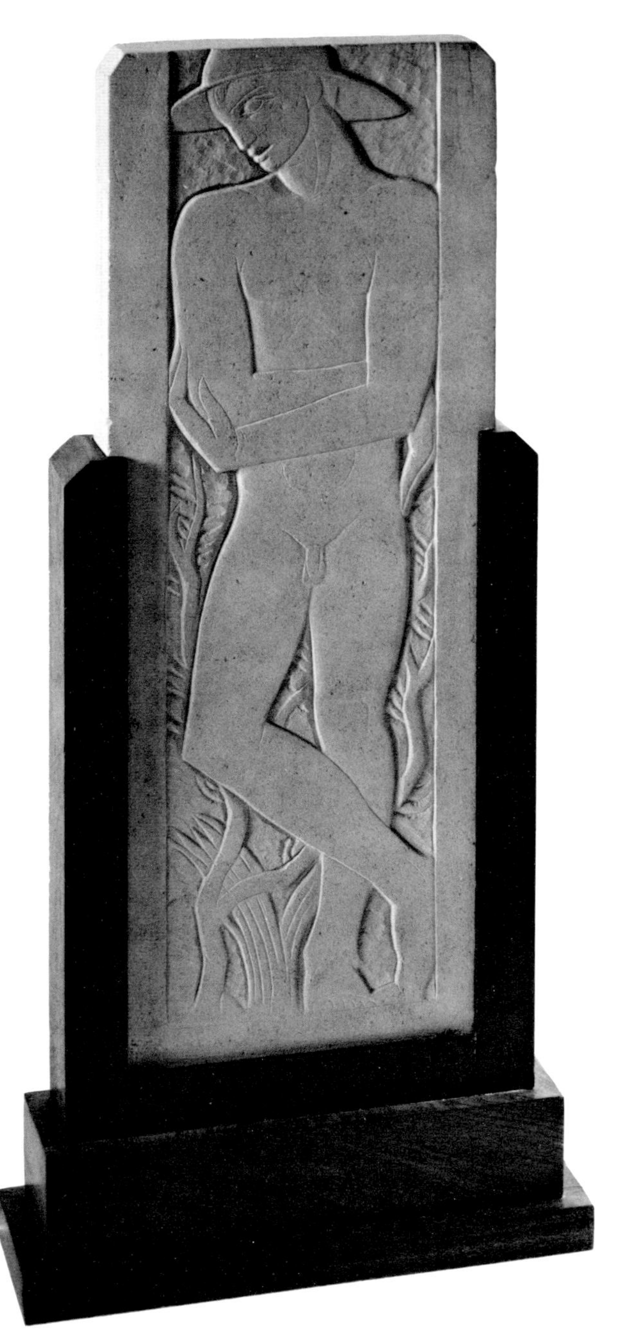
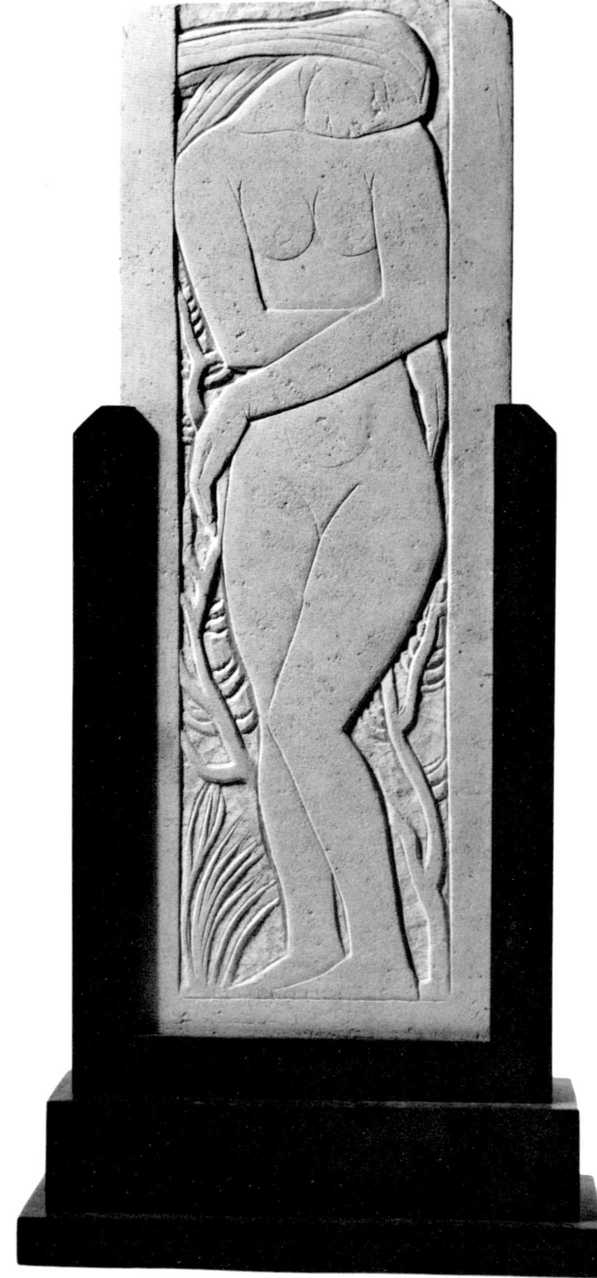

VII. The Late Works 1939–1956

139. *Adam*, 1948
Stone
16¾ x 6⅛ x 1¼
(42.5 x 15.6 x 3.2)
Estate of Monique Storrs Booz;
courtesy of Robert Schoelkopf
Gallery, Ltd., New York

140. *Eve*, 1948
Stone
16¾ x 6⅛ x 1⅜
(42.5 x 15.6 x 3.5)
Estate of Monique Storrs Booz;
courtesy of Robert Schoelkopf
Gallery, Ltd., New York

Impact of the Second World War

By 1938, John Storrs had received public recognition and the admiration of his peers in the art world. He had been made a Chevalier of the French Legion of Honor and, in 1937, his show of paintings and sculptures at the Galerie Jeanne-Myrbor in Paris was attended by a number of celebrated artists.[1] His career, however, was not really flourishing. As he later described his situation: "After 1933, as you know, the bottom fell out of building and in sculpture in general, and by 1938 I felt quite restless and lost. . . . And then came the war. . . ."[2]

In May 1939, the Storrs family sailed from America to France on the *SS Champlain*.[3] On September 2, at the Château de Chantecaille, they learned that war had been declared. They canceled their trip back to the United States and made preparations to stay at Chantecaille for the duration of the war. What John Storrs did not know, and did not expect, was that he would never again return to America.

Enlisting as a driver for the Red Cross, Storrs transported the sick and wounded in his shaky, second-hand Rolls Royce. On December 23, 1941, just before Christmas, he was arrested by German forces at his château, taken to Orléans to spend the night in military prison, and the next day taken to prison at Compiègne.[4] Informers had said that he had a wireless set directly connected to the enemy.[5] Although this accusation was unfounded, Storrs' daughter, Monique, was a member of the official Gaullist underground in charge of the French Resistance.[6]

During his internment in Front-Stalag 122, Compiègne, Storrs suffered from chronic bronchitis and dysentery. He spent much time in the prison hospital and then in the general hospital in Compiègne. Often there was no food or heat, although his wife and daughter smuggled in packages on their permitted semi-monthly visits. However, the psychological pain was more difficult for him than the physical hardships. Storrs was an artist whose acute visual sensitivity made the sights that surrounded him in Stalag 122 unbearable. He could not shut them out—and he would remain obsessed by what he had seen in Compiègne for the rest of his life.

Storrs was released after six months internment in June 1942.[7] Back at the Château de Chantecaille, weakened and in poor health, Storrs broke his hip while working in the garden. This necessitated surgery in Blois and six months of relative inactivity. By 1943, he had lost forty pounds.[8] The hardships and the bombings in the Loire region continued. From this period there is a pensive and rather sad

141. *The Gardener's Daughter,
Chantecaille*, c. 1943
Pencil on paper
9 x 8½ (22.9 x 21.6)
Collection of Arie L. Kopelman

portrait sketch, *The Gardener's Daughter, Chantecaille* (Fig. 141), which attests to the quality of Storrs' art even in the midst of extreme difficulty and adversity.

In July 1944, Storrs was again arrested with his daughter, this time because of Monique's work in the French Resistance. Father and daughter were taken to Blois, where they were imprisoned by the Gestapo for three weeks. Monique was kept in solitary confinement. They were liberated when the first American troops arrived. Monique then joined the American forces of General Patton as an interpreter. For her bravery, heroism, and service she received the Croix de Guerre, the Distinguished Service Cross, and the British Silver Star.[9]

After the war, Storrs could not exorcise the images of imprisonment, of his fellow prisoners humiliated, sick, and dying. His diary entry for March 9, 1946 reads:

finished a drawing in pencil of a young negro that died on a straw bag on the floor at the foot of my cot at the hospital of our camp, at Compageine. We couldn't keep the covers on him & when he died there was nothing but a sheet that half covered his fine nude body. I did not have the heart to make a skitch, at the time, but all day long as I lay in my bed I gazed at him and the monumental atitude of his dieing.[10]

This is only one of several such entries in Storrs' 1946 diary, where he recapitulates the sickness and death that surrounded him in Compiègne and writes that he has done drawings of the scenes.

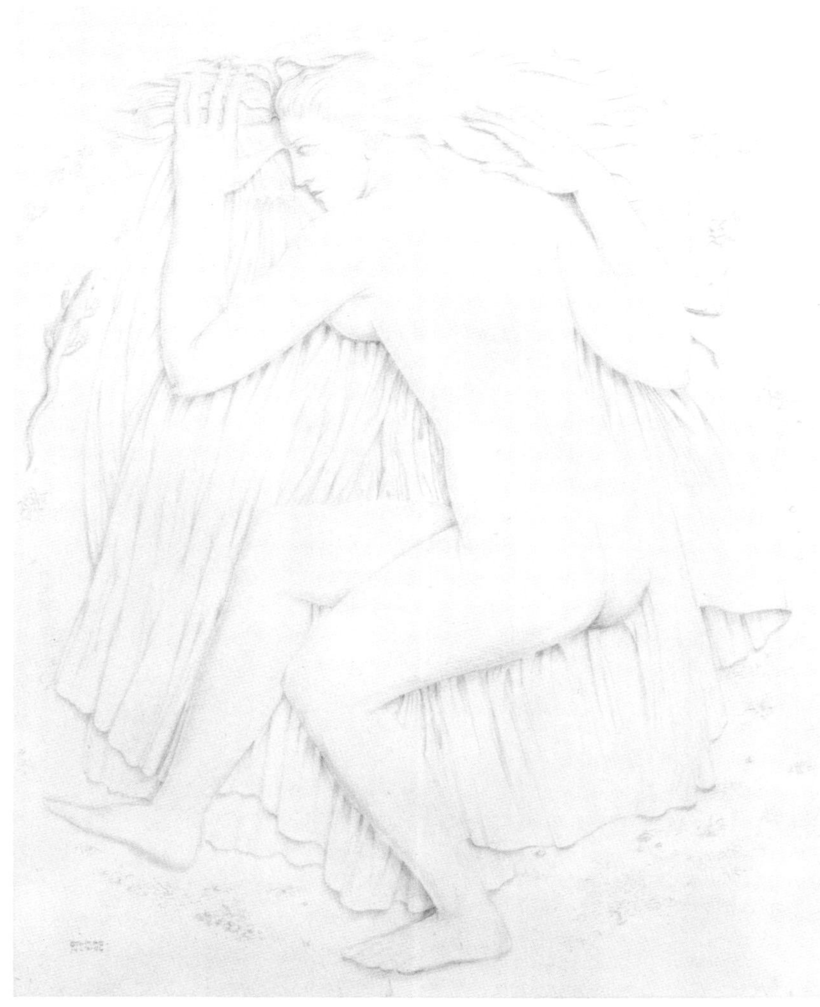

Storrs' 1946 diary is depressing in its general tone, although he continued to do drawings and began painting outdoors.[11] Materials for sculpture were still difficult to obtain, as were the services needed to finish or produce sculpture. "Since the war," Storrs wrote, "it is almost impossible to get things done in sculpture, whereas canvas and color can be had, and then I no longer have the physical strength for standing up all day as one must for sculpture."[12]

A striking example of Storrs' 1946 drawings is *Nude and Lizard* (*Spring*) (Fig. 142).[13] Given his turbulent state of mind, it is not surprising that the nude, both in posture and facial expression, shows a fear and anxiety far beyond that which would ordinarily have been aroused by a small lizard. The exquisite line is a hardened reprise of the refined, elegant drawing style that Storrs had developed around 1928–31.

In 1948, Storrs was again modeling in clay and executing numerous incised and carved reliefs in stone. At this point, he felt that the silhouette of any form in his sculpture was more important than the sum of all the exterior details and that the form was in essence the

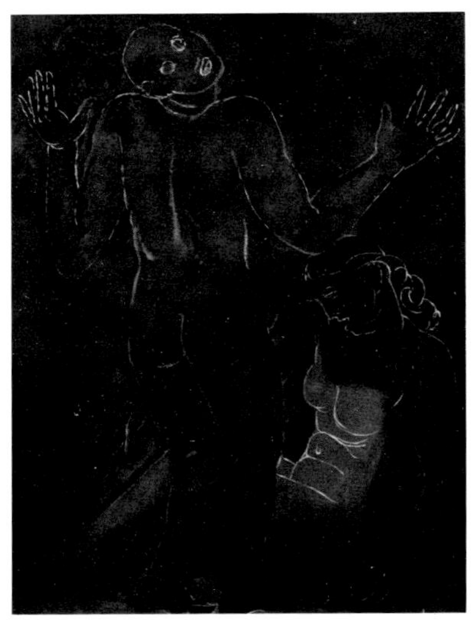

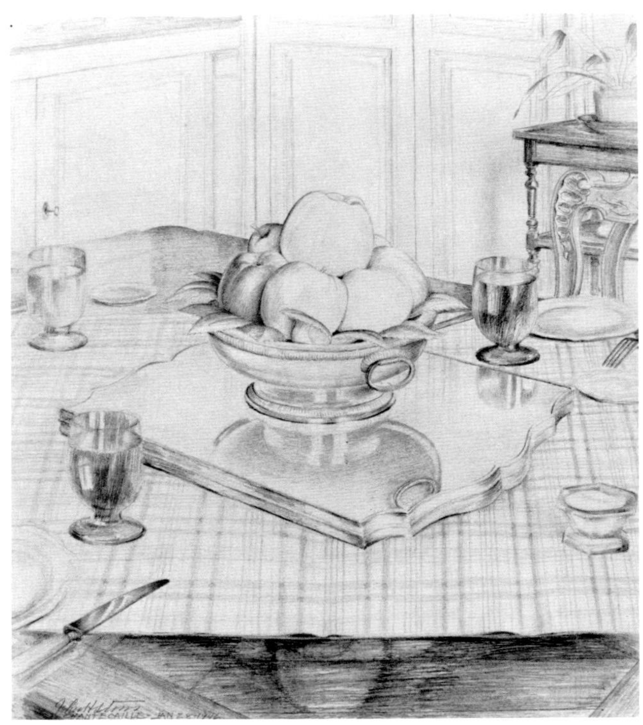

aggregate of its silhouettes.[14] His reliefs were chiefly figurative and the male and female figures tended to be elongated, somewhat nervous in line and pose, and more mannered. These characteristics constitute what can be regarded as Storrs' late style and they appear in his freestanding sculptures as well as in his numerous stone reliefs. One typical example of Storrs' late style in sculpture is *Adam* (Fig. 139) of 1948, a shallow relief incised and carved in stone. Originally, there was a figure of *Eve* on the reverse side of the stone but Storrs decided to saw the thick stone in two; thus *Eve* (Fig. 140), separated from *Adam*, exists as a pendant relief sculpture.[15]

Storrs' late paintings are essentially of two basic types, either paintings of a terrifying surreal quality that reflect his psychological and spiritual reactions to the war (Fig. 143), or, conversely, paintings in which he explores anew the comforts and basic realities of his life and surroundings at Chantecaille. In a 1946 pencil drawing (Fig. 144), the pleasures of the table at the Château de Chantecaille, and the fruit of the Loire Valley, piled in a silver bowl, are celebrated in a quiet, restrained manner.

Fighting bouts of depression, Storrs continued to work in his studio and outdoors at Chantecaille. His 1948 *Self-Portrait* shows him aging and tired (Fig. 145). In his 1950 diary, he lamented: "because of the world tension my nerves are like they were at the camp at C. It is a terrible state to be in—having a hard time controlling my thoughts—can't sleep, eat or work."[16] The worsening world situation, as noted in an earlier diary entry, referred to the beginning of the war in Korea.[17]

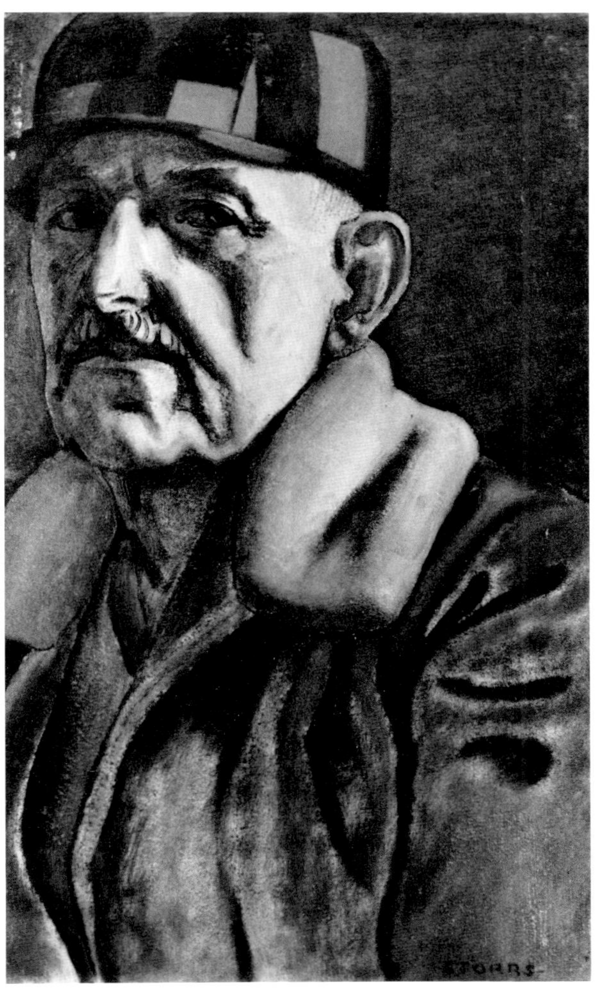

In 1949, Storrs had exhibited paintings and sculpture in a one-artist exhibition at the Municipal Library in Orléans, but nothing was sold.[18] In 1951, he tried to assess his life's work and he judged it harshly:

As I look around my studio the statues are in bronze or stone or plaster & the paintings are on canvas. You can touch & feal their reality—but their reality for me is not the bronze or stone but is still the qaulity of life & beauty I tried to put into them & not always with very great success. A reality I thought I saw & fealt and which I can never forget, but for which I have not found forms & color to adequately express.[19]

A Critical Reappraisal

John Storrs died of cancer in 1956, at the age of seventy-one, and was buried in Mer, France. His art would have had little impact after his death were it not for that phenomenon we call "taste." Despite the fact that after the Chicago World's Fair of 1933 Storrs' works were exhibited, his name was rarely mentioned in the art world. The

121   The Late Works

general impression was that he had dropped out of things during the
1930s. It was, of course, in this period that the stylistic movement we
today call Art Deco, the movement with which Storrs' sculptures are
so intimately connected, was considered in advanced circles to be
retardataire. The newly acclaimed International Style opposed surface
decoration on buildings; and sculpture, it was felt, should not be combined with architecture; if used at all, it should be isolated from
the structure.[20]

Opportunities to execute sculpture in conjunction with commercial building projects were scarce. From 1930 to 1950, there was little
commercial building of any consequence, first due to the Depression,
then the war, and then the recovery from the war. As for Storrs'
more abstract, experimental sculpture, it too fell victim to the vagaries
of taste, for in the 1940s and 1950s it was Abstract Expressionism that
attracted the attention of avant-garde artists and critics. And the chief
contribution and energy of the Abstract Expressionist movement was
perceived as being in the direction of painting, not sculpture.

An appreciation of John Storrs' work slowly grew in the 1960s and
and has continued to the present. As Minimal and Conceptual art blos-
somed, Storrs' sculptures, with their clean, spare, architectonic forms,
came to be viewed as logical and progressive. Moreover, it was also in
this period that Art Deco began to enjoy a renewed appreciation, a
revision of taste that brought Storrs' work increasing recognition.

It was at the 1963 Whitney Museum of American Art exhibition
"The Decade of the Armory Show: New Directions in American Art"
that Storrs' sculpture attracted the attention of art dealers. Edith
Halpert was a significant force in promoting his work at the Downtown Gallery; she held one-artist shows of his sculpture in 1965 and
of his paintings, drawings, and prints in 1967.[21] Then, in 1969, a
large retrospective exhibition was held at The Corcoran Gallery of
Art.[22] Storrs' work has gained further exposure through the dedicated
efforts of Robert Schoelkopf, the art dealer who became responsible
for the John Storrs estate in 1970. Important articles on Storrs, such as
those by Edward Bryant and Hilton Kramer, began to appear in the
1960s[23] and, in recent years, a good number of Storrs' works have
been recovered so that his art as a whole can be viewed more compre-
hensively than ever before.

Today, a new generation of artists is reappraising Storrs' art,
not only in terms of its formal simplicity, but also for its multileveled
emotional and spiritual content.[24] The works of John Storrs always
reveal more symbolic content and emotional expressiveness than
immediately meets the eye. So striking in their simplicity and force,
they gradually disclose the multiple layers of significant thought
that led to their creation.

Notes

1. The invitation to the exhibition "Peintures et Sculptures de John Storrs," Galerie Jeanne Bucher-Myrbor, May 20–June 2, 1937, is in AAA, JSP, 8, Exhibition catalogs (5th folder thus marked); no listing of the works shown has yet been located. Concerning those who attended the show, Storrs' entry, May 20, 1937, AAA, JSP, 1, Diary 1937, reads: "a show of my things at the gal Jenne Bucher—Bill Bullitt came also some of my artist socalled freinds—which encluded Osenfant, Lurca Lipsachtz—Leger Marcoussis—Zervos—Man Ray Jacque Villon—Max Ernest—Joan Miro—Hans Arp, Chauvin etc. Jacque Villon being the only real freind."

2. Storrs to Charles E. Luntz, August 8, 1946, photocopy in the possession of the author.

3. Much of the material, dates, and events of John Storrs' war experiences are based on a nine-page document written by Marguerite Storrs, "The Chronological Story of the Trio," a history of the Storrs family from May 25, 1939, to January 1, 1945; AAA, JSP, 1, Biography & Chronology. Although Marguerite Storrs dramatized this family history, the events are substantiated by John Storrs' entries, AAA, JSP, 1, Diary 1941 and Diary 1942.

4. Storrs' entry, written across the dates of January 4–6, 1942, AAA, JSP, 1, Diary 1942, gives this sequence of events.

5. Related to me by Robert Schoelkopf from his past discussions with Monique Storrs Booz.

6. Ibid.

7. AAA, JSP, 10, Miscellaneous (2nd folder thus marked). Storrs' official release states that he was interned from December 12, 1941 to June 26, 1942. His entry, June 28, 1942, AAA, JSP, 1, Diary 1942, reads, "a free man again!"

8. Storrs to Charles E. Luntz, August 8, 1946 (see n. 2 above) says, "By 1943 I had lost over forty pounds in weight." Marguerite Storrs, "The Chronological History of the Trio," AAA, JSP, 1, Biography & Chronology, reports that his weight dropped from 160 to 100 pounds.

9. Monique Storrs Booz died in June 1985. It was not until the eulogies given at her funeral that most of us became aware of the honors she had received.

10. Entry, March 9, 1946, AAA, JSP, 1, Diary 1946.

11. Storrs began painting both indoors and outdoors in March 1946; see especially his entries for March 15, 19, 26, 1946, AAA, JSP, 1, Diary 1946.

12. Storrs to Charles E. Luntz, August 8, 1946 (see n. 2 above).

13. Entry, March 14, 1946, AAA, JSP, 1, Diary 1946: ". . . finished a pencil drawing of 'spring,' the back view of a young nude woman laying on a rumpled sheet on the ground surrounded by the first sprouting of grass & small flowers & watching a lizard."

14. Entry, April 2, 1949, AAA, JSP, 1, Diary 1949: "Before going to sleep I thought that: for the expresion, as a whole, the siloette of any form is more important than the sum of all its exterior details—just as any form *is* the sum of its siloetts."

15. See the entries from January 31, 1948, through February 20, 1948, for a description of his work on this relief; AAA, JSP, 1, Diary 1948.

16. Entry beginning December 11, 1950, AAA, JSP, 1, Diary 1950.

17. Entry of June 27, 1950, AAA, JSP, 1, Diary 1950.

18. *John Storrs—Peintures Récents—Sculpture*, exhibition catalogue, with essay by Roger Toulouse, copy inserted in the John Storrs Scrapbook, Robert Schoelkopf Gallery, Ltd., New York. For lack of sales, see Storrs' entry, June 7, 1949, AAA, JSP, 1, Diary 1949.

19. Entry, August 25, 1951, AAA, JSP, 1, Diary 1951.

20. See Henry-Russell Hitchcock and Philip Johnson, *The International Style* (reprint, New York: W.W. Norton & Company, 1966), esp. pp. 73–74.

21. Downtown Gallery, New York, "John Storrs," March 23–April 17, 1965, and "John Storrs," April 18–May 13, 1967.

22. May 3–June 9, 1969; there was no catalogue for this exhibition, although what appears to be a preliminary checklist is in the museum files.

23. Edward Bryant, "Rediscovery: John Storrs," *Art in America*, 57 (May–June 1969), pp. 66–71. Hilton Kramer, "Assimilation of the Modern Movement: John Storrs Paintings from the '30's On View," *The New York Times*, April 22, 1967, p. 26, and "The Rediscovery of Storrs," *The New York Times*, December 13, 1970, section 2, p. 25; this latter article is reprinted as "The Return of John Storrs," in Kramer, *The Age of the Avant-Garde: An Art Chronicle of 1956–1972* (New York: Farrar, Straus and Giroux, 1973), pp. 296–98.

24. Among contemporary artists, the painter Robert Moskowitz has directly responded to the poetic and psychological reverberations of Storrs' sculptures and paintings. Although he cannot be specific, Moskowitz views his 1975 *Wrigley Building (Chicago)* in terms of similarities and relationships to Storrs' work; interview with the author, July 9, 1984. As concerned with architecture as Storrs, Moskowitz found it interesting that in the early 1930s Storrs was making paintings of his sculptures and playing with them in settings to see how they would look in space. In this context, Moskowitz chose two of Storrs' works—*The Idol (Figure in a Circular Room)* (Fig. 125) and *Architectural Form No. 3* (Figs. 82, 83) to hang along with his own works in the exhibition "Artists Choose Artists III," CDS Gallery, New York, 1984. (Moskowitz noted, however, that Storrs was his second choice—he first tried to borrow a painting by Pieter Saenredam, the seventeenth-century Dutch painter of architectural interiors.)

Chronology

1885

Born John Henry Bradley Storrs, in
Chicago, the last of seven children
of David W. Storrs, Chicago architect and real estate developer, and
Hannah Harrington Storrs of Kings-
ton, Canada.

1887

Family moves to their third home in
Chicago, 6732 Wentworth Avenue;
D.W. Storrs rebuilds the house.
William Storrs dies at age nine of
scarlet fever contracted at school.
As the only surviving son, John is
not allowed to attend school.

1889

Begins violin lessons (through 1896).

1893

Visits the World's Columbian Exposition in Chicago.

1894

First sculpture, a plasteline relief of
Napoleon, created during a conva-
lescence from illness.

Enters a normal school near home,
still unable to read or write.

1897

Two dated geometric watercolors.

1899–1900

Attends Catholic boarding school in
Indiana, called The University of
Notre Dame, a preparatory school
for the University.

1900

Beloved seafaring grandfather,
Captain Jeremiah Harrington, dies.

Summer. Enters Culver Military
Academy.

Fall. Enters the Chicago Manual
Training School (part of University
High School).

1903

Spends summer at the Culver Naval
(formerly Military) Academy.

1904

Draws cartoons for *The University
High School Weekly*. Becomes staff
artist.

Scheduled to graduate from University High School, but lacks credits.
Creates and teaches an advanced
class in architectural drawing in
order to gain sufficient credits; class
supervised by Frederick Newton
Williams.

September. Visits World's Fair in
St. Louis, Missouri.

1905

Art editor of *The Correlator*, yearbook of the senior class of University High School; graduation
from University High School.

Embarks on a trip to Europe with a
Chicago friend, Sidney Jenkins.
Sails from New York City; takes
pictures with new Kodak camera.
Travels to England, Holland, Bel-
gium, and Germany.

Fall. With Sidney Jenkins, joins
sister Mary, who is studying music
in Berlin. Begins vocal lessons.
Meets his sister Mary's close friend
Maud Allan, an interpretive
dancer.

Attends numerous concerts and
operas in Berlin, including a dance
performance by Maud Allan.
Decides to study art seriously; at
Allan's suggestion, goes to study

with her friend, the sculptor Arthur Bock in Hamburg; accepted as an apprentice for a six-month trial period.

1906

Spring. Terminates study with Arthur Bock.

Summer. Travels with family in Europe.

Fall. Lives in Paris; enrolls in the Académie Julian; either withdraws almost immediately or never attends opening classes.

Probably studies with Richard Miller at Académie Montparnasse; fellow American students are Walter Cole and Irving Heitkamp.

1907

January–March. Enrolled in the Académie Franklin.

March. Lives with the Irving Heitkamp family; also living there is J.H. Duval, a music and art critic, who gives him a card of introduction to Gino Severini.

Summer. Travels to Italy, Turkey, Egypt, Spain, and Greece with Irving Heitkamp.

Sister Mary marries Arthur Olaf Andersen, a composer, in Chicago.

Fall. Back in Paris. Probable time of first meeting with Gino Severini and, possibly, Antoine Bourdelle.

November. Sails from France, arrives in New York City. Travels to Boston and then to Chicago.

1908

January. Begins work in his father's real eastate office, collecting rents and attempting to rent apartments. Begins night classes at the Chicago Academy of Fine Arts and classes at the School of the Art Institute of Chicago.

Four months study in the sculpture class of Charles J. Mulligan.

Purchases Japanese prints at Carson Pirie Scott department store exhibition, including works by Hiroshige, Hokusai, and Utamaro.

1909

Continues to work in D.W. Storrs' real estate office.

January–July. Attends classes at the School of the Art Institute of Chicago.

Fall. Enrolls in the School of the Museum of Fine Arts, Boston. Studies sculpture with Bela Pratt and is acquainted with Loredo Taft. Attracted to works by Rodin, Greek and Roman antiquities, and Japanese pottery at Museum of Fine Arts.

Begins collecting Grueby and Dedham pottery.

1910

January. Begins to make his own pottery.

February. Still enrolled in the School of the Museum of Fine Arts. Takes a studio with fellow art student Henry Hoyt.

April. Back visiting his family in Chicago. Attends a vocal performance given by his sister Mary, and draws a sketch of a Wrightian home on the program.

May. Spends a day at the Dedham Pottery Works in Dedham, Massachusetts.

June. Travels in New England and then to New York City.

Fall. Enrolls at the school of the Pennsylvania Academy of the Fine Arts. Studies sculpture under Charles Grafly and painting and drawing with Daniel Garber. Immediately placed in the advanced painting class by Thomas Anschutz, chief instructor and head of the faculty.

1911

Spring. Wins the Stewardson Prize given by the Department of Sculpture of the Pennsylvania Academy of the Fine Arts for a half life-sized figure done from the model in a time limit of eighteen hours.

Determines to return to Paris to study sculpture. Arrives there in September.

Visits Irving Heitkamp in Étaples; goes to see H.O. Tanner and his wife, who live nearby.

October. Enrolls at the Académie Colarossi and studies with Paul Bartlett and Jean-Antoine Injalbert. Also enrolls at the Académie de la Grand Chaumière; studies with Lucien Simon.

1912

Continues enrollment at the Académies Colarossi and la Grand Chaumière until June.

April. Shares his studio with Howard Smith, a painter in Paris on a scholarship from the School of the Museum of Fine Arts, Boston.

July. Returns to Chicago at his parents' request.

October. Returns to Paris with his father, mother, and nephew Peter Andersen.

1913

May have studied at the Académie Julian in early part of the year.

Meets and corresponds with Marguerite De Ville Chabrol of Orléans, a novelist and correspondent for *Paris Temps*.

June 19. First recorded correspondence with Rodin's secretary. Probably begins studies with Rodin at this time, although it is possible such studies began as early as the fall of 1912.

July. Hannah Storrs dies and is buried in Père Lachaise Cemetery, Paris.

August. First recorded etching.

1914

August. Beginning of World War I. Stays with the family of his fiancée, Marguerite De Ville Chabrol, in Orléans.

September 14. Marries Marguerite Chabrol.

Engaged in hospital and ambulance work.

1915

Goes to Chicago for three months. Takes a delayed honeymoon trip, accompanied by D.W. Storrs, to the Canadian Rockies, Santa Fe, Kansas City, Denver, and Mexico. Attracted to American Indian Art, which he probably begins to collect at this time.

Commissioned to make medal and poster for the Association Nationale pour la Protection des Veuves et Orphelins de la Guerre, a charitable institution in Paris.

1916

Lives in Chicago with his wife and D.W. Storrs.

Brief correspondence with Theodore Roosevelt.

June. Sails for France.

August. Tries to arrange a Rodin exhibition with Martin Birnbaum, director of the Berlin Photographic Company, New York.

Begins to write poetry seriously.

1917

August. Beginning of recorded correspondence with journalist Louise Bryant, who remains a lifelong friend and champion of Storrs' works.

November 17. Death of Rodin. At the request of Rodin's family and Léonce Bénédite, later director of the Musée Rodin, executes a deathbed portrait in drypoint which is later transformed into a lithograph.

October. *The Masses* publishes Storrs' etchings with an accompanying article on his work by Louise Bryant.

1918

April. *The Liberator* publishes his poem "Music."

Goes to see Antoine Bourdelle's frescoes at the Théâtre des Champs-Elysées, Paris.

Meets Jessie Dismorr, who acquaints him with activities of the Vorticists.

October. One of his woodcuts used on the front cover of *The Liberator*, which continues to publish his work.

November. Birth of his only child, Monique, in Orléans.

Starts portrait bust of Viscount Inouye, Japanese ambassador to England.

1919

January. The first issue of the experimental magazine *Playboy* publishes a woodcut by and description of Storrs; other woodcuts are published in future issues.

May 31. Attends centennial commemorative program honoring Walt Whitman in Paris.

June. Studies for two weeks at the Académie Julian. Creates large, abstract, inlaid, three-figure composition, *Action, Inaction, and Reaction*.

December 15. The interior design firm of Ruhlmann et Laurent makes inquiries concerning the price of the bronze *Horses' Heads*.

1920

Ruhlmann et Laurent make further inquiries about several sculptures.

Receives commission from Aero Club of France for a monument to commemorate Wilbur Wright's test flight at Le Mans, France.

Death of D.W. Storrs. John Storrs contests will, which requires him to spend eight months each year in the United States in order to obtain his full income from the estate.

1921

Loses suit to contest his father's will; refuses to comply with the residency restrictions.

July. Visits Florence and probably the Tuscan hill towns.

Purchases fifteenth-century Château de Chantecaille, Mer, Loir-et-Cher, which he retains throughout his life.

Begins to buy and sell antiques, antiquities, and occasionally art, the proceeds often used to help fellow artists.

Fall. Marsden Hartley stays with the Storrs at the Château de Chantecaille.

1922

January–April. Sees Jacques Lipchitz frequently.

Visits Salon des Indépendants, where he speaks with Gertrude Stein and Alice B. Toklas.

February. Visits Ossip Zadkine. Severini leaves paintings with Storrs to sell.

March. Working on *Auto Tower* sculpture.

October. Wilbur Wright monument dedicated at Camp d'Auvours, near Le Mans. Portrait of Viscount Inouye in polished silvered bronze completed.

1923

Ezra Pound selects photographs of Storrs' sculpture for publication in *The Little Review*; winter 1922 issue has photographs of his sculptures and his article "Museums or Artists."

February. Arrives New York. With Louise Bryant, goes to see Joseph Stella's paintings and visits William and Marguerite Zorach.

March. Charles Sheeler photographs Storrs' sculpture in New York.

Creates set for actress-singer Georgette Leblanc Maeterlinck's *Histoires de Coeur*, one of the musical programs in the *Soirées Intimes* held at her theater at 47 Washington Square South. Remaining programs in March and April have sets by Joseph Stella, Léon Bakst, and André Chotin.

1924–25

Summer. Chicago architect Barry Byrne visits Storrs in Paris and purchases two sculptures; Byrne is probably accompanied by the sculptor Alfonso Ianelli.

Within the next twelve months has social and professional encounters with Jacques Lipchitz, Man Ray, Marcel Duchamp, Tristan Tzara, Jean Cocteau, Ezra Pound, George Biddle, and Marsden Hartley.

1926

May. Correspondence with Paris firms concerning fabrication of mixed metal sculptures.

June. Goes to Vienna to visit his friend John Miller, who has suffered a nervous breakdown. Corresponds with Alfred Adler concerning Miller's condition.

1927

November. Arrives New York from France, en route to Chicago.

Earliest possible date for his first meeting with Frank Lloyd Wright.

1928

Commissioned to make a statue of *Ceres* for the top of the Chicago Board of Trade Building, a pioneering skyscraper in the Art Deco style. Takes an apartment in Chicago.

Creates rug designs executed by the New Age Artists and Workers Association under the direction of Ralph R. Pearson and Zoltan Hecht.

1929

February. Elected to active membership in American Union of Decorative Artists and Craftsmen, New York.

Meets Buckminster Fuller in Chicago and, through him, Isamu Noguchi.

March. Accepts commission to execute life-sized bronze statues of *Night* and *Day* for "The Centaurs," Alfred Hamill's estate, redesigned by architect David Adler.

June. The American Battle Monuments Commission approves Storrs' proposal to prepare preliminary drawings and execute models for reliefs for the U.S. Naval Monument to be erected in Brest, France.

July. Travels in Ireland in connection with future sculptural work for the Church of Christ the King in Cork.

October. The Building Committee of the Board of Trade, Chicago, approves small model of *Ceres* sent from France.

December. Begins sketches for monumental statue of *Christ* for entrance of the Church of Christ the King.

1930

January–February, Paris.

March, New York. Visits Alfred Stieglitz at his An American Place gallery.

Late March–early April. Providence, Rhode Island, at the Gorham Bronze Foundry, to check the full-scale aluminum statue of *Ceres* for the Board of Trade Building.

May. Again visits Stieglitz, who wishes to show his work; no exhibition materializes.

June. Dedication of the Chicago Board of Trade Building.

Travels to Vienna.

December, Chicago. Begins to paint seriously.

1932

January. Signs contract with Chicago World's Fair (A Century of Progress) committee for sculpture in Hall of Science; to include a free-standing group at the head of the north ramp, four panels of bas-reliefs for the north wall, and two bas-reliefs for the rostrum.

February, Philadelphia and New York.

March, Chicago.

Summer, France.

November. First correspondence from Alexander Calder, who wishes to meet Storrs and invites him to see his *Circus*.

1933

January. Plans for Hall of Science speaker's rostrum at A Century of Progress exhibition cancelled.

February. Signs contract for a statue of *The Legislative Branch* for the exterior of the Federal Building at A Century of Progress.

1934

March. Begins working for the Public Works of Art Project at $38.25 per week.

1935

First correspondence with the General Alloys Company, Boston, concerning the casting of metal sculptures.

March. Pays $25 to save his *Knowledge Combatting Ignorance*, monumental statue created for A Century of Progress, from the wreckers.

1936

October. Stays in Orléans for winter with family. Honored as Chevalier of the Legion of Honor by the French government.

1937

Enters (and loses) U.S. Treasury Department competition for statues outside the Apex Building in the Federal Triangle, Washington, D.C.

August 15. Dedication of the U.S. Naval Monument, Brest, France.

1938

Fulfills commission from Mrs. James Ward Thorne for two miniature female nudes, *Summer* and *Winter*, for placement in one of the miniature rooms that form part of Mrs. Thorne's collection of such rooms at The Art Institute of Chicago.

1939

Last trip to the United States; returns to France in May.

1941

Transports wounded to hospitals in Orléans area.

July 4. Destruction of the U.S. Naval Monument at Brest by German forces.

December 23. Arrested by Germans at Château de Chantecaille. Taken to Blois and then to military prison in Orléans.

December 24. Imprisoned in Compiègne, Front-Stalag 122.

1942

January–March. In military hospital with bronchitis. Three days after return to prison, rehospitalized with dysentery. After two weeks, sent back to prison camp.

June 11. First notation in diaries of drawings done in prison camp. June. Released from prison camp.

December. Operated on for broken hip in Blois.

1944

Works on drawings and prints at the Château de Chantecaille.

January. Begins series of woodcuts to illustrate poems by Edgar Allan Poe.

July 19. Arrested by Gestapo with daughter, Monique, who has been active in the French underground, and imprisoned in Blois.

August 7. Liberated from prison. Monique Storrs joins General George Patton's American forces as guide and interpreter.

1945

July. Monique receives Croix de Guerre.

1946–1953

Works on sculptures, drawings, and paintings; has local exhibitions in museums in the Loire Valley.

1954

Makes last attempt to contest D.W. Storrs' will.

Elected president of the École de la Loire, a group of artists working in the Loire Valley.

1956

Dies of cancer at the Château de Chantecaille. Buried at Mer, Loir-et-Cher.

Selected Exhibitions and Bibliography

Exhibitions are listed in chronological order; an asterisk denotes a one- or two-artist exhibition. Reviews and related documents are listed alphabetically by author or, lacking author, by title, immediately following each exhibition and are indicated with a bullet (·). Books and articles unrelated to exhibitions are listed at the end of each year. In cases where newspaper articles or other material have been taken from archival scrapbooks or papers, it has not been possible to supply all reference data.

1913

Société du Salon d'Automne. "Salon d'Automne IIe Exposition de 1913" (catalogue).

1914

Société Nationale des Beaux-Arts, Salon de 1914. "XXIVe Exposition" (catalogue).

· Mowrer, Paul Scott. "Work of Two Chicago Artists in Paris." *The Chicago Daily News*, May 9, 1914, p. 13.

1915

Panama-Pacific International Exposition, San Francisco. February 20–December 4 (catalogue).

1917

The Art Institute of Chicago. "Exhibition of Etchings under the Management of the Chicago Society of Etchers." February 1–March 4 (catalogue).

Galerie du Luxembourg, Paris. "Première Exposition de L'Arc-en-Ciel Groupe Franco-Anglo-Americain." December 5–29 (catalogue, with preface by Francis Carco).

· "French, American and British Art Exhibition." *New York Herald* (European edition), December 2, 1917, p. 2.

· "Striking Art Exhibit Opens in Latin Quarter." *New York Herald* (European edition), December 6, 1917, p. 2.

"American Sculptor Chosen to Design French War Medal." *Buffalo Express*, April 26, 1917 (?).

Bryant, Louise. "John Storrs." *The Masses*, 9 (October 1917), p. 21.

1918

The Art Institute of Chicago. "Exhibition of Etchings under the Management of the Chicago Society of Etchers." March 25–May 1 (catalogue).

Storrs, John. "Music." *The Liberator*, 1 (April 1918), p. 11.

1919

Musée National du Luxembourg, Paris. "Exposition des Artistes de l'École Américaine." October–November (catalogue, with preface by Léonce Bénédite).

"Playboys and Playgirls." *Playboy*, 1 (January 1919), p. 34.

1920

*Galerie des Feuillets d'Art, Paris. "Exposition des Peintures de Henry Ottman et des Sculptures de John Storrs." January 19–31 (catalogue).

*Folsom Galleries, New York. "John Storrs." December 9–24 (catalogue, with essay by Marc Debrol [Marguerite De Ville Chabrol Storrs]).

· Ackerman, Phyllis. "New York Art Letter." *Star*, December 19, 1920.

• "Art: Exhibitions of Paintings." *The New York Times*, December 19, 1920, section 6, p. 10.

• "Art News and Comment: Modern Primitives by John Storrs." *The Christian Science Monitor*, December 20, 1920, p. 12.

• Boswell, Peyton. "Happenings in the World of Art: Modern Trend in Sculpture Exhibition." *New York American*, December 19, 1920, p. 4.

• Cortissoz, Royal. "Two Persuasive Types of the Modernist Movement: John Storrs, A New American Sculptor and Wood Engraver." *New York Herald Tribune*, December 19, 1920, section 3, p. 7.

• "Exhibitions Now On: John Stoors [sic] at the Folsom Galleries." *American Art News*, 19 (December 18, 1920), p. 2.

• Field, Hamilton Easter. "The Art of John Storrs." *The Arts*, 1 (January 1921), pp. 22–23.

• ———. "When Is a Whistler Not a Whistler? Roerich and Storrs, Russian and American." *The Brooklyn Daily Eagle*, December 26, 1920, section 3, p. 6.

• McBride, Henry. "Modern Art." *The Dial*, 70 (February 1921), pp. 234–36.

• ———. "News and Reviews of the World of Art—Interesting Exhibitions: Mr. John Storrs Making First Appearance in the Folsom Galleries." *New York Herald*, December 19, 1920, section 3, p. 9.

Ervine, St. John. "A London Letter." *New York Evening Post*, December 24, 1920, *The Literary Review*, p. 7.

Patterson, Augusta Owen. "Arts and Decoration." *Town & Country*, 77 (January 10, 1921), p. 27.

Tyrrell, Henry. "Why This Queer Sculpture Is Art." *New York World*, November 28, 1920, *The World Magazine*, p. 9.

1921

*Arts Club of Chicago. "Exhibition of Sculpture and Wood Engravings by John Storrs." January 21–February 4 (catalogue). Traveled to the Milwaukee Art Institute.

• "John Storrs." *Chicago Evening Post*, January 25, 1921, *Magazine of the Art World*.

• K., J. "Modernist in Art Exhibits at Institute." *The Milwaukee Journal*, February 20, 1921.

Brown-Robertson Gallery, New York. "Wood Block Prints with the Provincetown Printers." ? –April 16 (catalogue).

"An Artist Who Celebrates Wright and Whitman." *Current Opinion*, 70 (February 1921), p. 245.

Davis, Charles Belmont. "The Roulette Wheel of Literature." *Vanity Fair*, 16 (April 1921), p. 61.

Gilbert, Paul T. "Fortune or No, Storrs Will Go Back to France." *Chicago Evening Post*, January 20, 1921, p. 1.

Sawyer, Phil. "Leaving Fortune, Sculptor Storrs Returns to Paris." *Chicago Tribune* (European edition), March 28, 1921.

1922

Storrs, John. "Museums or Artists." *The Little Review*, 9 (Winter 1922), p. 63.

1923

*Société Anonyme, New York. "Exhibition of Sculpture by John Storrs." February 23–March 22 (brochure, with essay by André Salmon). Traveled to the Arts Club of Chicago.

• Brook, Alexander. "John Storrs at the Société Anonyme." *The Arts*, 3 (March 1923), pp. 211–12.

• F., R. "New York Art News: John Storrs' Sculpture." *The Christian Science Monitor*, March 8, 1923, p. 6.

• McBride, Henry. "Abstract Sculpture by John Storrs." *New York Herald*, March 4, 1923, section 7, p. 7.

• Read, Helen Appleton. "News and Views on Current Art: Storr's [sic] Sculpture a Vindication for Cubism." *The Brooklyn Daily Eagle*, March 4, 1923, section B, p. 2.

"Critics Would Shoot Storrs, Leader of Sculpture Rebels." *The World*, March 18, 1923.

1924

L'École Speciale d'Architecture, Paris. "L'Architecture et les Arts Qui s'y Rattachent." March 22–April 30 (catalogue).

• Kahn, Gustave. "L'Exposition d'un Groupe Hollandais 'De Styl' Surprend par l'Audace. . . ." *Quotidien*, April 18, 1924.

1925

Galerie Briant-Robert, Paris. "Exposition de 6 Peintres Américains—2 Sculpteurs Américains." January 19–February 19 (brochure, with text by Léonce Rosenberg).

• Bal, Georges. "American Art Is Shown in Paris Display." *New York Herald Tribune* (European edition), January 20, 1925, p. 5.

• MacDougall, Allan Ross. "Plays and Personalities in Paris." *Arts and Decoration*, 22 (April 1925), pp. 46–47.

• "Modern U.S. Art On View Here." *Paris Tribune*, January 20, 1925, p. 2.

Edgar Miller's House at the End of the Street, Chicago. "A Loaned Exhibition of Modern Art." March 1–April 10.

G., F. "Round the Studios." *New York Herald Tribune* (European edition), January 25, 1925, p. 4.

Lennon, R.A. "Two Works of Art in Odd Adventure." *The Art World Magazine*, March 3, 1925, p. 8.

1926

Galerie Jean Charpentier, Paris. "Artistes Américains de France." Organized by l'Association Française d'Expansion et des Échanges Artistiques. October 25–November 14.

Galerie Durand-Ruel, Paris. "Groupe de Peintres et Sculpteurs Américains de Paris." Organized by the American Art Association. November 2–26.

The Brooklyn Museum, New York. "An International Exhibition of Modern Art." Organized by the Société Anonyme. November 19, 1926–January 1, 1927 (catalogue by Katherine S. Dreier). Traveled to The Anderson Galleries, New York; Albright Art Gallery, Buffalo; and Art Gallery of Toronto.

1927

Steinway Hall, New York. "Machine Age Exposition." Organized by *The Little Review*. May 16–28 (catalogue).

Jacques Seligman et Fils, Paris. "Salon of American Arts." July 2–14.

The Art Institute of Chicago. "The Fortieth Annual Exhibition of American Paintings and Sculpture." October 27–December 14 (catalogue).

Arts Club of Chicago. "Sculpture by John Storrs." December 11–31 (catalogue, with introduction by Maurice Reynal).

*M. Knoedler & Company, New York. Exhibition of sculpture, prints, and drawings. December 17–29.

Bulliet, C.J. "John Storrs in Role of Miracle Worker." *Chicago Evening Post*, December 20, 1927, *Magazine of the Art World*.

1928

*The Brummer Gallery, New York. "Storrs." February 1–25 (catalogue).

• J[ewell], E[dward] A[lden]. "A Complex Art Fabric." *The New York Times*, February 12, 1928, section 8, p. 14.

Huddleston, Sisley. *Paris Salons, Cafés, Studios*. Philadelphia and London: J.B. Lippincott Company, 1928.

1929

The California Palace of the Legion of Honor, San Francisco. "Contemporary American Sculpture." Organized by The National Sculpture Society. April–October (catalogue).

*Albert Roullier Art Galleries, Chicago. "An Exhibition of Original Drawings in Pencil and Silver Point By the American Sculptor John Storrs." April 9–26 (catalogue, with introduction by Maurice Reynal).

• Bulliet, C.J. "Storrs' Silver Point and Lepere's Needle." *Chicago Evening Post*, April 16, 1929.

• Ellis, Maude Martin. "John Storrs Holds Local Exhibit." *Chicago Sunday Tribune*, April 14, 1929.

L'Effort Moderne, Paris. "Oeuvres Anciennes et Nouvelles." May 22–June 22.

The Art Institute of Chicago. "Forty-Second Annual Exhibition of Paintings and Sculpture." October 24–December 8 (catalogue).

• "Sanely Modernist Works Win Main Prizes at Chicago's Annual." *The Art Digest*, 4 (November 1, 1929), pp. 5–6.

Rindge, Agnes M. *Sculpture*. New York: Payson and Clarke Ltd., 1929.

1930

Hampson, Philip. "Ancient Goddess in Modern Form to Command City." *Chicago Sunday Tribune*, May 4, 1930, section 2, p. 14.

1931

*Chester H. Johnson Galleries, Chicago. "Paintings by John Storrs." March 13–? (catalogue).

• Bulliet, C.J. "John Storrs Makes Debut as Painter." *Chicago Evening Post*, March 17, 1931, *Magazine of the Art World*, p. 2.

• J[ewett], E[leanor]. "Paintings by Storrs." *Chicago Tribune*, March 22, 1931.

• "Storrs, Cubist Sculptor, Takes Up Brush." *The Art Digest*, 5 (April 1, 1931), p. 9.

The Art Institute of Chicago. "The Eleventh International Exhibition: Water Colors, Pastels, Drawings, Monotypes and Miniatures." April 30–May 31 (catalogue).

———. "The Forty-Fourth Annual Exhibition of American Paintings and Sculpture." October 29–December 13 (catalogue).

• "Chicago's Annual Draws Eyes of Fighters for American Art." *The Art Digest*, 6 (November 1, 1931), pp. 3–4.

Albert Roullier Art Galleries, Chicago. "An Exhibition of Original Drawings and Lithographs by Modern Masters." November 10–30.

1932

Society of Arts and Crafts, Detroit. "American Contemporary Paintings and Sculpture." March 31–April 23 (catalogue).

Sweeney, James Johnson. "Barry Byrne and New Forms in Church Construction." *Creative Art*, 2 (September 1932), pp. 61–65.

1933

The Art Institute of Chicago. "Thirty-Seventh Annual Exhibition by Artists of Chicago and Vicinity." January 12–March 5 (catalogue).

Whitney Museum of American Art, New York. "Paintings and Prints by Chicago Artists." February 28–March 30 (catalogue).

Arts Club of Chicago. "Annual Exhibition by the Professional Members." April 23–May 13 (catalogue).

The Art Institute of Chicago. "A Century of Progress Exhibition of Paintings and Sculpture." June 1–November 1 (catalogue).

Whitney Museum of American Art, New York. "First Biennial Exhibition of Contemporary American Sculpture, Watercolors and Prints." December 5, 1933–January 11, 1934 (catalogue, with foreword by Juliana Force).

The Museum of Modern Art, New York. "Painting and Sculpture from 16 American Cities." December 13, 1933–January 17, 1934 (catalogue).

1934

Pennsylvania Academy of the Fine Arts, Philadelphia. "129th Annual Exhibition." January 28–February 25 (catalogue).

The Art Institute of Chicago. "The Thirteenth International Exhibition: Water Colors, Pastels, Drawings and Monotypes." March 29–April 29 (catalogue).

Bulliet, C.J. "Miró Going a Bit Hard in New York." *The Chicago Daily News*, March 17, 1934, p. 6.

Cahill, Holger and Alfred H. Barr, Jr., eds. *Art in America in Modern Times*. New York: Reynal & Hitchcock, 1934.

Ricker, Jewett E., ed. *Sculpture at A Century of Progress: Chicago, 1933, 1934*. Chicago: 1934.

1935

The Brooklyn Museum, New York. "The Eighth Biennial Exhibition of Water Colors, Pastels and Drawings by American and Foreign Artists." February 1–28 (catalogue, with foreword by Herbert B. Tschudy).

Whitney Museum of American Art, New York. "Abstract Painting in America." February 12–March 22 (catalogue).

*Albert Roullier Art Galleries, Chicago. "An Exhibition by John Storrs: Sculpture, Painting and Drawing." February 15–March 1.

• Bulliet, C.J. "Around the Galleries: John Storrs Vigorous Abstracts." *The Chicago Daily News*, February 16, 1935, p. 10.

• ———. "Around the Galleries: John Storrs, Realist." *The Chicago Daily News*, February 23, 1935, p. 15.

• Jewett, Eleanor. "Storrs Exhibit Is Remarkable In Color Work." *Chicago Tribune*, February 16, 1935.

1936

*Albert Roullier Art Galleries, Chicago. "An Exhibition of Sculpture, Portraits, Original Drawings, Paintings by John Storrs." ? –January.

• Bulliet, C.J. "Around the Galleries: Three Sculptures by John Storrs." *The Chicago Daily News*, January 18, 1936, section 3, p. 4.

1937

*Galerie Jeanne Bucher-Myrbor, Paris. "Peintures et Sculptures de John Storrs." May 20–June 2.

Musée du Jeu de Paume, Paris. "Origines et Développement de l'Art International Indépendant." July 30–October 31 (catalogue).

1938

Carnegie Institute, Pittsburgh. "An Exhibition of American Sculpture." May 5–June 19 (catalogue).

Rich, Daniel Catton. *The Charles H. and Mary F.S. Worcester Collection of Paintings, Sculpture and Drawings*. Chicago: The Lakeside Press, 1938.

1939

*Albert Roullier Art Galleries, Chicago. "Five New Sculptures by John Storrs." January 28–February 11 (announcement-checklist).

The Art Institute of Chicago. "Half a Century of American Art." November 16, 1939–January 7, 1940 (catalogue).

1940

Arts Club of Chicago. "Annual Exhibition by the Professional Members." May 12–June 5 (catalogue).

1941

Thorne, Mrs. James Ward. *American Rooms in Miniature*. Chicago: The Art Institute of Chicago, 1941.

1948

Hôtel de Ville, Romorantin, France. "Exposition Artistique 1948" (catalogue).

1949

Philadelphia Museum of Art. "3rd Sculpture International." May 15–September 11 (checklist).

Bibliothèque Municipale, Orléans. "John Storrs Peintures Récentes—Sculptures." May 23–June 7 (brochure, with text by Roger Toulouse).

Château Dunois, Beaugency, France. "3me Exposition Artistique Régionale." July 31–September 4 (catalogue, with essay by Marc Debrol [Marguerite De Ville Chabrol Storrs]).

1950

Dreier, Katherine S., and Marcel Duchamp; George Heard Hamilton, ed. *Collection of the Société Anonyme: Museum of Modern Art 1920*. New Haven, Connecticut: Yale University Art Gallery, 1950.

1953

Musée des Beaux-Arts d'Orléans. "Exposition d'Art Religieux—Contemporain." September–October (catalogue, with text by Jacqueline Pruvost).

1954

"37me Exposition des Beaux-Arts de l'École de la Loire" (catalogue, without indication of institution).

Miller, Lucy Key. "Famed Goddess of Grain Statue Modeled by Girl of 14." *Chicago Tribune*, April 21, 1954, section 3, p. 2.

Walter, Don. "John Storrs: Misfortune and Fame in France." *The Stars and Stripes*, October 21, 1954, p. 11.

1955

Galerie Charpentier 76, Paris. "École de Paris 1955" (catalogue, with introduction by Raymond Nacenta and texts by Robert Ducroquet and Pierre Mazars).

1956

"Monsieur Storr [sic]." *La Renaissance du Loir et Cher*, May 5, 1956.

"Designer of Ceres: John Storrs Dies; Famed as Sculptor." *The Chicago Daily News*, April 24, 1956.

"John B. Storrs Dies; Chicago-Born Sculptor." [Chicago] *Sun-Times*, April 24, 1956.

"John B. Storrs, Sculptor, 71." *New York Herald Tribune*, April 26, 1956, p. 16.

"John Storrs Dies; A Pupil of Rodin." *The New York Times*, April 26, 1956, p. 33.

1961

Byrne, Barry. "To the Editor of Liturgical Arts." *Liturgical Arts*, 30 (November 1961), p. 55.

Delany, Patrick M. "Church Art in Ireland Today." *Liturgical Arts*, 29 (August 1961), pp. 86–89.

1963

Whitney Museum of American Art, New York. "The Decade of the Armory Show: New Directions in American Art." February 27–April 14 (catalogue, with text by Lloyd Goodrich).

1965

*Downtown Gallery, New York. "John Storrs." March 23–April 17 (catalogue).

• "Art Tour: The Galleries—A Critical Guide: John Storrs." *New York Herald Tribune*, March 27, 1965, p. 9.

• B[rowne], R[osalind]. "John Storrs." *Art News*, 64 (April 1965), p. 15.

• G[rossberg], J[acob]. "John Storrs." *Arts Magazine*, 39 (May–June 1965), p. 68.

• Preston, Stuart. "John Storrs." *The New York Times*, March 27, 1965, p. 23.

National Collection of Fine Arts, Smithsonian Institution, Washington, D.C. "Roots of Abstract Art in America, 1910–1930." December 2, 1965–January 9, 1966 (catalogue, with introduction by Adelyn D. Breeskin).

• Ahlander, Leslie Judd. "American Roots in Abstract Art." *The Christian Science Monitor*, January 7, 1966, p. 4.

1966

Zabriskie Gallery, New York. "The American Sculptor, 1900–1930." April 5–30 (checklist).

• Kramer, Hilton. "The American Sculptor, 1900–1930." *The New York Times*, April 23, 1966, p. 27.

"Acquisition." *Des Moines Art Center Bulletin* (September 1966), n.p.

1967

*Downtown Gallery, New York. "John Storrs." April 18–May 13 (catalogue).

• Kramer, Hilton. "Assimilation of the Modern Movement: John Storrs Paintings from '30's On View." *The New York Times*, April 22, 1967, p. 26.

• Murphy, Bernard. "Gallery Hopping: John Storrs." *News Sentinel*, May 4, 1967, p. 9.

The Leicester Galleries, London, in association with the Downtown Gallery, New York. "Six Decades of American Art." July (catalogue, with introductions by John I.H. Baur and Bryan Robertson).

Kay, Jane H. "John Storrs: Remembrance of an Artist Past." *The Chicago Daily News*, June 10, 1967, *Panorama*, p. 6.

Rose, Barbara. *American Painting Since 1900: A Critical History*. New York: Frederick A. Praeger, 1967.

1968

The University of Connecticut Museum of Art, Storrs. "Edith Halpert and the Downtown Gallery." May 25–September 1 (catalogue, with introduction by Marvin S. Sadik).

Chappell, Sally Anderson. "Barry Byrne: Architecture and Writings." Ph.D. dissertation, Northwestern University, Evanston, Illinois, 1968.

Craven, Wayne. *Sculpture in America*. New York: Thomas Y. Crowell Company, 1968.

Tarbell, Roberta K. "John Storrs and Max Weber: Early Life and Work." M.A. thesis, University of Delaware, Wilmington, 1968.

1969

*The Corcoran Gallery of Art, Washington, D.C. "John Storrs." May 3–June 9.

• Forgey, Benjamin. "Art: The Work of John Storrs, a Long-Forgotten Hero." *The Washington Star*, May 18, 1969, section D, p. 13.

Bryant, Edward. "Rediscovery: John Storrs." *Art in America*, 57 (May–June 1969), pp. 66–71.

1970

Finch College Museum of Art, New York. "Art Deco." October 14–November 30 (catalogue, with introduction by Elaine H. Varian and text by Judith Applegate).

*Robert Schoelkopf Gallery, New York. "John Storrs: Paintings, Sculpture, Drawings." November 21–December 24 (checklist).

• Kramer, Hilton. "The Rediscovery of Storrs." *The New York Times*, December 13, 1970, section 2, p. 25.

• Pincus-Witten, Robert. "John Storrs." *Artforum*, 9 (February 1971), p. 76.

1972

*Robert Schoelkopf Gallery, New York. "John Storrs: Drawings & Prints." November 4–30 (checklist).

• Mellow, James R. "John Storrs." *The New York Times*, November 25, 1972, p. 23.

Museum of Art, Carnegie Institute, Pittsburgh. "Forerunners of American Abstraction." November 18, 1971–January 9, 1972 (catalogue, with foreword by Leon Anthony Arkus and introduction by Herdis Bull Teilman).

• Miller, Donald. "John Storrs 1 of 8 Showing at Museum." *Pittsburgh Post-Gazette*, January 5, 1972, p. 28.

Lipchitz, Jacques, with H.H. Arnason. *My Life in Sculpture.* New York: The Viking Press, 1972.

1973

Kramer, Hilton. *The Age of the Avant-Garde: An Art Chronicle of 1956–1972.* New York: Farrar, Straus and Giroux, 1973.

1974

Heckscher Museum, Huntington, New York. "Art Deco and Its Origins." September 22–November 3 (catalogue, with texts by Donald Harris Dwyer and Priscilla de F. Williams).

Davidson, Abraham A. "John Storrs: Early Sculptor of the Machine Age." *Artforum*, 13 (November 1974), pp. 41–45.

Lerner, Abram, ed. *The Hirshhorn Museum and Sculpture Garden.* New York: Harry N. Abrams, 1974.

1975

*Robert Schoelkopf Gallery, New York. "John Storrs." March 4–29 (checklist).

• André, Michael. "John Storrs." *Art News*, 74 (May 1975), p. 94.

Delaware Art Museum, Wilmington. "Avant-Garde Painting & Sculpture in America 1910–25." April 4–May 18 (catalogue, edited by William Innes Homer, with text on Storrs by Susan E. Strickler).

• Kramer, Hilton. "A Fresh Look at Early American Modernists." *The New York Times*, April 27, 1975, section 2, p. 31.

Terry Dintenfass, New York, "Shapes of Industry: First Images in American Art." November 4–29 (catalogue, with text by Roxana Barry).

1976

Whitney Museum of American Art, New York. "200 Years of American Sculpture." March 16–September 26 (catalogue, with texts by various authors).

• Kramer, Hilton. "A Monumental Muddle of American Sculpture." *The New York Times*, March 28, 1976, section D, p. 1.

• Rose, Barbara. "American Sculpture: The First Two Hundred Years." *Vogue*, 166 (July 1976), p. 40.

National Collection of Fine Arts, Smithsonian Institution, Washington, D.C. "America as Art." April 30–November 7 (catalogue, with text by Joshua C. Taylor).

*Museum of Contemporary Art, Chicago. "John Storrs (1885–1956): A Retrospective Exhibition of Sculpture." November 13, 1976–January 2, 1977 (catalogue, with text by Judith Russi Kirshner).

• Artner, Alan G. "Storrs and Dawson: Pairing of Shows in Worthwhile Review." *Chicago Tribune*, November 21, 1976, section 6, p. 45.

• ————."Three Mavericks and Their Art." *Chicago Tribune*, November 21, 1976, *Magazine*, section 9, p. 60.

• Forwalter, John. "Honored in Retrospectives." *The Post-Tribune*, December 7, 1976, section A, p. 8.

The Detroit Institute of Arts. "Arts and Crafts in Detroit 1906–1976: The Movement, The Society, The School." November 26, 1976–January 16, 1977 (catalogue).

Frackman, Noel. "John Storrs and the Origins of Art Deco." M.A. thesis, Institute of Fine Arts, New York University, 1976.

1977

Centre Georges Pompidou, Paris. "Paris—New York." June 1–September 19 (catalogue).

Teilman, Herdis Bull. "Three Early American Sculptors." *Carnegie Magazine*, 51 (March 1977), pp. 113–18.

1978

*Robert Schoelkopf Gallery, New York. "John Storrs: Paintings of the Thirties." October 21–November 18 (checklist).

1979

*Robert Schoelkopf Gallery, New York. "John Storrs: Painting and Sculpture of the Thirties." April 29–May 26 (checklist).

• Ashbery, John. "Action in the North Atlantic." *New York*, 12 (May 21, 1979), pp. 70–71.

Allen Memorial Art Museum, Oberlin College, Oberlin, Ohio. "École to Deco: Small Sculptures from a Private Collection." May 8–September 2 (catalogue, with entries on Storrs' sculptures by Donna K. White).

Rutgers University Art Gallery, New Brunswick, New Jersey. "Vanguard American Sculpture: 1913–1939." September 16–November 4 (catalogue, with texts by Joan M. Marter, Roberta K. Tarbell, and Jeffrey Wechsler). Traveled.

Albright-Knox Art Gallery, Buffalo, New York. "Constructivism and the Geometric Tradition: Selections from the McCrory Corporation Collection." October 14–November 25 (catalogue, with text by Willy Rotzler). Traveled.

The Art Institute of Chicago. "100 Artists 100 Years: Alumni of the School of the Art Institute of Chicago." November 23, 1979–January 20, 1980 (catalogue, with texts by Donald J. Irving, Katherine Kuh, and Norman L. Rice).

Bourdon, David. "Art: American Figurative Sculpture." *Architectural Digest*, 36 (November 1979), pp. 158–63.

McCoy, Garnett. "An Archivist's Choice: Ten of the Best." *Archives of American Art Journal*, 19 (1979), pp. 2–18.

Nash, Steven A., with Katy Kline, Charlotta Kotik, and Emese Wood. *Albright-Knox Art Gallery: Painting and Sculpture from Antiquity to 1942.* New York: Rizzoli International Publications, 1979.

1980

*Sterling and Francine Clark Art Institute, Williamstown, Massachusetts. "John Storrs & John Flannagan: Sculpture & Works on Paper." November 7–December 28 (catalogue, with texts by Jennifer Gordon, Laurie McGavin, Sally Mills, and Ann Rosenthal).

Haskell, Barbara. *Marsden Hartley* (exhibition catalogue). New York: Whitney Museum of American Art in association with New York University Press, 1980.

Russell, Jennifer, and Patterson Sims. "Masterpieces from the Whitney Museum of American Art." *The Magazine Antiques*, 117 (March 1980), pp. 614–25.

1981

The Drawing Center, New York. "Sculptors' Drawings Over Six Centuries 1400–1950." March 21–June 20 (catalogue, with text by Colin Eisler and notes on Storrs' drawing by Donna J. Hassler).

Stamford Museum and Nature Center, Stamford, Connecticut. "Classic Americans: XX Century Painters & Sculptors." June 14–September 7 (checklist, with foreword by Robert Metzger).

1982

Musée d'Art Moderne de la Ville de Paris. "Léger and the Modern Spirit: An Avant-Garde Alternative to Non-Objective Art (1918–1931)." March 17–June 6 (catalogue, with texts by various authors). Traveled.

Bohan, Ruth L. *The Société Anonyme's Brooklyn Exhibition: Katherine Dreier and Modernism in America*. Ann Arbor, Michigan: UMI Research Press, 1982.

Gardner, Virginia. *"Friend and Lover": The Life of Louise Bryant*. New York: Horizon Press, 1982.

1983

*Robert Schoelkopf Gallery, New York. "John Storrs: Paintings, Sculpture and Drawings." January 4–26 (checklist).

• Russell, John. "Art: John Storrs." *The New York Times*, January 7, 1983, section C, p. 23.

Museum of Art, Carnegie Institute, Pittsburgh. "Abstract Painting and Sculpture in America 1927–1944." November 5–December 31 (catalogue, edited by John R. Lane and Susan C. Larsen, with text on John Storrs by Noel Frackman). Traveled.

• Smith, Roberta. "Abstraction Then, for Now." *The Village Voice*, July 31, 1984, p. 78.

Bach, Ira J., and Mary Lackritz Gray. *A Guide to Chicago's Public Sculpture*. Chicago and London: The University of Chicago Press, 1983.

Henderson, Linda Dalrymple. *The Fourth Dimension and Non-Euclidean Geometry in Modern Art*. Princeton, New Jersey: Princeton University Press, 1983.

Schweizer, Paul D. "Skyscraper Sculpture: John Storrs Acquired by the Museum." *Munson-Williams-Proctor Institute Bulletin* (November 1983), n.p.

1984

CDS Gallery, New York. "Artists Choose Artists III." May 23–June 30 (catalogue, with text by Donald B. Kuspit, Storrs' works selected by Robert Moskowitz).

Whitney Museum of American Art, New York. "Print Acquisitions 1974–1984." August 29–November 25 (catalogue, with text by Judith Goldman).

The Museum of Modern Art, New York. "'Primitivism' in 20th Century Art: Affinity of the Tribal and the Modern." September 27, 1984–January 15, 1985 (catalogue, edited by William Rubin, with texts by various authors). Traveled.

Munson-Williams-Proctor Institute Museum of Art, Utica, New York. "Order and Enigma." October 13–December 2 (catalogue, with text by Sarah A. Clark-Langager). Traveled.

Herbert, Robert L., Eleanor S. Apter, and Elise K. Kenney, eds. *The Société Anonyme and the Dreier Bequest at Yale University: A Catalogue Raisonné*. New Haven and London: Yale University Press, 1984.

1985

The Metropolitan Museum of Art and the American Federation of Arts, New York. "The Figure in 20th Century American Art." Circulated February 1985–June 1986 (catalogue, with text by Lowry Sims).

Norton Gallery and School of Art, West Palm Beach, Florida. "The Fine Line: Drawing with Silver in America." March 23–May 5 (catalogue, with introduction by Agnes Mongan and text by Bruce Weber). Traveled.

Yale University Art Gallery, New Haven, Connecticut. "Art for the Masses 1911–1917: A Radical Magazine and Its Graphics." Circulated April 21, 1985–March 9, 1986 (catalogue, with text by Rebecca Zurier).

The Museum of Modern Art, New York. "Contrasts of Form: Geometric Abstract Art 1910–1980." October 7, 1985–January 7, 1986 (catalogue, with introduction by John Elderfield and text by Magdalena Dabrowski).

duPont, Diana, Katherine Church Holland, Garna Garren Muller, and Laura L. Sueoka. *San Francisco Museum of Modern Art: The Painting and Sculpture Collection*. New York: Hudson Hills Press in association with the San Francisco Museum of Modern Art, 1985.

Gurney, George. *Sculpture and the Federal Triangle*. Washington, D.C.: Smithsonian Institution Press, 1985.

Sims, Patterson. *Whitney Museum of American Art: Selected Works from the Permanent Collection*. New York: Whitney Museum of American Art in association with W.W. Norton & Company, 1985.

Works in the Exhibition

Dimensions are in inches, followed by centimeters; height precedes width precedes depth. For sculpture, dimensions are given without the base; "polychromed" refers to the application of more than one color, "painted" to a single color. Unless otherwise indicated, works are in the Estate of Monique Storrs Booz and are lent by courtesy of Robert Schoelkopf Gallery, Ltd., New York. An asterisk indicates that a work will be shown at the Whitney Museum of American Art only.

Sculpture

Head on Column, 1913
Bronze, 9⅛ x 1⅝ x 2¼
  (23.2 x 4.1 x 5.6)

Howard E. Smith, 1913
Bronze, 14½ x 6 x 4½
  (36.8 x 15.2 x 11.4)
Private collection

Dancing Woman on a Column, 1914
Bronze, 10 x 1¼ x 1¼
  (25.4 x 3.2 x 3.2)

Morning, 1915
Bronze, 16¾ x 8¾ x 9
  (42.5 x 22.2 x 22.9)

Horses' Heads, 1917–19
Bronze, 13½ x 9 x 4½
  (34.3 x 22.9 x 11.4)
The Corcoran Gallery of Art,
  Washington, D.C.; Bequest of
  George Biddle

Abstract Forms No. 1, c. 1917–19
Stone and marble, 34⅝ x 3¼ x 7½
  (87.9 x 8.3 x 19.1)
The Newark Museum, New Jersey;
  Charles W. Englehart Bequest
  Fund and The Members' Fund

Abstract Forms No. 2, c. 1917–19
Stone, 19¹¹⁄₁₆ x 8¾ x 5 ⅝
  (50 x 22.2 x 14.3)
Weatherspoon Art Gallery, University of North Carolina at Greensboro; Gift of Jefferson Standard
  Life Insurance Company

Egyptian Mother and Child,
  c. 1917–19
Painted terra-cotta, 6⅜ x 2⅜ x 7⅜
  (16.2 x 6 x 18.7)

* *Stone Panel with Black Marble
  Inlay,* c. 1917–20
Stone and marble, 60½ x 15¼ x 1¾
  (153.7 x 38.7 x 4.4)
The Museum of Modern Art, New
  York; Walter J. Reinemann Fund

Dance (Dancers), 1918
Polychromed terra-cotta, 9 x 2⅞ x 3
  (22.9 x 7.3 x 7.6)

* *Modern Madonna,* c. 1918
Polychromed terra-cotta,
  11⅛ x 3¾ x 2⅜ (28.3 x 9.5 x 6)
Collection of Mr. and Mrs.
  Alvin S. Lane

* *Untitled (The Dancer),* c. 1918
Polychromed terra-cotta, 4¾ x 4 x 4
  (12.1 x 10.2 x 10.2)
Yale University Art Gallery,
  New Haven, Connecticut;
  Bequest of Katherine S. Dreier
  to the Collection Société Anonyme

Winged Woman, c. 1918
Wood, 14⅛ x 11¼ x 3⅛
  (35.9 x 28.6 x 7.9)

Four-Sided Figurative Column,
  c. 1918–19
Stone, 23⅜ x 7½ x 6⅛
  (59.4 x 19.1 x 15.6)

Abstraction, 1919
Painted terra-cotta, 4¾ x 2¾ x 2
  (12.1 x 7 x 5.1)

Action, Inaction, and Reaction, 1919
Stone with enamel, 41¾ x 17¼ x 8
 (105 x 43.8 x 20.3)
Musée Régional, Arts et Traditions
 de l'Orléanais, Château Dunois,
 Beaugency, France

Egyptian Head, 1919
Bronze, 7 x 7 x 4½
 (17.8 x 17.8 x 11.4)

Gendarme, 1919
Stone with enamel,
 41½ x 11½ x 14½
 (105.4 x 29.2 x 36.8)
Musée Régional, Arts et Traditions
 de l'Orléanais, Château Dunois,
 Beaugency, France

Joan of Arc, 1919
Terra-cotta with traces of gilding,
 9¹³⁄₁₆ x 4¼ x 2¼
 (24.9 x 10.8 x 5.7)
Allen Memorial Art Museum,
 Oberlin College, Ohio;
 Friends of Art Fund

* *Standing Gendarme*, 1919
Painted plaster, 9¼ x 2⅛ x 3¼
 (23.5 x 5.4 x 8.3)

* *Figurative Abstraction*, c. 1919
Marble, 20½ x 12½ x 6
 (52.1 x 31.8 x 15.2)
Sheldon Memorial Art Gallery,
 University of Nebraska, Lincoln;
 Gift of Mrs. Olga N. Sheldon

Nude Man, c. 1919
Stone, 30¾ x 10½ x 10½
 (78.1 x 26.7 x 26.7)
Des Moines Art Center;
 James D. Edmundson Fund

Pietà, c. 1919
Polychromed marble, 11 x 9¾ x 5¼
 (27.9 x 24.8 x 13.3)

Winged Horse, c. 1919
Bronze, 13¼ x 15 x 2½
 (33.7 x 38.1 x 6.4)
Collection of John and Fay Stern

The Abbot, 1920
Bronze, 17⅛ x 8¼ x 12⅝
 (43.5 x 21 x 32.1)
The Hirshhorn Museum and
 Sculpture Garden, Smithsonian
 Institution, Washington, D.C.;
 Gift of Joseph H. Hirshhorn

Le Sergent de Ville (*Gendarme*),
 c. 1920
Bronze with silver gilt,
 13¼ x 5¼ x 5¼
 (33.7 x 13.3 x 13.3)
The Corcoran Gallery of Art, Washington, D.C.; W.A. Clark Fund

Le Sergent de Ville (*Gendarme*),
 c. 1920
Bronze with silver gilt,
 9 x 2¼ x 3⅝ (22.9 x 5.7 x 9.2)
Collection of Mr. and Mrs.
 George Blow

Untitled, c. 1920
Terra-cotta, 12 x 1¾ x 3½
 (30.5 x 4.4 x 8.9)

Untitled (*Study for Figure*), c. 1920
 (cast c.1935)
Polychromed steel, 6¹³⁄₁₆ x 2½ x 1⅞
 (17.3 x 6.4 x 4.8)

Untitled (*Study for Figure*), c. 1920
Wood, 6¾ x 2⅝ x 1¹⁵⁄₁₆
 (17.1 x 6.6 x 4.9)

Auto Tower (*Industrial Forms*),
 1922
Painted plaster, 12⅞ x 3¼ x 2¾
 (32.7 x 8.3 x 7)

My Daughter in Winter Costume,
 c. 1922
Stone, 17 x 6½ x 5
 (43.2 x 16.5 x 12.7)
Collection of John P. Axelrod

Architectural Form, c. 1923
Stone, 19¾ x 3¼ x 3
 (50.2 x 8.3 x 7.6)

Architectural Form No. 3, c. 1923
Stone, 19¾ x 3¼ x 3¼
 (50.2 x 8.3 x 8.3)
Collection of Mr. and Mrs.
 Meyer Potamkin

Study in Architectural Forms, c. 1923
Marble, 66 x 10¾ x 3
 (167.6 x 27.3 x 7.6)
Collection of Mr. and Mrs.
 Barney A. Ebsworth

Study in Form (*Architectural Form*),
 c. 1923
Stone, 19½ x 3⅛ x 3¼
 (49.5 x 7.9 x 8.3)
San Francisco Museum of Modern
 Art; Purchased through a gift of
 Julian and Jean Aberbach

Study in Form No. 1, c. 1923
Stone, 19¾ x 3¼ x 3⅛
 (50.2 x 8.3 x 7.9)

Study in Form No. 2, c. 1923
Stone, 19 x 3¼ x 3¼
 (48.3 x 8.3 x 8.3)
Collection of Abby and
 B.H. Friedman

Study in Form No. 4, c. 1923
Stone, 18⅜ x 3⅛ x 3
 (46.7 x 7.9 x 7.6)

Study in Form (*Forms in Space*),
 1924
Bronze, 20 x 12⅛ x 2⅜
 (50.8 x 30.8 x 6)
Hirshhorn Museum and Sculpture
 Garden, Smithsonian Institution,
 Washington, D.C.; Gift of
 Joseph H. Hirshhorn

Forms in Space, c. 1924
Aluminum, brass, copper, and wood,
 28½ x 5½ x 5¼
 (72.4 x 14 x 13.3)
Whitney Museum of American
 Art, New York; Gift of
 Charles Simon   77.58

Forms in Space, c. 1924
Brass, copper, and steel,
 9⅛ x 1¾ x 2 (23.2 x 4.4 x 5.1)
The Museum of Modern Art, New
 York; The Riklis Collection of the
 McCrory Corporation (fractional
 gift)

**Forms in Space No. 1*, c. 1924
Marble, 76¾ x 12⅝ x 8⅝
 (194.9 x 32.1 x 21.9)
Whitney Museum of American Art,
 New York; 50th Anniversary Gift
 of Mr. and Mrs. B.H. Friedman
 in honor of Gertrude Vanderbilt
 Whitney, Flora Whitney Miller,
 and Flora Miller Biddle   84.37

Study in Form, c. 1924
Steel, copper, and brass, 9⅛ x 4⅞
 x 3⅛ (23.2 x 12.4 x 17.9)

Study in Form (*Forms in Space*),
 c. 1924
Wood, 20¼ x 12¼ x 2¹⁄₁₆
 (51.4 x 31.1 x 5.2)
Private collection

*Study in Pure Form (Forms in
  Space No. 4)*, c. 1924
Steel, copper, and brass,
  12¼ x 3 x 1½ (31.1 x 7.6 x 3.8)
Munson-Williams-Proctor Institute
  Museum of Art, Utica, New York

New York, c. 1925
Bronze and steel, 21 x 4 x 1½
  (53.3 x 10.2 x 3.8)
Indianapolis Museum of Art;
  Director's Discretionary Fund

Relief of Female Head, c. 1925
Terra-cotta, 9 x 6½ x ⅝
  (22.9 x 16.5 x 1.6)

Man's Head, 1926
Bronze, 13 x 8¼ x 9¼
  (33 x 21 x 23.5)
The Art Center, South Bend,
  Indiana; Gift of Dr. and Mrs.
  Norval Green

**Study in Architectural Forms*, 1927
Steel, 31 x 6 x 5
  (78.7 x 15.2 x 12.7)
Collection of Mr. and Mrs.
  Raymond D. Nasher

Bust of Ceres, c. 1929
Bronze, 7¼ x 6⅜ x 3⅝
  (18.4 x 16.2 x 9.2)

Ceres, c. 1929
Steel, 26 x 6½ x 5
  (66 x 16.5 x 12.7)
The Art Institute of Chicago;
  Gift of John N. Stern

*Relief of Female Head (Profile of
  Marguerite Storrs)*, c. 1930
Marble, 7⅜ x 7¼ x 1¼
  (18.7 x 18.4 x 3.2)

Industrial Forms No. 2, 1931–35
Polychromed terra-cotta,
  9 x 5¾ x 3½ (22.9 x 14.6 x 8.9)
Collection of Mr. and Mrs.
  Barney A. Ebsworth

Abstract Figure, c. 1934
Bronze, 33¾ x 9¾ x 13
  (85.7 x 24.8 x 33)
Collection of Jack Titelman

Composition Around Two Voids,
  c. 1934
Steel, 20 x 10 x 6
  (50.8 x 25.4 x 15.2)
Whitney Museum of American Art,
  New York; Gift of Monique
  Storrs Booz   65.34

Untitled, c. 1935
Terra-cotta and stone, 8⅝ x 6½ x 2
  (21.9 x 16.5 x 5.1)

Untitled, 1936
Stone, 10¹⁄₁₆ x 8⅛ x 2
  (25.6 x 20.6 x 5.1)

Opposing Forms, c. 1936
Bronze, 9¾ x 10⅛ x 1½
  (24.8 x 25.7 x 3.8)
Collection of Harry L. Koenigsberg

Assemblage in Shadow Box, c. 1937
Steel, brass, and copper,
  13¾ x 11¾ x 2
  (34.9 x 29.8 x 5.1)

Open Window with Figures, c. 1939
Bronze, 10½ x 12⅜ x 2⅜
  (26.7 x 31.4 x 6)

Tête-à-Tête, c. 1939
Bronze, 11 x 11½ x 2¼
  (27.9 x 29.2 x 5.7)
The Metropolitan Museum of Art,
  New York; Purchase, Edward C.
  Moore, Jr. Gift and Rogers Fund

Untitled, c. 1940
Polychromed terra-cotta,
  6½ x 15⅞ x 1½
  (16.5 x 40.3 x 3.8)
The Lannan Foundation,
  Lake Worth, Florida

Adam, 1948
Stone, 16¾ x 6⅛ x 1¼
  (42.5 x 15.6 x 3.2)

Eve, 1948
Stone, 16¾ x 6⅛ x 1⅜
  (42.5 x 15.6 x 3.5)

The Three Graces, c. 1950
Painted stone, 13¾ x 7⅛ x 1¼
  (34.9 x 18.1 x 3.2)

Drawings

Mme. Jane Bathori, Chantant, 1918
Ink on paper, 5¼ x 4¾
  (13.3 x 12.1) sight

Self-Portrait, 1918
Ink on paper, 10 x 8
  (25.4 x 20.3)
Collection of Carole and
  Richard Rifkind

Le Sergent de Ville (Gendarme),
  1918
Watercolor and ink on paper, 10 x 7
  (25.4 x 17.8)

Untitled, 1918
Ink on paper, 15¾ x 18¾
  (40 x 47.6) sight
Private collection

Soldier, c. 1918
Pencil on paper, 14¾ x 11
  (37.5 x 27.9)

Man with the Crutch, c. 1919
Ink and watercolor on paper,
  9¾ x 5¾ (24.8 x 14.6)
Private collection

War Widow, c. 1919
Ink on paper, 8 x 4¾
  (20.3 x 12.1) sight
Private collection

Machine Form, 1920
Ink and pencil on paper,
  11⅝ x 8⅞ (29.5 x 22.5)
Yale University Art Gallery, New
  Haven, Connecticut; Gift of
  Collection Société Anonyme

*Study for Auto Tower (Industrial
  Forms)*, 1920
Pencil and ink on paper, 12⅛ x 9
  (30.8 x 22.9)
Collection of Mr. and Mrs.
  Alvin S. Lane

Seated Figure, c. 1920
Ink on paper, 7¹¹⁄₁₆ x 4½
  (19.5 x 11.4)
Yale University Art Gallery, New
  Haven, Connecticut; Gift of
  Collection Société Anonyme

Study for a Metal Sculpture, 1922
Ink on paper, 6¹³⁄₁₆ x 4⁵⁄₁₆ (17.3 x 11)
Yale University Art Gallery,
  New Haven, Connecticut;
  Anonymous gift

Drawing for Study in Form (Forms in Space), 1923
Ink on paper, 10¼ x 8¼ (26.1 x 21)

Study for a Sculpture (Forms in Space), 1923
Ink on paper, 10¾ x 8¾ (27.3 x 22.2)
The Museum of Modern Art, New York; The Riklis Collection of the McCrory Corporation (fractional gift)

Design for Fabrication of Abstract Metal Sculpture, c. 1924–25
Ink on paper, 15⅜ x 10¾ (39.1 x 27.3)
Collection of Raymond J. Learsy

Study for a Tower, c. 1925
Ink and pencil on paper, 12⅝ x 9⅞ (32.1 x 25.1)
Hirshhorn Museum and Sculpture Garden, Smithsonian Institution, Washington, D.C.; Museum Purchase

Nude Girl on Louis XIII Chair, 1927
Silverpoint on paper, 13 x 10⅛ (33 x 25.7)

Bust of a Woman Leaning on Her Elbow (Sleeper), 1928
Silverpoint on paper, 13 x 10⅞ (33 x 27.6)
The Art Institute of Chicago; Charles H. Worcester Collection

Study for a Monumental Tower with Sculptural Decorations, c. 1928
Ink on paper, 16 x 6⁹⁄₁₆ (40.6 x 16.7)
The St. Louis Art Museum, Missouri; Purchase, Friends Fund

Profile of Woman with Cork-Screw Curls, 1929
Silverpoint on paper, 13⅜ x 10¼ (34 x 26)

Study for Architectural Sculpture, 1929
Silverpoint on paper, 13¼ x 10¼ (33.7 x 26)

Ceres, c. 1929
Pencil on paper, 14¾ x 6⅝ (37.5 x 16.8)
Collection of Stephens Inc., Little Rock, Arkansas

Study for Christ, for the façade of the Church of Christ the King, Cork, Ireland, c. 1929
Pencil on paper, 29 x 23 (73.7 x 58.4)

Female Head in Turban, c. 1930
Silverpoint on paper, 12¾ x 10⅛ (32.4 x 25.7)
Private collection

Male Model on Back, 1931
Silverpoint on paper, 12⅞ x 9¾ (32.7 x 24.8)

Study for Hall of Science Reliefs, 1933 Chicago World's Fair: Man and Industry, 1932
Pencil on paper, 13 x 9¾ (22.9 x 24.8)

Study for Hall of Science Reliefs, 1933 Chicago World's Fair: Man Moving Rock, 1932
Pencil on paper, 12¾ x 9¾ (32.4 x 24.8)

Study for Hall of Science Reliefs, 1933 Chicago World's Fair: Man with Cogwheel, 1932
Colored pencil and pencil on paper, 11½ x 8½ (29.2 x 21.6)

Study for Hall of Science Reliefs, 1933 Chicago World's Fair: Woman Watering Plants, 1932
Pencil on paper, 14¾ x 11⅜ (37.5 x 28.9)

Study for Hall of Science Reliefs, 1933 Chicago World's Fair: Woman with Plumb Line, 1932
Colored pencil and pencil on paper, 10½ x 9½ (26.7 x 24.1)

Study for Hall of Science Reliefs, 1933 Chicago World's Fair: Female Study, Woman with Retort, c. 1932
Pencil on paper, 14½ x 11½ (36.8 x 29.2)

Study for Hall of Science Reliefs, 1933 Chicago World's Fair: Male Study, Man with Cogwheel, c. 1932
Pencil on paper, 14½ x 11½ (36.8 x 29.2)

Study for Hall of Science Reliefs, 1933 Chicago World's Fair: Woman Holding Retort, c. 1932
Colored pencil and pencil on paper, 11¾ x 9¼ (29.8 x 23.5)

Study for Left-hand Panels of Speaker's Rostrum, Hall of Science, 1933 Chicago World's Fair, c. 1932
Pencil on paper, 10 x 13 (25.4 x 33)
Collection of Edward R. Downe, Jr.

Abstract Forms (25–12–33), 1933
Colored pencil and pencil on paper, 9 x 5½ (22.9 x 14)

Abstract Forms (28–12–33), 1933
Colored pencil and pencil on paper, 9 x 5½ (22.9 x 14)

Study for Cock of the Morning, 1933
Pencil on paper, 9¼ x 6 (23.5 x 15.2)

Abstract Forms (26–12–36), 1936
Colored pencil and pencil on paper, 7⅜ x 6¾ (18.7 x 17.1)

Entwined Abstract Forms, c. 1936
Colored pencil on paper, 7 x 9¾ (17.8 x 24.8)

Study for Sculpture (Personages), 1937
Pencil on paper, 9¼ x 5⅞ (23.5 x 14.9)
Collection of Mr. and Mrs. Alvin S. Lane

China—Japan, 1938
Pencil on paper, 10⅞ x 8⁵⁄₁₆ (27.6 x 21.1)

Sculpture Studies (including Tête-à-Tête), 1939
Pencil and typewriter ink on paper, 11 x 8⅞ (27.9 x 22.5)

Dr. Soler, Compiègne, Sta. 122, 1942
Silverpoint on paper, 9⅞ x 8 (25.1 x 20.3)

Oise Front, Stalag, Compiègne, France, 1942
Silverpoint on paper, 4⅛ x 7 (10.5 x 17.8)

Captain Jean Ravaut, c. 1942
Silverpoint on paper, 7 x 4
 (17.8 x 10.2)

Dr. Sterling, c. 1942
Silverpoint on paper, 9¾ x 8⅝
 (24.8 x 22)

General Nicolas Golejewski, 333,
 c. 1942
Silverpoint on paper, 9¾ x 8⅛
 (24.8 x 20.6)

Floor Plan (9–3–43), 1943
Pencil on paper, 9½ x 12⁹⁄₁₆
 (24.1 x 31.9)

Floor Plan (12–3–43), 1943
Pencil on paper, 9½ x 12⁹⁄₁₆
 (24.1 x 31.9)

Floor Plan (28–2–43), 1943
Pencil on paper, 12⁹⁄₁₆ x 9½
 (31.9 x 24.1)

Man in Bowtie with Mustache, 1943
Pencil on paper, 11 x 9 (28 x 22.9)

Self-Portrait, 1943
Pencil, 7¼ x 7 (18.4 x 17.8)

Study for Church (8–3–43), 1943
Pencil on paper, 12⁹⁄₁₆ x 9⁷⁄₁₆
 (31.9 x 24)

*Study for Church with Statue of
 Bishop (8–3–43)*, 1943
Pencil on paper, 12⁹⁄₁₆ x 9⁷⁄₁₆
 (31.9 x 24)

*The Gardener's Daughter,
 Chantecaille*, c. 1943
Pencil on paper, 9 x 8½
 (22.9 x 21.6)
Collection of Arie L. Kopelman

Fruit in a Silver Dish, 1946
Pencil on paper, 14¾ x 12⅝
 (37.5 x 32.1)

Nude and Lizard (Spring), 1946
Pencil on paper, 12¾ x 9⅞
 (32.4 x 25.1)
Yale University Art Gallery, New
 Haven, Connecticut; Director's
 Purchase

Seated Man, Arms Raised, 1946
Pencil on paper, 12⅞ x 10
 (32.7 x 25.4)

Chantecaille, 1947
Pencil on paper, 12¾ x 9¹⁵⁄₁₆
 (7 x 25.2)

Prints

Scaffoldings, 1913
Etching: sheet, 18¾ x 6½
 (47.6 x 16.5); image, 9¾ x 3⅛
 (24.8 x 7.9)

Self-Portrait, 1914
Etching and acquatint: sheet,
 12¾ x 10 (32.4 x 25.4); image,
 7 x 4⅞ (17.8 x 12.4)

Romantic Night (Eagle), 1916
Woodcut: sheet, 9¾ x 7⅞
 (24.8 x 20); image, 4 x 4
 (10.2 x 10.2)
Whitney Museum of American Art,
 New York; Purchase, with funds
 from the John I.H. Baur
 Purchase Fund   82.33

Beauty and the Beast (Femme Nue),
 1917
Woodcut: sheet, 7 x 5¾
 (17.8 x 14.6); image, 5¼ x 3¼
 (13.3 x 8.3)

Spirit of Walt Whitman, 1917
Woodcut: sheet, 15¾ x 11
 (40 x 27.9); image, 9¹⁄₁₆ x 8³⁄₁₆
 (23 x 20.8)
University Art Museum, The
 University of New Mexico,
 Albuquerque

The Spirit of the Night, c. 1917
Woodcut: sheet, 11⅜ x 8⅛
 (28.9 x 20.6); image, 6½ x 6⁷⁄₁₆
 (16.5 x 16.4)
Whitney Museum of American Art,
 New York; Gift of the Robert
 Schoelkopf Gallery, Ltd.   80.23

Coming from the Bath, c. 1917–18
Stamp and woodcut: sheet,
 31¼ x 21⅞ (79.4 x 55.6); image,
 29¾ x 15 (75.6 x 38.1)

Beauty and the Beast (Femme Nue),
 1918
Woodcut: sheet, 10⅞ x 10¼
 (27.6 x 26) irregular; image,
 5⁵⁄₁₆ x 3¼ (13.5 x 8.3)
Whitney Museum of American Art,
 New York; Purchase, with funds
 from the John I.H. Baur
 Purchase Fund   82.32

Three Soldiers, 1918
Woodcut: sheet, 11⅛ x 7½
 (28.3 x 19.1); image, 4⅜ x 4⅜
 (11.1 x 11.1)

War, 1918
Woodcut: sheet, 11⅜ x 10
 (28.9 x 25.4); image, 8 x 6⅜
 (20 x 16.2)

*Woman's Face in Three-Quarter
 View (White Face on Black)*,
 1918
Woodcut: sheet, 13 x 9½ (33 x 24);
 image, 10⅝ x 8⅜ (27 x 21.3)

Self-Portrait, c. 1918
Woodcut: sheet, 15 x 10¾
 (38.1 x 27.3); image, 10 x 10
 (25.4 x 25.4)

*Woman's Face in Three-Quarter
 View (Black Face on Black)*,
 c. 1918
Woodcut: sheet, 15¾ x 11
 (40 x 28); image, 10⅝ x 8⅜
 (27 x 21.3)

Reclining Figure Under a Tree
 (unpublished illustration for
 Walt Whitman's *Song of Myself*),
 c. 1918–20
Woodcut: sheet, 11⅛ x 8⅞
 (28.3 x 22.5); image, 6⅜ x 6⅜
 (16.2 x 16.2)
Yale University Art Gallery,
 New Haven, Connecticut; Alan
 Evarts Forster, B.A. 1906, Fund

Embracing Couple, 1919
Woodcut: sheet, 11¼ x 7½
 (28.6 x 19.1); image, 4⅜ x 4⅜
 (11.1 x 11.1)

Man's Head, 1919
Woodcut: sheet, 9¾ x 7⅞
 (24.8 x 20); image, 4¼ x 4¼
 (10.8 x 10.8)

Family, 1919 – 20
Woodcut: sheet, 9⅝ x 13⅛
 (24.4 x 33.3); image, 6¼ x 6¼
 (15.9 x 15.9)

*Folsom Galleries Announcement
 (Black Letters on White Ground)*,
 1920
Woodcut: sheet, 5½ x 5 (14 x 12.7);
 image, 2¾ x 2¾ (7 x 7)

*Folsom Galleries Announcement
 (White Letters on Black Ground)*,
 1920
Woodcut: sheet, 5½ x 5½ (14 x 14);
 image, 2¾ x 2¾ (7 x 7)

Profile Head with Cap, 1920
Woodcut: sheet, 5⅞ x 6
  (14.9 x 15.2); image, 4⅜ x 4⅜
  (11.1 x 11.1)

Grain of Wood, c. 1920
Woodcut: sheet, 15¾ x 11
  (40 x 27.9); image, 10 x 10
  (25.4 x 25.4)

Joan of Arc, c. 1920
Woodcut: sheet, 7⅞ x 11⅛
  (20 x 28.3); image, 5¹⁄₁₆ x 5¹³⁄₁₆
  (12.9 x 14.8)
National Museum of American Art,
  Smithsonian Institution, Washington, D.C.; Museum Purchase

Grays and Black, c. 1935
Lithograph: sheet, 19¾ x 13⅛
  (50.2 x 33.3); image, 16¾ x 11¾
  (42.5 x 29.8)
National Museum of American Art,
  Smithsonian Institution, Washington, D. C.

Paintings

Man and Woman, 1930
Oil on canvas, 14 x 12
  (35.6 x 30.5)
Collection of Harvey and
  Françoise Rambach

Double Entry, 1931
Oil on canvas, 45½ x 30¼
  (115.6 x 76.8)
Collection of Mr. and Mrs.
  Barney Ebsworth

Monologue, 1931
Oil on canvas, 57¼ x 38¼
  (145.4 x 97.2)
Collection of Raymond J. Learsy

Politics, 1931
Oil on canvas, 40 x 40
  (101.6 x 101.6)

Portrait of an Aristocrat, 1931
Oil on canvas, 44 x 30
  (111.8 x 76.2)
Collection of Edward R. Downe, Jr.

Room 13, c. 1931
Oil on wood, 16 x 13½
  (40.6 x 34.3)
Private collection

Abstract No. 1, 1932
Oil on masonite, 58 x 45
  (147.3 x 114.3)
The Museum of Fine Arts, Houston;
  Museum purchase

Genesis, 1932
Oil on board, 31¾ x 26
  (80.6 x 66)
Private collection

Green and White Sculpture, 1932
Oil on canvas, 32 x 25½
  (81.3 x 64.8)
Collection of Edward R. Downe, Jr.

The Battle, 1936
Oil on canvas, 34 x 49
  (86.4 x 124.5)
Private collection

*The Idol (Figure in a Circular
  Room)*, 1936
Oil on canvas, 25½ x 31½
  (64.8 x 80)
Collection of Edward R. Downe, Jr.

Untitled, 1936
Oil on masonite, 43 x 42½
  (109.2 x 108)
Private collection

Composition, Abstract Forms, 1937
Oil on canvas, 12 x 18 (30.5 x 45.7)
Jordan-Volpe Gallery, Inc.,
  New York

Walking on the Grass, 1937
Oil on canvas, 12⅛ x 18
  (30.8 x 45.7)
Collection of Mr. and Mrs.
  Alvin S. Lane

Photograph Credits

Photographs accompanying this text have been supplied, in the majority of cases, by the owners or custodians of the works, as cited in the captions. The following list applies to photographs for which an additional acknowledgment is due. Numerical citations refer to figures.

Archives of American Art, Smithsonian Institution, Washington, D.C.: 4, 6, 7, 15, 23, 39, 45, 73, 98, 99, 100, 101, 103, 126, 127, 128

Armen Photographers: 42

© Copyright 1986 by The Barnes Foundation: 124

The Richard W. Bock Sculpture Collection, Greenville College, Greenville, Illinois: 57, 58

Bonney: Frontispiece

Jay Brooks: 8, 117

The Francis Barry Byrne Collection, Chicago Historical Society: 96, 97

Chicago Board of Trade: 89

Geoffrey Clements: 1, 27, 31, 32, 105, 130, 132

eeva-inkeri: 2, 10a, 10b, 12, 34, 61, 72a, 72b, 74, 78, 86, 94, 107, 111, 112, 113, 116, 139, 141, 143

Paul Galgiani: 66

Hedrich-Blessing: 87

Peter A. Juley: 29

A. Mewbourn: 110

Otto E. Nelson: 79

Edward Owen: 14, 17

Timothy Rub: 63

John D. Schiff: 16a, 16b, 22, 30, 48, 49, 51, 59, 68, 106, 109, 114, 115, 140, 145, 151

Arthur Siegel: 5

James Steinkamp, Murphy/Jahn Architects: 90

Soichi Sunami: 55

Joseph Szaszfai: 67, 142

Bob Thall: 84

Jerry L. Thompson: 28, 54, 62

University of Illinois at Chicago, The Library Manuscript Collection: 129

Malcolm Varon: 76

Tom Van Eynde: 20, 21, 35, 37, 46, 52, 60, 85, 95, 120, 121, 131, 138

Ellen Page Wilson: 125

The Frank Lloyd Wright Memorial Foundation: 65, 150